THE END

Fundamentalism
and the Struggle for
the Temple Mount

OF DAYS

Gershom Gorenberg

THE FREE PRESS

NEW YORK   LONDON   TORONTO   SYDNEY   SINGAPORE

*f*P

THE FREE PRESS
A Division of Simon & Schuster Inc.
1230 Avenue of the Americas
New York, NY 10020

THE FREE PRESS and colophon are trademarks
of Simon & Schuster Inc.
Designed by Edith Fowler
Manufactured in the United States of America

10   9   8   7   6   5   4   3   2   1

Library of Congress Cataloging-in-Publication Data

Gorenberg, Gershom.
    The end of days : fundamentalism and the struggle for
  the Temple Mount / Gershom Gorenberg.
        p.   cm.
    Includes bibliographical references (p.) and index.
      1. Temple Mount (Jerusalem).   2. Religious fundamentalism—Political
  aspects—Jerusalem.   3. Judaism—Relations.   4. Christianity and other
  religions.   5. Islam—Relations.   I. Title: Fundamentalism and the struggle
  for the Temple Mount.   II. Title.
  DS109.28.G67   2000
  933—dc21   00-064649

  ISBN 0-684-87179-3

In Judi's memory

CONTENTS

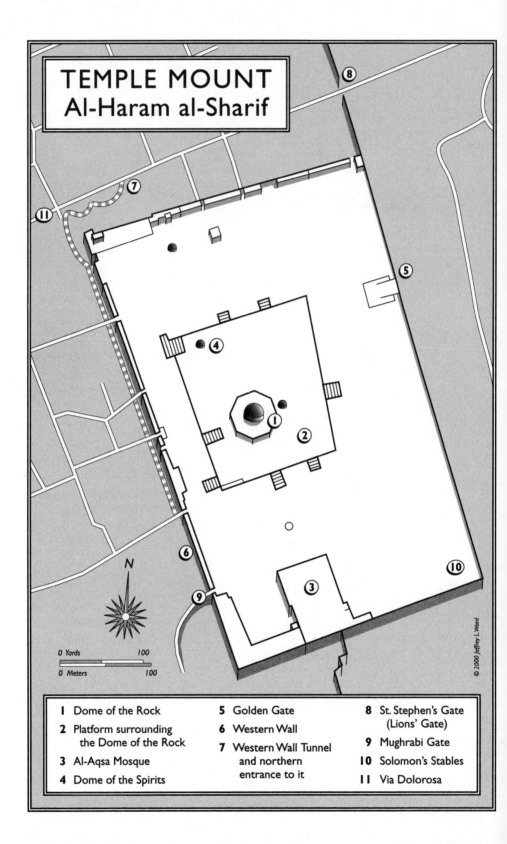

TEMPLE MOUNT
Al-Haram al-Sharif

N

0 Yards 100
0 Meters 100

© 2000 Jeffrey L. Ward

1 Dome of the Rock
2 Platform surrounding the Dome of the Rock
3 Al-Aqsa Mosque
4 Dome of the Spirits
5 Golden Gate
6 Western Wall
7 Western Wall Tunnel and northern entrance to it
8 St. Stephen's Gate (Lions' Gate)
9 Mughrabi Gate
10 Solomon's Stables
11 Via Dolorosa

The Beginning is Nigh

THE BELL TOLLED at midmorning, summoning the faithful to their church. They trooped down the hillside silently; they'd abjured unnecessary speech, along with sex and liquor. Some stopped to pour out food they wouldn't need, covering the path with flour.

The members of the Movement for the Restoration of the Ten Commandments, a shoot sprung from the trunk of Catholicism, had expected the world to end in 1992, in 1995, and on the last day of 1999. Despite their prophecies' failures, they'd continued recruiting new members. Now, on March 17, 2000, they knew the Virgin Mary was about to come to take them to heaven. They'd celebrated, slaughtering three bulls, at their compound at Kanungu in the fertile hills of south Uganda; they'd burned clothes and money, vestiges of earthly life. Inside the building, waiting, they sang and chanted. Someone nailed shut the doors and windows.

The End came in a flash of gasoline-fed flames.

Afterward, local police guessed that 530 people died in the fire. The dead were hard to count, since ashes were all that was left of many bodies. Within days, police found some four hundred more corpses

1

buried in pits at Kanungu and other sect compounds. The signs were that they'd been stabbed, strangled, or poisoned in the weeks before the fire, though neighbors had heard nothing, no cries of resistance.

Ugandan officials described the case as mass murder, rather than mass suicide. They posited that the sects' leaders had escaped, taking the wealth of the members; warrants were issued for their arrest. An AP report referred to Credonia Mwerinde, who founded the movement after seeing visions of the Virgin, as a "huckster" and "charlatan." It fit a common description of "cults" that predict the End—con-man leader, duped followers. Perhaps that was less frightening than another possibility: that hoping for history's end and the kingdom of God, sane people had killed or had willingly died, based on beliefs an inch or three away from those of established religions. But in the first days after the fire, it was impossible to prove either explanation of the catastrophe. The witnesses had left this life.

One thing should be clear: A certain sigh of relief elsewhere in the world at the start of 2000 had been altogether premature. In the months before the turn of the millennium, media reports and security agency assessments warned that religious groups might commit violence to help the End begin. At the same time, newspapers carried updates on concerns that the Y2K bug would stop computers at midnight, December 31, 1999. That whiff of techno-apocalypse helped merge the two concerns. So did the use of "millennium" to refer both to the Christian belief in God's kingdom on earth and to the biggest New Year's party ever. It was easy to get the impression that anyone predicting the End was expecting it that midnight, and that if anyone acted on the belief, that's when he'd do so. But the magic minute passed, the computers didn't even hiccup, and no "cultists" killed themselves. Ergo, the religious concerns were misplaced, just like the technological ones.

Just two and a half months later, fire swept through a Ugandan church. Reading the reports in Jerusalem, I was sickened, but not surprised.

As a journalist and an associate of the Center for Millennial Studies, I study people who believe we are living in history's final days. Popular depictions of such people are often simplistic, drawing too great a separation between "doomsday cults" and mainstream society.

The fact is that millions of quite rational men and women, belonging to established religious movements around the globe, look forward to history's conclusion, to be followed by the establishment of a perfected era. They draw support from ideas deeply embedded in Western religion and culture. You don't need to go to central Africa to find them; they live in American suburbs; they work in insurance offices and high-tech startups. Some are influential leaders of America's Christian right.

Likewise, the fear that any outburst of violence would occur on January 1 was mistaken: It fed exaggerated concerns about that day, and overlooked more serious risks afterward. In fact, the Uganda tragedy fit a pattern familiar to researchers: The deaths came as a delayed reaction, after reality repeatedly defied prophecy. Worse, there was no reason to assume that the Ugandan case would be the last outburst of violence linked to expectations of the End. The turn of the millennium marked not the end of the danger, but the beginning of a dangerous time.

Living where I do, I take that danger seriously. If there's any place in the world where belief in the End is a powerful force in real-life events, it's the Holy Land. The territory today shared and contested by Jews and Palestinians is the stage of myth in Christianity, Judaism, and even Islam. When a great drama is played out here, the temptation to match events with the script of the Last Days can be irresistible. For a century just such a drama has been acted out, compelling the world's attention—and firing expectations in all three religions among those who hope for the End.

The impact of such belief on a complex national and religious struggle has received too little attention. It underlies the apocalyptic foreign policy promoted by many on the American religious right: support for Israel based on certainty that the Jewish state plays a crucial role in a fundamentalist Christian script for the End. In Israel, belief in final redemption has driven the most dedicated opponents of peace agreements. Among Muslims, expectation of the final Hour helps feed exaggerated fears about Israel's actions in Jerusalem. Belief in the approaching End has influenced crucial events in the Arab-Israeli conflict. Time and again, it has been the rationale behind apparently irrational bloodshed, and undermined efforts at peacemaking. In the worst case, desire for history's finale has the potential to spark all-out war in the Middle East.

And here's the paradox: The world's resolute refusal to end doesn't mute expectations; it turns them up. In the years to come, therefore, hope for the End will continue to exert political influence— and its potential to set off violence will only increase. That hope is more than a fantasy; it has the power to affect our world. The purpose of this book is to show why.

I CAME TO JERUSALEM from California in 1977. I was a year out of college. I came to study Judaism in the Holy City for a year, but I had a one-way ticket. I had nothing written down for the future. I fell in love with the place and, surprising myself, I stayed.

The America of my childhood had been the arena of outrageous hope: We could change the world, completely, by tomorrow. When I was fifteen, spending a summer as a volunteer in a legal aid office on the poor side of Los Angeles, I sat with friends on the floor of the house we shared, and we talked about what America would look like after the revolution. We had, of course, little clue as to what "revolution" meant, besides a mood expressed half by having long hair and half by spending a summer in south Los Angeles, suburban kids right-eously slumming. At the university where I later studied, on the coast south of San Francisco, the mood of the sixties lasted halfway into the seventies. Fellow students had programs for remaking humanity: Marxism, lesbian feminism, offbeat spirituality. By the time I left for Israel, the mood of extravagant hope had passed, leaving a dry hang-over in many mouths. My last year in America I spent in Berkeley. The town's telephone poles were the public notice boards, covered in countless layers of announcements. Already, flyers advertising new kinds of psychological therapy and meditation had buried all the fa-mous calls to protest. My older sister, who'd thrilled me by getting ar-rested at a campus demonstration when I was in eighth grade, now commuted to a job she hated.

Through college, my own commitment to Jewish tradition deep-ened. There were many reasons, but two messages of that tradition matter for this story. One was messianism: faith that a time would come when war would end, oppression evaporate. Irreligious or anti-religious as my left-wing friends often were, it seemed obvious that this hope was the mother of their hopes. If we believed that the world should be radically different than it was, religion was responsible. The second message had the opposite import: People were inherently capable of both good and evil; that's what made them human. No change in the regime, class structure, or relations between the sexes would change that. Therefore, anyone hawking a program for a perfected world was selling a hollow promise. The two messages didn't live peacefully with each other, but both struck me as true.

In Israel, political passion had not gone out of fashion. Strangers argued politics on the bus. In a society where very little was rude, it was rude to phone someone during the evening TV news: The news *mattered.* There were a dozen political parties in parliament; banks and HMOs had party labels, even the soccer teams belonged to parties. Egyptian President Anwar al-Sadat visited Jerusalem in 1977, offering peace in return for the Sinai Peninsula. Everyone I knew, it seemed, went to demonstrations for or against. Simply deciding to live in the country rather than returning to an easier life in California would be a political statement. Eventually, I succumbed, trading my tourist visa for an immigrant's papers. After several years of study, in yeshivah (Talmudic seminary) and graduate school, I began a career as a journalist.

I wrote regularly on religion and politics. In particular, the ultra-nationalist Orthodox settlers of the West Bank gripped my attention. They were changing the map of the occupied territories, but they were also imposing a new map of Judaism. The settlers' ideology was messianism: The creation of Israel fulfilled prophecy, and the conquest of the West Bank was another step toward final redemption. They claimed to know God's program for history, and their place in it. For the most extreme, that hubris freed them of all moral constraints: In the mid-eighties, a group of settlers was arrested and convicted of terrorist acts against Palestinians and of plotting to destroy the Dome of the Rock, the Muslim shrine at the center of the Temple Mount in Jerusalem. A central member of the group, Yehudah Etzion, told me after his release that "we saw ourselves as God's messengers, asking what He would want us to do."

This isn't where faith has to end up. But I wanted to lay bare at least part of the reasons that it sometimes does. In the process, I widened my focus to include all three of the religions that call Jerusalem sacred. I've listened to Muslim sheikhs explain how verses in the Koran foretell Israel's destruction, and to American evangelical ministers who insist on their deep love for Israel and nevertheless eagerly await apocalyptic battles on Israel's soil so terrible that the dry river beds will, they predict, fill with rivers of blood. I also came to realize that the center of my story had to be the Temple Mount. What happens at that one spot, more than anywhere else, quickens expectations of the End in three religions. And at that spot, the danger of provoking catastrophe is greatest.

Which is also an old story: A Jewish text records the debate of sages 1,800 years ago on why Cain murdered Abel. By naming what drove Cain to kill, each sage meant to identify the source of human violence. According to one, a twin sister was born with Abel; the brothers fought over who'd possess the only available woman. Another sage argued that the brothers agreed to divide everything in the world between them. One promptly claimed the clothes on his brother's back and ordered him to strip; the other claimed the ground under his brother's feet and shouted, "Fly." Blows followed, then blood.

The third sage, a Rabbi Levi, also said the brothers agreed to split the world. But then, he said, one claimed the land where the Temple would be built, the other insisted it was his, and "Cain rose up against his brother Abel, and slew him."

The history of fratricide began, said Rabbi Levi, in an argument over who would own religion. It began with a fight over the Temple Mount.

ONE

CATTLEMEN OF
THE APOCALYPSE

And death shall have no dominion.

—DYLAN THOMAS

MELODY, THE COW that could have brought God's kingdom on earth, or set the entire Middle East ablaze, or both, depending on who you ask, has her head stuck between the gray bars of the cowshed and is munching hay and corncobs.

At late afternoon in the Jezreel Valley in northern Israel, the hot moist unmoving air could poach a person for dinner. The cows stand on slats that let their droppings fall into a vat below. In the milking room, Gilad Jubi, dairyman of the Kfar Hasidim agricultural school, works with teenage boys in rubber aprons slipping nozzles on udders. A shovel lies in the farmyard next to a rusty wheelbarrow. The scene seems pastoral, not apocalyptic, fit for William Carlos Williams, not St. John the Divine. The friend I brought from Jerusalem, a young born-again American Christian who grew up on a Pennsylvania dairy farm, tells me that his dad once turned on the machine that liquefies the manure under the slats to pump it out, and ten cows dropped dead, asphyxiated by nitrogen that wafted up. The most dangerous thing around is dung. Only the backdrop hints at divine fury: Above Kfar Hasidim looms Mt. Carmel, where Elijah slaughtered the prophets of

Baal. Driving up from the city, we stopped at the ancient ruins of Megiddo, whose name came out as Armageddon in the Book of Revelation and gave the West a title for history's ultimate battle, to be feared or hoped for or disbelieved, depending on your wont. Myth hangs over the countryside like the afternoon mist.

The Holsteins are black and white. But Melody is deep red, from her wet nose almost to the tip of her tail. She looks like an adman's concept: the one bit of furious color on a black and white page. The color says she matters. It's her color that threatened to undo the delicate division of holy space in Jerusalem and to set Jews and Muslim at war. Her color made her the unlikely herald of apocalypse for evangelical Christians around the globe. "The red heifer"—as one U.S. evangelical website voiced the mood—"is but another piece in the prophetic timetable which is moving closer to the end of the age and the return of Messiah."

Melody's birth in August 1996 seemed to defy nature: Her mother was a black and white Holstein. In fact, Jubi says he'd had trouble breeding the dairy cow, and finally imported semen, from Switzerland, he thinks, from a red breed of beef cattle. But "red" cows are normally splotched. An entirely crimson one is extraordinary: The *Mishneh Torah,* Moses Maimonides' twelfth-century code of Jewish law, records that just nine cows in history have fit the Book of Numbers' requirements for sacrificing as a "red heifer." Yet the rare offering was essential to maintaining worship in the Temple in Jerusalem. The tenth cow, Maimonides asserts, will arrive in the time of the messiah. That's when Jewish tradition foresees the Third Temple being built on the Temple Mount.

Kfar Hasidim is an Orthodox Jewish school. Up from the cowshed is a storehouse with the words "End of Days Square" painted on the eave. In a fading mural on the wall, a wolf lies down with a sheep, a lion cuddles with an antelope. A sign on the door reads:

> *Subjects studied here:*
> *The king messiah*
> *The Kingdom of Israel*
> *"And it will come to pass in the end of days"*

Not surprisingly, the boys in the dairy talked about the new calf, and one mentioned it to his father, school rabbi Shmaria Shore.

Shore, still not sure if this is really *his* story, if he belongs in it, takes pains to deny the report, published during the media storm Melody set off, that his son ran home saying, "Dad, a red heifer, a red heifer," almost as if he was announcing the coming of the messiah. Fact is, Shore didn't pay much attention when his son mentioned the calf. Two weeks later, when the subject came up again, he dropped by the dairy. She was red, but there were white hairs on her udders. Shore wasn't sure, but to be safe he told Jubi not to apply the cream that removes a cow's horns: To fulfill the requirements of Numbers 19, the heifer must be in mint condition. Seeking advice, he called the state-appointed regional rabbi, who was uninterested. So he phoned someone who would know whether the calf qualified, and would care: Rabbi Yisrael Ariel, founder of the Temple Institute in Jerusalem's Old City and a central figure in the movement on the far edge of Israel's religious right dedicated to establishing the Third Temple— not as faraway hope, but as a practical program, a pressing need. Finding a red heifer is one precondition to building the Temple. Another, it's generally assumed, is removing the Dome of the Rock from the Temple Mount.

Ariel said he'd come with a colleague to look Melody over. Instead, Shore recalls, "two or three minibuses" arrived one March day, and fifteen or twenty people, the Who's Who of the Temple movement, piled out. Ariel came, as did Yehudah Etzion, who had spent years in prison as the ideologue of the terrorist underground organized by West Bank settlers in the 1980s; and Adir Zik, an announcer on the settlers' pirate radio station known for his fiery rhetoric. Jubi let the cow out, Ariel and his colleagues examined her and ruled that, so far, she fit the requirements. The question was whether she'd stay red till the third year of her life, as required to serve for the sacrifice. Someone passed out wine to toast, "To life." In a snapshot, schoolboys and black-jacketed rabbis are dancing in a circle in the farmyard as if at a wedding.

The next day, a newspaper broke the story. Zik spoke about the red heifer on his radio show. The madness about Melody had begun.

One of the first calls came from an Israeli TV anchorman: how about bringing Melody to the studio? Shore refused; he didn't like the media circus. It didn't matter. Press photographers arrived. The rabbi, sans calf, appeared on national TV. The *Boston Globe*'s man did a story, and other American correspondents followed. In the next few months, Shore says, a CNN crew made a pilgrimage to the red heifer, as did crews from ABC and CBS, and from Japan, Holland, France.

If much of the world's media reported on Melody in a bemused tone, as a story about the strange things people believe, not everyone saw the cow as a joke. On the opinion page of the influential Israeli daily *Ha'aretz,* columnist David Landau argued that the security services should see the red heifer as "a four-legged bomb" potentially more dangerous than any terrorist: "It's equal, in its ability to set the entire region on fire, to the power of non-conventional weapons in the hands of Iranian ayatollahs." Landau, it happens, is doubly unusual: an Orthodox journalist in the often stridently secular Israeli press, and a proponent of peace in the mostly hawkish world of Israeli religious Orthodoxy. He understood the expectations of building the Temple that the cow could inspire among Jewish religious nationalists, and its potential for inciting war with the Muslim world. "A bullet in the head," he wrote, "is, according to the best traditions, the solution of security services in such cases . . ."

Too shrill? As Landau alluded, the nameless agents of Israel's Shin Bet domestic security force, caught offguard by the assassination of Prime Minister Yitzhak Rabin in November 1995, had underestimated the power of faith in the past. At Kfar Hasidim, Melody was moved from the cowshed to "solitary confinement" in the school's petting zoo, where she could be kept slightly safer from the visitors arriving daily. A dog was posted to guard her. It couldn't guard against sprouting white hairs.

UNQUESTIONABLY, the reactions to Melody seem bizarre. But there are three very solid reasons for the fears and hopes she engendered: the past, the present, and most of all the future.

Numbers 19 is one of the most opaque sections in scripture. A red heifer, "faultless, wherein is no blemish, and upon which never came a yoke," is to be slaughtered, and its body burned entirely to ash. Paradoxically, this sacrifice must be performed outside the Temple, yet the heifer's ash becomes the key to the sanctuary: It alone can cleanse a man or woman tainted by contact with human death.

For, says the biblical text, anyone who touches a corpse, or bone, or grave, anyone who even enters the same room as a dead body, is rendered impure, and must not enter the Temple. Yet proximity to death is an unavoidable part of life, and sacrifice was how Israelites served God. So to free a person of impurity, says Numbers, mix the heifer's cinder with water, and sprinkle the mixture on him. As Jewish tradition read those verses, the heifer really had to be faultless. Two white hairs would disqualify it. The rarest possible beast was essential to purify a priest who'd attended his own father's burial, or to allow any Israelite who'd been in the presence of a corpse to share in the sacrificial cult.

Presumably, the ritual seemed reasonable three thousand years ago. Impurity, as a modern Bible scholar points out, was a real thing, and was contagious, virulent, an affliction of the soul. The rite of the red heifer, writes Tel Aviv University's Baruch Schwartz, meant that "God will dwell among and protect His people" only if death has no dominion in the sanctuary. Our modern minds get half a fingerhold on the blank rockface of the idea, but no more. We can't climb up it. Which puts us in good company: By the classical era, first-century sage Yohanan ben Zakkai asserted that the commandments of Numbers 19 were beyond human grasp, to be performed only out of obedience and love for God—another concept many moderns find distant.

The last ashes of the last red heifer ran out sometime after the Romans razed the Temple in Jerusalem in the year 70. Every Jew became impure by reason of presumed contact with death which, practically speaking, didn't matter much because there was no sanctuary to enter and sacrifice had ceased being the center of Judaism. The tenth heifer logically belonged to the imagined time of the messiah because a rebuilt temple also did.

Except that today, the absent ashes of the red heifer have a new function. They are a crucial factor in the political and strategic balance of the Middle East.

Over nineteen hundred years have passed since the Temple's destruction, but its location—give or take a few crucial meters—is still a hard physical reality. It is the most contested piece of real estate on earth: a thirty-five-acre not-quite-rectangular enclosure on the southeast corner of the Old City of Jerusalem. If the mountain of the Lord doesn't look much like a mountain, it's because of earthworks carried out by the Herod the Great, the Roman-appointed vassal king of Judea, in the first century B.C.E.* Herod expanded the Temple court-yards, at the top of the hill known as Mt. Moriah, presumably because the appearance of glorifying God would glorify himself. To do so, he built huge retaining walls, turning the hill into a stone box. In princi-ple, the Temple Mount remains the most sacred site in Judaism. In practice, the place to which Jews have come to worship for centuries is the base of one of Herod's retaining structures, the Western Wall, or, as it was once commonly called, the Wailing Wall, in reference to Jews mourning for the ruined sanctuary. The stones are huge. At the bot-tom the crevices are packed with the crumpled notes of prayer pushed into them by worshipers.

But the Mount itself isn't in ruins. As Al-Haram al-Sharif, the Noble Sanctuary, it is the third-holiest site in Islam. Near its center stands the Dome of the Rock—a gilded half-sphere rising from an oc-tagonal base. The protuberance of bedrock inside the shrine tradition-ally marks the spot where Muhammad ascended to heaven on his nighttime journey from Mecca nearly fourteen hundred years ago. It probably also marks—a shimmering uncertainty is part of the land-scape—the location of the Holy of Holies, the sacred core of the Jew-ish Temple. At the southern end of the esplanade is Al-Aqsa Mosque. To confuse matters, the name has a double meaning: Today any Mus-lim, at least in Jerusalem and the West Bank and Israel, will insist that the entirety of the Haram is Al-Aqsa, including the open squares be-tween the shrines and the olive grove north of the Dome, all sacred ground.

Perhaps human beings should recognize that God's mountain could have more than one name, more than one path up it. In practice, packing two kinds of sanctity into one place is like stuffing it with two volatile chemicals. A glance at the Mount testifies that any effort to build the Temple where it once stood—the one place where Jewish tradition says it can be built again—would mean removing shrines sa-cred to hundreds of millions of Muslims, from Morocco to Indonesia.

* *The following abbreviations are used for dates: B.C.E.—Before Common Era (rather than B.C.); C.E.—Common Era (rather than A.D.)*

An attempt to dedicate even a piece of the enclosure to Jewish prayer would mean slicing that piece out of the Islamic precincts.

On June 7, 1967, the third day of the Six-Day War, Israeli troops took East Jerusalem, bringing the Temple Mount under Jewish rule for the first time since the year 70. Israel's leaders decided to leave the Mount, Al-Haram al-Sharif, in Muslim hands. The decision kept the ingredients for holy war apart, just barely. Instead of the Mount, the Western Wall drew Jewish pilgrimage.

Yet the separation made by the civil government would not have worked without a hand from Jewish religious authorities. From the Six-Day War on, Israel's leading rabbis have overwhelmingly ruled that Jews should not enter the gates of the Mount. One of the most commonly cited reasons—even if the sages have not always explained their decree in full—is that under religious law, every Jew is presumed to have had contact with the dead. For lack of a red heifer's ashes, there is simply nothing to be done about it: no way for Jews to purify themselves to enter the sacred square, no way for Judaism to reclaim the Mount, no way to rebuild the Temple. Government officials and military leaders could only regard the requirement for the missing heifer as a stroke of sheer good fortune preventing conflict over the Mount.

In any legal system, a technical ruling can mask deeper consider-ations. The statement issued by Israel's Chief Rabbinate in the sum-mer of 1967 ends with the prayer that "the Holy One Blessed be He will speed our full Redemption, and we will joyously . . . visit His sanc-tuary and serve with a full heart, quickly and in our days." Decoded in traditional manner, that would mean that the Temple will be rebuilt only when God sends his messiah: in a future for which the faithful should pray and wait. Conquering the real estate isn't enough.

Unless the future is *now*. Unless the waiting is over, unless history is literally drawing to its climax, ancient prophecies coming true be-fore our eyes.

That idea, too, can strike the modern mind as foreign, but this time the distance is an illusion. Belief in the End is part of our lives. Tens of millions of people speak of it openly in the traditional language of religion. Widespread predictions that the year 2000 marked the hour were only one expression of that belief. After the year is past, the last of the three zeros clicked over to 1, it's likely to grow stronger. Many more people, even those who laugh at religious language, have held a fragment of a hope that they are living at history's dénouement. Some, for instance, would have at least an embarrassed memory of a tremble on hearing words like:

> *We are stardust*
> *We are golden*
> *And we've got to get ourselves*
> *Back to the garden.*

The idea that human beings are in exile from the Garden, that we're on the verge of returning, wasn't born in the 1960s. Pause before you mock.

The concept of an End of Days, in which God's kingdom will be established on earth, exists in Christianity, Judaism, and Islam, though it's often suppressed in all three faiths. If there's one thing that has made it difficult to repress that subversive idea today, it is the existence of the state of Israel. The creation of Israel in 1948 and its conquest of Jerusalem in 1967 aren't ordinary history: For those inclined to hear them, they're divine proclamations that the hour is near. For literalists, the venue for the final events is Jerusalem—and at its center, the Temple Mount.

This may be myth, but the Mount is not a mythical spot. It is in the midst of a very earthly city. It is a short stroll from the business districts of West and East Jerusalem. The dispute over who owns the Mount is one of the most intractable issues of real-world Middle Eastern politics. The conflict is intense because of the Mount's place in history—but even more because of its place in the future. For a small but growing group of Jews on the Israeli religious right, every day since 1967 has been a missed opportunity to begin building the Third Temple. For a far larger number of conservative Christians elsewhere in the world—and particularly in the United States—building that Temple is an essential condition for the Second Coming. And for many Muslims, any attempt to destroy the shrines of Al-Aqsa is a sign that the Hour is at hand.

Should such beliefs matter to anyone else? In 1984, the Shin Bet stumbled onto the Jewish settler underground's plot to blow up the

Dome of the Rock. One of the group's leaders explained that among the "spiritual difficulties" that kept them from carrying out the attack was that it is forbidden to enter the Temple Mount because of impurity caused by contact with the dead—that is, they lacked the ash of a red heifer. In a verdict in the case, one judge wrote that if the plan had been carried out, it would have "exposed the State of Israel and the entire Jewish people to a new Holocaust." The danger hasn't gone away: The Temple Mount is potentially a detonator of full-scale war, and a few people trying to rush the End could set it off.

JOURNALISTS WEREN'T ALONE in coming to see Melody. The first to flock to see her were the ultra-Orthodox, the Jews who most vehemently criticize modernity. The ultra-Orthodox traditionally reject any human efforts to bring redemption. For that reason, they opposed the establishment of Israel. But the red calf was all right, she was a proper miracle, a sign God could be ready to act Himself. Other Israelis followed. By Passover, a month after the first news reports, visitors were arriving in droves, seven or ten or twelve cars at once arriving at the gate of the agricultural school.

Interior Minister Eli Suissa didn't visit Melody, but he did comment on her. Suissa's ultra-Orthodox Shas party is usually moderate on the issue of Israeli-Palestinian relations. Suissa stands out as the hawk of the party. In a speech to right-wing professors, he repeated the rabbinic position since 1967, saying that he wasn't interested in Jewish control of the Temple Mount for religious reasons. But, he added, "when use is made of the red cow that's been discovered, and the people of Israel can be purified through its ashes, I'll change my mind." That is, the status quo could remain in force until Melody reached her third year and became the full-grown heifer required by scripture.

That detail didn't escape the foreign visitors—mostly born-again Christians—who were pulling up at Kfar Hasidim. There were days when three tourist buses arrived, or five, or ten. A group of one hundred clergymen from Texas met with Shore and asked when the cow would be ready. In two years, he answered, when it was in the third year of its life. Immediately, Shore says, they got very excited, and winked at each other, and started talking about the year 2000: Melody would be ready on time.

Reverend Irvin Baxter, a Pentecostal minister from Richmond, Indiana, made Melody the cover story in his *Endtime* magazine, which provides "World Events from a Biblical Perspective," then published a follow-up article when he was able to come and visit himself. To his 40,000 Christian subscribers, he explained Maimonides' view that the tenth red heifer would be offered in the messiah's time—and then noted that under the diplomatic schedule then in effect for the Oslo accords, "the final status of Jerusalem and the Temple Mount is to be settled by May of 1999. It's in 1999 that Melody will be three years of age . . ." In other words, the calf, the medieval Jewish sage, and the Israel-PLO peace agreement all proved that the Temple would be in place for the End Times to begin by the millennium's end. Televangelist Jack Van Impe likewise noted that "scripture requires the red heifer be sacrificed at the age of three," and asked breathlessly, "Could Melody's ashes be used for Temple purification ceremonies as early as 2000?"

Here and there such enthusiasm sparked complaints. In his Internet newsletter, Dallas televangelist Zola Levitt said he'd received too many letters about the calf. "If the Christian community had as much concern about the Lord, salvation, prophecy, and correct doctrine in churches as it has about the red heifer, we would be fine Christians," he wrote. Apparently Levitt's objections to interest in the Temple didn't go too far; the same newsletter carried an upbeat interview with Gershon Salomon, leader of an Israeli group dedicated to building the Temple. The writer suggested that Salomon's efforts were part of "the fulfillment of biblical prophecy [which] marches onward, moving inexorably toward the Second Coming of the Messiah." But Levitt—a Jew-turned-Christian-fundamentalist who promotes proselytizing to the Jews along with support for Israel and rejection of the Mideast peace process—had another beef: The rabbis wouldn't come through. "With their almost pathological insistence on the letter of the law, I suspect they will reject the heifer," he said. The polemic against "legalism," a shopworn standard of theological anti-Judaism, gained a new use—"the law" could keep the Jews from fulfilling their role of building a Temple to facilitate the Christian apocalypse, and once again the Jews would fail Jesus.

The concerns in other quarters were different. Early in the summer of 1999, I dropped in at the offices of the Al-Aqsa Association, a group linked to the radical wing of the Islamic Movement in Israel, to see Ahmad Agbariya. The office is on the main street of Umm al-Fahm, an Israeli Arab town a half-hour drive from Kfar Hasidim (drive south past Armageddon and turn right). Green flags and banners on the street proclaim, "Islam is the solution" and "There is no god but God." Agbariya is in charge of the association's efforts to develop the mosques at Al-Haram al-Sharif. Three large, framed photos of the holy site decorate his office; in one, taken on a Friday during the holy month of Ramadan, rows of worshipers fill every inch of outdoor space. The Jews, he told me, "intend to build the Third Temple." Was there a target date, I asked. "All I know is that three years ago they said a red heifer had been born," he said, "and that in three years they'd start building. Three years will be up in August 1999."

Agbariya wasn't the only one worried. *Deflecting the Arrows from the Book, "The Life of the Community of Islam,"* an Islamic tract on the approaching apocalypse published in Cairo, also discusses "the red cow . . . born recently in Haifa, in what they call Israel." What that event portends, explains author Amin Jamal al-Din, is that the appearance of the Antichrist—a sign of darkness before the final dawn in Islam as in Christianity—"is an arrow's shot away or closer." For when the cow "reaches its full development in the third year of its life, it will be sacrificed at the Temple of Solomon, and the person who will do this will be their king, their redeemer, the Antichrist." Jamal al-Din and Irvin Baxter agreed on one thing: The folks with the cow had a star role on the stage of the End.

RABBI SHMARIA SHORE is miscast in that role. He didn't ask for it, but then neither did he choose to escape it. He's fragmented.

We meet one day in a Jerusalem café frequented by professors, artists, writers. The waitresses are in tanktops. If Shore, a thin man with a long steel-gray beard and a white button-down shirt—the standard attire of an Orthodox rabbi—feels misplaced, he doesn't show it. He begins conversations in Hebrew, but his accent is as American as mine, and I switch to English. When he changes languages, I hear a cadence—a vowel stretched in diffuse amazement at the world, a consonant rounded off at the end of a word—familiar from another time: the sixties, dorm rooms, and campus coffee shops.

The former Steven Shore grew up in New Haven, Connecticut. Black Panther founder Bobby Seale's murder trial opened in the city in tandem with the Chicago 8 trial, Shore tells me, as the start of his own biography. "In high school I was radical, I was against the war. . . . There were four days of protests, with tear gas on the New Haven Green. And the prosecutor was one of my parents' best friends." From there, with the help of Antioch College's work-study program, he began a tour of the era's last blazing. He spent four months in Berkeley, where he worked in a school for disturbed boys; he took classes in Zen. In the summer of '72 he lived in a Boston commune that ran an organic restaurant. "Every night we'd go do something else, Sufi dancing, or yoga, or things I wouldn't want to mention." But he was torn between "the sincere part and the feeling people were just having fun. Like the drug scene. . . . By my first year of college, I'd read a lot, you know, Aldous Huxley's *Doors of Perception*. And then I remember one guy saying to another what are you doing tonight, and he says, 'Watching a movie and taking acid.' " The world wanted to change, the rabbi across the table tells me, but there was a dark side. "Woodstock—people romanticized it, but three people died."

He studied for a year in Grenoble—philosophy at the university, Christianity with a Jesuit group. He was, it seems to me, a spiritual bungee jumper: "I really got into French culture. I wouldn't speak English." In a visit to Lucerne, a divinity student asked him if he was Catholic or Protestant. "I told him 'Jewish.' He pulled out a book in Hebrew. I didn't know Hebrew." By the next summer, he was in Israel—"instead of going to Nepal," he says. The journey from antiwar protests to Merkaz Harav yeshivah, the talmudic institute that inspired the West Bank settlement movement, he would argue, is not as long as it seems. Religious Zionism, the kind of Orthodox Judaism he chose, asserts that human beings are acting to bring the world's final redemption. Jews returning to their land and building a state is a piece of that. "There's a basic feeling that the world is progressing toward something. What's nice is it exists not only on a Jewish level. . . . Communism also believes in perfection of the world. 'Getting better, all the time,' as John Lennon said. It was electrifying to be in the world in

Cambridge in the summer of '72. There was a feeling that something was about to happen." The distance between him and the other man he could have been—living, say, in a Boston burb with a collection of old Joni Mitchell albums and the jazz he played on his Antioch radio show—was the small extra willingness to throw oneself into a new hope rather than say that hoping for a world perfected here and now had proved extravagant.

But the cow was a problem. He'd point out to visitors that it might not fit the biblical requirements. He'd tell Christian groups that if they wanted to see proof of the messiah's approach they should look at the boys from Russia and Ethiopia in his school, Jews returning from four corners of the earth. The "Redemption is not just technical. It reflects spiritual changes in the Jewish people and the whole world. It's not as if God is wringing his hands because a red heifer hasn't been born yet." The teachings he follows put building the Temple only at the very end of the spiritual process. He still doesn't like shallowness.

Yet when Melody was born, he did not say, as he quotes his spiritual master Rabbi Tzvi Yehudah Kook responding to reports of a red calf twenty years ago, "Nu, so there are brown cows in the world." He called the Temple Institute. When I ask why, he answers slowly. You can know people best by their contradictions, and this is one of Shore's contradictions. "Whether this was *the* red heifer, or just to study about the red heifer, I had the responsibility to find out if it was kosher. I was doing my duty." Melody solved the problem. By the age of a year and a half, she sprouted a clump of white hairs at the tip of her tail. The story was published, but news of a letdown travels more quietly than reports producing high anxiety. Jubi moved her to the cowshed, and removed her horns.

Yet under instructions from Shore, he used semen from a red bull to inseminate her. Shore's teachers taught that people acting in the world are bringing the messiah, and that the Temple would be built. They also said to wait for God's time to build it. Put one foot on the gas pedal of sacred history, they said, and one on the brake. As happens in movements to perfect the world, the machine bucks and bursts out of control.

■

THE COWS ON THE SCREEN graze on barely rolling pastureland. They're red—some appear pure red—and there are lots of them. The sky is gray, the occasional tree is barren of leaves. On the audio, two men speak in strong southern accents, over the cattle's low grunts. We see a young calf, and Reverend Clyde Lott's voice says, "This is really an extraordinary heifer, from the standpoint of her length of body, her massiveness, her stoutness of bone . . . the quality of the hair she has on her, it is the color that rabbis are looking for."

Lott knows cows the way he knows to walk or speak; the knowing is bred into him. Knowledge of what rabbis want in a cow has come more recently. He passes in front of the camera, a square-faced, silver-haired man, his wide shoulders hunching in a sweatshirt insufficient for Nebraska at winter's end. He tells Reverend Guy Garner to swing the camera at a calf which, he says, "from a color standpoint, is very very close to what is required to be a Numbers 19 heifer . . . a heifer to meet all the qualifications of *parah adumah,* from the Babylonian tractate of Parah Adumah," the Hebrew words battered by his drawl. "Not all of these will go but there are some individuals here who will be selected to go to Israel," he tells us. With the help of jumbo jets and contributions from born-again American Christians who deeply love Israel, Clyde Lott and Guy Garner are ready to drive hundreds—eventually thousands—of head of cattle onto the set for the End of Days.

Lott, son and grandson of cattlemen, grew up on a farm in Mississippi. By his twenties, he was on the success track on what he calls the "high-tech" side of farming, producing show cattle, "the highest of the highest quality," exhibited in shows across the Southeast. He sold hundreds of champions. He was also, it seems, dissatisfied.

Lott was raised a Southern Baptist, a tradition that, he says, "didn't put a lot of moral restraints on my life . . . I realized there had to be quite a bit of improving in my life." One night he attended a Pentecostal church—part of the branch of Christianity that combines biblical literalism with an all-out religious enthusiasm, a certainty that in these Last Days, men and women have direct access to the Holy Spirit. Swept up by the Spirit, Pentecostals "talk in tongues"—speaking what are for them the inspired words of unknown languages and what for outsiders is babble—and practice faith healing. Often they hear what

God wants of them. Their exultation and willingness to hear the Voice from without inspires disdain even from other conservative Protestants—and has turned Pentecostalism into what may be the quickest-growing form of Christianity around the globe. Lott went home "and got down by my bed, and repented, and felt the Holy Spirit enter into me."

Soon after, he began a correspondence course that led him to ordination in the Pentecostal Assemblies of Jesus Christ. The course was for himself; he's never served as a pastor, though he's a gifted preacher: A fundraising video shows him shout out extemporaneous prayer, fists pounding the air, then switch to a sermon voice that reminds one of the look of well-finished wood, polished to a sheen but with the natural grain showing.

At the end of the 1980s, Lott recalls, "there was a wave of prophecy preaching going through Mississippi, and the question was when is Israel going to build the Temple." For that, Lott knew, a red heifer was needed. Yet studying his scripture one night he hit Genesis 30,* where Jacob tells his father-in-law Laban what he'll take as salary after having received both Leah and Rachel in marriage: "I will pass through all thy flock today, removing from thence all the speckled and spotted cattle . . ." Or so says the King James version—in which, Lott didn't realize, a crucial word is easily misunderstood. If the Israelites' original cattle were speckled and spotted, the cattleman-preacher wondered, how'd they ever get a red heifer?

The question weighed on him for months. Until one day, when he was working in the field and a piece of equipment broke down and Lott got in his car to head for town, the car took him instead to the state capital of Jackson, where he strode uninvited into the office of Ray Manning, international trade director for the State of Mississippi. Lott enjoys telling of the "cold shock" on the official's face at seeing him, straight from the hay field, dirty, smelly. The bizarre meeting eventually produced a letter to the agriculture attaché at the U.S. embassy in Athens, responsible in his specialty for the entire Middle East.

---

* *Full citations for biblical references appear in the endnotes. Citations from the Hebrew Bible ("Old Testament") are from the 1917 Jewish Publication Society translation; in Christian contexts, from the King James version. New Testament citations are from the King James version.*

Manning explained that he'd been approached by a cattle producer who'd made this offer: "Red Angus cattle suitable for Old Testament Biblical sacrifices, will have no blemish or off color hair, genetically red . . . also excellent beef quality."

What Lott did has a logic. Cattle-raising today is biotech. It was his life's work. But did it *mean* anything? Lott isn't the only technical person pulled to the vision of Temple-building because it promises that a technical skill is essential to the world's salvation. Nor is he the only one in our technological age to read the Bible itself as a tech manual, installation instructions for the final, fantastic upgrade of the universe.

The letter bounced from Athens back to New York to the U.S. embassy in Tel Aviv to Israel's Religious Affairs Ministry to the Temple Institute in Jerusalem's Old City, where it landed on Rabbi Chaim Richman's desk. It moved from the Mississippi biblical literalist to the Israeli fringe group either by chance or, as Lott and his partners for a number of years at the Temple Institute would see it, by the unswerving hand of Providence.

CHAIM RICHMAN grew up in Massachusetts in a Jewish home with little religion. Under circumstances he won't discuss—Richman possesses the ideologue's certainty that what matters is the cause, not himself—he became Orthodox and gained a rabbinic education. By 1982 he'd moved to Israel, and sometime afterward joined the staff of the Temple Institute—part of a self-imagined vanguard who will restore the Jews to their proper status in the world as "a sign that God exists" by virtue of performing sacrifices at a rebuilt Temple.

Richman speaks in an anxious, sarcastic voice that hovers precisely between mocking himself and taunting his listener. Thin, dark-haired, sidecurls tucked behind his ears, gazing through small wire-framed glasses with amazement at how the world has misunderstood him, he is Woody Allen's counterlife, the ultra-Orthodox Jew as whom Allen has imagined himself on-screen. "I don't have to apologize for . . ." is the standard way he half-apologetically starts ideas about the Jews' place in the world. Fact is, he likes to quote Allen, among others. "Israel has been here fifty-one years. The question, to paraphrase Jack Nicholson, is 'Is this as good as it gets?' The Bible says the Jews are the chosen people. Does that mean we're the best pediatricians and Wall Street brokers?" he says, explaining the need for a Temple.

Lott's letter set off several months of phone conversations, after which the Pentecostal cattleman arrived in Jerusalem in 1990 to meet Richman and Rabbi Ariel. As Lott tells the story, Richman asked him how many cows would have to be imported to produce a red heifer in Israel. Two hundred, Lott replied. And how much would they cost? For the high-quality cows needed, Lott estimated, $2,000 a head. Richman translated for Ariel, who speaks no English; the two rabbis spoke furiously in Hebrew; Lott asked what the problem was. Twenty thousand per cow is a lot, Richman said. No, $2,000, Lott repeated, adding, "We're not trying to take advantage of you as you turn to God." Again, Richman translated and the rabbis talked furiously.

Then Richman told him a two-thousand-year-old story, preserved in the Talmud and other rabbinic texts, of a wealthy gentile named Dama, son of Netina, who lived in Ashkelon. In the version of the story that Richman told to Lott, a delegation of rabbis went to Dama to buy a jewel for the high priest's breastplate, in the days when the Temple stood. They offered one hundred gold dinars; Dama refused, saying the key to the lockbox was under his sleeping father's pillow. The rabbis assumed that was a negotiating ploy, steadily raised their offer to one thousand pieces of gold, and finally left. Soon after, Dama caught up to them and announced that his father had awoken and he could sell the jewel. So the rabbis counted out one thousand coins, but Dama would only take the original hundred. Here, as Lott recalls the story, Dama says he doesn't want "to take advantage of you when you turn to God." His reward: God causes a red heifer to be born in his herd.

That's not the only version of the tale, part of a cycle that celebrates Dama the idolator as the paragon of honoring one's father. In the ancient texts the hero says nothing of God, only of not wanting to make a profit from filial respect—and eventually he makes good his loss by selling the red heifer. But the version Lott was told, with the pious gentile who takes a tenth of what he could get, fit the hour. For Richman and Ariel, Lott became a walking literary allusion. As for

Lott, he'd later tell Christian audiences back home that *every* time Israel needed a red heifer, it had come from a gentile. In conversation, he stresses that "God has called gentile people to help Israel" many times—Hiram, who helped Solomon build his Temple; Oskar Schindler . . .

That was the first of Lott's trips to Israel. He and Richman began exploring the country, looking for the right spot to raise red cows. The search first took them to the Golan Heights, then to the West Bank: precisely the areas whose future would be determined in peace talks, precisely the land whose conquest by Israel—in the eyes of both Israeli religious rightists and countless conservative Christians abroad—had signaled fulfillment of biblical prophecies of the End of Days.

Back in Mississippi, Lott fasted and prayed, "seeking God's face" for guidance. Strangers called him: a preacher who'd found Lott's name on his desk and who'd had a vision of a valley where the cows should go; an expert on grasses who offered a strain of alfalfa grass whose roots would dive toward hidden underground water and make wilderness bloom. For Lott, those miracles showed he was being guided by God. That's the kind of certain faith that has fed media stories suggesting he was one more kook in the turn-of-the-millennium American landscape. Another exegesis makes more sense: Lott's name was getting out, people who'd never met him were inspired by his plan, in one significant swath of American society he was not nuts but cold sane.

On a quest for perfect pastures, Lott, Richman, and Ariel visited the West Bank settlements of Shiloh and Elon Moreh, then moved on to the Jordan Valley. Afterward Ariel pointed out that they'd inadvertently retraced, in reverse, the Israelites' footsteps as they'd entered the land under Joshua—another sign they were on the right track. "Yasser Arafat," Lott later explained to potential supporters back home, "is trying to take possession of this land. . . . Now there is a plan to take this land, fence it and take it out of disputed status. . . . It is now Israel's." Christians would help Israel stake that claim. "We feel"—Lott likes the first person plural—"that God is going to directly involve his Church."

In 1994, Richman visited Mississippi, a country undoubtedly more foreign for him than Israel ever was. Lott took him to the barn and showed him four heifers. One caught his attention. Richman stared, moved back, checked her from another side, examined the young animal for fifteen minutes, and finally declared: "You see that heifer. That heifer is going to change the world"—the first cow in two thousand years to satisfy Numbers 19. Lott had proved he could deliver. Richman, though, apparently still wanted a heifer born and raised in Israel, to insure it remained unblemished.

In the meantime, Lott's idea was changing form. Israeli growers, he'd found, were raising the wrong cattle for producing meat. He felt "guided by the hand of God" to change that. Rather than bringing a few hundred Red Angus to Israel, he'd bring fifty thousand. The "restoration of Israel"—the term Christians concerned with the End have used for generations to refer to the prophesied return of the Jews to their land—must also, he decided, be the "restoration" of Israel's livestock industry.

Lott gave up his family farm. At a Nebraska ranch, he began raising Red Angus bred to the highest standards, which means, he explains, "marbling in the meat, white flakes through the flesh . . . easy calving, hardiness . . . longevity." To further the effort, the Association of Beef Cattle Breeders in Israel set up a professional board whose members included Lott, Richman, and several Israeli Agriculture Ministry officials. Ranchers who could take the cows were found. The "hosts" did not need to have any interest in red heifers for sacrifice. Lott was making an offer they couldn't refuse: He'd supply them with perfect beef cattle. In the spring of 1998, Canaan Land Restoration of Israel, Inc., a nonprofit body dedicated to bringing cattle to Israel, was established, with pastors scattered from California to Pennsylvania as officers and advisory board members. Lott appeared at churches, raising funds, and on Christian TV. Donation cards, adorned with sepia photos of grazing cows, allowed supporters to sponsor the purchase of "1 red heifer—$1,000.00," a half-heifer or quarter, or "1 air fare (1 cow)" at $341. A fundraising letter exhorted, "Remember, Gen. 12:2–3: 'I will bless those who bless you, and whoever curses you, I will curse' "—a verse often cited by evangelicals as a reason to support Israel—and expressed thanks for "this opportunity to share a portion of this monumental work that the God of Abraham, Isaac and Jacob is doing at the hands of these simple men of faith in these last days." The idea that Christians should "bless Israel" with cows had grown beyond one man's obsession.

GUY GARNER is a broad-built, relaxed man in his fifties, with an accent that erases the difference between "tie" and "tire"—the latter being what he sold for "twenty-something years," along with serving as pastor of the Apostolic Pentecostal Church of Porterdale, Georgia, until he gave up the business to commute to Israel and handle Canaan Land's affairs.

Garner admits to knowing little about cows. That's not what brought him in. On a Christian tour to Israel at the start of the nineties, he found himself in the Temple Institute's exhibition of utensils for the Third Temple, his group guided by Chaim Richman. Suddenly, "I felt that God called on me to . . . study Endtime prophecy." He devoted the next four years to studying scripture, praying, and fasting—and talking with Lott. Among the insights he gained, he told me in our first meeting, is that Daniel 7:4—a snippet of a vision that describes a lion with eagle's wings—actually forecasts the United States gaining independence from England: The lion is England, and the wings that are "plucked" off him and given a "man's heart" are America, whose symbol is an eagle. Earlier the same week, a pastor from the Midwest had presented precisely the same reading of Daniel to me as *his* revelation.

Finding the nations in Daniel's beasts is a spiritual concern shared by countless conservative Christians. What makes Garner unusual is his concern with the Bible's predictions of the role of agriculture, and particularly cattle, in the Last Days. He and his wife Jean arrived at my office with several yellow legal-pad pages with verses copied out by hand. "In that day shall thy cattle feed in large pastures," Garner cites Isaiah 30:23, and adds a gloss: "IN that day meaning = Last days, or end of the Holy Ghost dispensation of time."

The cows, Guy Garner stresses, are "a giveaway to the Jewish people." The growers get them and the calves they produce free of charge, with just two obligations: After a number of years, they must provide Canaan Land with the same number of young cows as they originally received. And along the way, Canaan Land has the right to examine every newborn calf, and to take any it judges to be "special"—likely to qualify as a red heifer and speed establishment of the Temple. "We've always said that those who bless Israel will be blessed," Jean Garner happily affirms. The couple's dedication is immense: Not only have they given up their business and church and moved thousands of miles from their children and grandchildren, they draw no salary from Canaan Land. "Lots of changes," I comment, and Jean Garner for once drops her smile and looks at me intently.

"Do you like changes?" she says.

"She doesn't like things to change," her husband adds.

Yet who is supposed to reap the real benefit of bringing red heifers to Israel? Garner's certainty he is helping Israel is sincere. But he has humbly cast himself as a bit character in an Endtime drama whose script is somewhat rougher on Jews than on born-again Christians. In fact, the Christians will safely exit to the wings, while on stage, the Jews will find themselves at the center of the apocalypse. To start things off, that demonic figure known to Christian theology as the Antichrist will appear and, as Garner explains, solve the problem of the Islamic shrines on the Temple Mount by negotiating "a peace, or false peace . . . that includes setting up the Temple." In the process, "the Muslim temple will come down." From there, the world plunges toward Armageddon. "It's not a pleasant thing to think about," Garner says glumly, "but God's going to do what He's going to do."

Speaking to me, Lott stressed that his thinking had shifted since he started out. Helping Israeli agriculture, not building the Temple or "trying to make Endtime," had become the focus. That stress could be a matter of the audience, a Jew, or of Lott's own contradictions. In his recorded fundraising talk, he explains that once the true Christians vanish from earth the moment before the apocalypse, ownership of the project will pass to the Jews left behind. What's more, thousands of embryos will be culled in advance from the new herds in Israel and frozen to protect them from history's final catastrophes. That way, following the Second Coming, "in the first one or two decades of [Jesus'] millennial reign, Israel will be able to take the embryos and place them in cows, so in one generation . . . they will have the greatest cow on the face of earth.

"What is going to come out of this," Lott concludes, "is the unfolding drama that God has been waiting for six thousand years to share with mankind to prove to world who He is. And he's chosen people just like us to be a part of the greatest Endtime plan that mankind could ever have experienced."

"I FEEL CLOSER TO HIM than I do to some of my own family," Clyde Lott once said of Chaim Richman. Yet at the end of 1998, the Jerusalem rabbi angrily broke his connection with Canaan Land Restoration. The immediate dispute was financial. A later letter from Richman suggests an additional cause for tension—an allegation that Lott had been filmed in a Florida church talking about spreading the Gospel in Israel.

But this was never a partnership made in heaven—and in that respect, it may be symbolic of the much wider alliance between some conservative Christians and pieces of the Israeli right. It's an alliance in which each side often assumes that the other is playing a role it doesn't understand itself, in which each often regards the other as an unknowing instrument for reaching a higher goal.

Take that verse in Genesis that originally worried Clyde Lott: "I will pass through all thy flock today, removing from thence all the speckled and spotted cattle," it says, and Lott wanted to know how such cattle could have produced red heifers. Except that in Hebrew, the verse says nothing of cows. It refers, unmistakably, to the offspring of sheep and goats—as any Orthodox Israeli schoolchild who was awake in second grade knows. In the English of King James's time, "cattle" meant any livestock, not specifically bovines. It is theoretically possible that neither Rabbi Richman nor Rabbi Ariel caught Lott's error when he told them what brought him, or that Richman still missed the mistake when he repeated the story in his pamphlet, *The Mystery of the Red Heifer: Divine Promise of Purity*, published in English. The alternative, read in the most favorable light, is that Richman regarded Lott's mistake as serving God's purpose. Asked about the matter, Richman responds, "I'm really not working with him. I just have no comment."

Richman speaks astringently of the "doormat theology" of Christians who see Israel as a stepping-stone to an apocalypse from whose horrors only Christians will be saved. An evangelical believer, he re-counts, once told him that when the events of the End begin, "I'm out of here"; Richman responded, "Jimmy, did you leave a forwarding address for *Time* magazine?" Speaking to me, he is equally dismissive of those who'd calculate the time of the End. Yet *The Mystery of the Red Heifer* concludes on a crescendo certain to inspire ecstasy in those wanting to find prophetic meaning in dates: In the Temple, the Levites had a psalm they sang for each day of the week. The Second Temple was destroyed on a Saturday night—and yet, says a rabbinic legend, the Levites inexplicably sang the song for Wednesday. Richman's answer to the riddle: Israel's troops took the Temple Mount on Wednesday, June 7, 1967. The Levites had really seen into the future, to the day that would mark the start of rebuilding the Temple and the birth of a "new era."

On the Christian side are those who want to "bless" Israel, and provide it with what they believe is the fuse for Armageddon. And perhaps also to convert the Israelis, another "blessing" since only the converted will make it through the Last Days.

Partnership or no, the work went on. In letters after the breakup, Richman said that "the Temple Institute has its own plans with regard to red heifers." Not that he sees removing the religious barrier of impurity as destabilizing Jerusalem. While he rejects the Muslim claim to the Temple Mount, he insists the Temple will come peacefully. Perhaps the Muslims will ask the Jews to build it.

And meanwhile Clyde Lott and Guy Garner, each in his own way, continued to prepare to bring whole herds to Israel to breed a red heifer. Unlike Melody, she will be no accident. The Jews will want to use her; so says prophecy. Prophecy, Guy Garner explains, is "history written in advance." He's not unusual in thinking so.

TWO

the history
of the future

It's a hard rain's a-gonna fall.

–BOB DYLAN

MY SON AND I are stretched out in a hammock between two trees in the backyard of the country house where we like to vacation. It's in the hills of the Galilee, away from the noise and exhaust of Jerusalem; from the yard we can see the town of Tiberias and all of Lake Kinneret—the Sea of Galilee—shimmering blue and the Golan Heights rising dark and green behind it. My ten-year-old son is reading *The Phantom Tollbooth* yet again and giggles occasionally. I'm reading *Nicolae: The Rise of Antichrist,* by Tim LaHaye and Jerry B. Jenkins. And suddenly I start laughing harder than my son, which I'm not supposed to do in the middle of a thriller about the end of the world, complete with nuclear war and famine and plague, and he wants to know what's funny, so I read him the paragraph where world-renowned journalist Buck Williams, in Jerusalem on a secret mission, learns that "he would find who he was looking for in Galilee, which didn't really exist anymore," a geographical point he repeats for emphasis two pages later.

"Dad, if the Galilee doesn't exist, where are we?" my son asks.

"Maybe we don't exist either."

A couple minutes later I'm giggling again: Now Buck has decided to make the three-hour journey to "Tiberius" (*sic*) by boat—one of the many touring boats that, in the book, ply the Jordan River. Which would be fine if the Jordan were really "deep and wide," as the song goes, but in reality it's a narrow trickle not fit for navigating.

The experience is jarring, like meeting someone who calls you by your name, insists he knows you, remembers you from a high school you didn't attend, a job you never had. I'm reading a book set largely in the country where I live—but not really, because the authors' Israel is a landscape of their imagination, and the characters called "Jews" might as well be named hobbits or warlocks. Israel and Jews are central to *Nicolae* and the other books of the hugely successful Left Behind series—but the country belongs to the map of a Christian myth; the people speak lines from a script foreign to flesh-and-blood Jews. In this respect as in others, the books faithfully represent the apocalyptic vision known by the unwieldly name of dispensational premillennialism—a vision that, among other things, misdirects relations between real-life Jews and born-again Christians, and in the worst case could bend the future of the Middle East.

Left Behind, the novel that gave the series its name, came out in 1995. Jenkins, a prolific ghostwriter, did the writing. LaHaye provided the framework of religious ideas. That's reason enough for the book to deserve attention, for in America's culture wars, Reverend Tim LaHaye has served as a general, a lesser-known comrade-in-arms to Jerry Falwell and Pat Robertson. LaHaye was a leader of the Moral Majority. He created the mid-eighties American Coalition for Traditional Values, an umbrella group dedicated to boosting the voting clout of the religious right. In 1987, he served briefly as cochairman of conservative Republican Jack Kemp's presidential campaign—resigning after a newspaper revealed that he'd called Catholicism "a false religion" and had written that the Jews' rejection of God was one reason for Jerusalem's troubles through history. He's still a member of the arch-conservative Council for National Policy. But his end-of-the-world novels may be his most successful effort yet to promote his views.

By early 2000, the first six Left Behind books had sold 11 million copies. And popularity was rising: The next LaHaye-Jenkins production, *The Indwelling*, had an initial print run of 2 million copies, most of it already sold in advance orders. Jenkins promised more installments, even as the pair pushed out a matching series for kids, and preparations proceeded for a movie version.

These numbers are readouts from a cultural weather station, revealing a storm front of religious feeling across much of America. Yet the data was long ignored. When *Assassins*, book number six in the series, was perched high on *The New York Times* bestseller list, top staffers at a major New York publishing house told me they'd never heard of it; scholars of American religion admitted to not having opened the Left Behind books. These were novels, not straightforward political or theological texts, put out by a religious publisher in Illinois, not a New York media giant. The weather report was coming from evangelical America, a cultural province that the rest of the country often treats as terra incognita.

When *Left Behind* opens, Captain Rayford Steele is piloting his 747 over the Atlantic and planning to make his move on his flight attendant, Hattie Durham. He has reason; his wife has become a religious zealot as a result of listening to Christian radio. The setting and syntax are airport fiction; the image is as old as the Book of Proverbs, where wisdom is personified as the woman to whom a man should remain faithful, and error is the seductive "strange woman" whose lips drip honey. But when Rayford strolls back into the plane's cabin, a terrified Hattie tells him that dozens of passengers have vanished—their clothes and jewelry left behind on their seats—in a single moment. Worldwide, we soon learn, millions are gone, including all young children, and fetuses out of wombs. Pilots have vanished from cockpits, their planes crashing; drivers have disappeared from behind the wheel, leaving highways strewn with piled-up cars. Among the missing are Rayford's wife and young son.

Those who remain are clueless to explain the disaster. But Rayford knows the truth, thanks to his wife's warnings, and so do readers. The disappearance is a stock scene, portrayed countless times before for the self-defined "Bible-believing" audience: in books and movies; in posters showing cars crash while their drivers float up toward heaven, in a comic strip where a near-crazed maternity nurse tells a doctor that the babies are all missing. Jesus has returned, the sincere believers and innocent babes have been physically lifted to heaven to meet him, and the rest of humanity has been left behind. The Rapture has taken place.

THE "RAPTURE OF THE CHURCH" is a phrase popularized by John Darby, a nineteenth-century British preacher. It's a key element of dispensational premillennialism—a theology that erects a complex scaffolding of interpretation around the Bible, yet claims to be nothing but the simple intent of scripture. The sources for the Rapture are Paul's New Testament epistles: In one he says that when "the Lord shall descend from heaven with a shout," living believers "shall be caught up . . . in the clouds, to meet with the Lord in the air." In another, the apostle prophesies that at the time of the Second Coming, "this corruptible shall put on incorruption." That dense language, Darby's disciples say, means that the End will begin with true Christians literally leaving the earth and gaining brand-new, immortal bodies. The word "Rapture" describes the joy of the believers—but the rest of humanity is about to face apocalyptic terror, seven years' worth, before God's kingdom on earth is established.

The burden of Jenkins and LaHaye's books is to make that terror real, tell what it would look like if it began today, in the world of jumbo jets and laptop computers, because another key tenet of Darby's premillennialism is that we're on the very verge of it happening, perhaps before you get to the period at the end of this sentence.

"Real" is a relative term. The Rapture is just the first of umpteen events in the Left Behind books that take place because the doctrine says they must. This is realism for people already living in unsettled expectation, or for those open to persuasion that the End is near. For the believers, the books offer not just the boon of imagining how it would all look, but the delicious satisfaction of being proven right. Emphasis in the original: " 'What a sweet, sweet woman,' " Rayford thinks when he finds his wife has vanished. " 'I never deserved her, never loved her enough.' . . . And Rayford cried himself to sleep." A half-hearted pastor, Bruce Barnes, who has failed to make the cosmic grade, now rues that he didn't want to tell people that "Jesus is the only way to God," that he didn't want them to "lump me with the weirdoes." The "weirdoes" have won.

As for other readers, they get a sermon as serialized suspense story: This is what awaits you here on earth after the Rapture—the Tribulation. Yes, you'll have a last chance to make the "transaction" of accepting the true faith. But you're still likely to die, for the disasters of the Book of Revelation must play themselves out.

By the end of the first book, a thirty-three-year-old Romanian politician named Nicolae Carpathia has turned the United Nations into the Global Community, a one-world government with its headquarters in the city of New Babylon outside Baghdad. His rise, we're told, fulfills the Book of Revelation's prophecy of the white horse of the apocalypse. At the opening of *Nicolae,* the third book in the series, Carpathia crushes real and alleged opposition with nuclear arms: That's the red horse, war, to be followed by the black horse and pale horse—famine and plague. Those are also the first four of Revelation's "seven seals." The sixth seal is the "Wrath of the Lamb," an earthquake that defies natural law by shaking the entire earth. Driving through Chicago suburbs in his all-options Land Rover, Buck sees the earth swallow cars and houses. Rayford, who has improbably become the Antichrist's personal pilot, is in midair, and sees the moon turn blood-red, as meteors scourge the earth. By Tribulation's halfway point, at the end of *Assassins,* we meet demon locusts and millions of ghostly horsemen, and half of the world's population is dead.

Jenkins and LaHaye would insist that today's believers won't even be around when all this happens. But as they describe it, the Tribulation backs up much of the American far-right agenda right now. Not only is the United Nations a tool for the Antichrist, there really is a conspiracy of world bankers, and it brings him to power. The only resistance to the despot is offered by America's militia movement. Survivalists are right: The Tribulation saints protect themselves by building a well-stocked underground shelter. The Antichrist promotes abortion and ecumenicalism, both part of a demonic program. The line between today and Tribulation is blurry; we live with one foot in the time of the End and tomorrow's evil gives moral force to today's urgent activism.

All of which makes eerie reading of the last pages of *Assassins:* Rayford, in Jerusalem and armed with a high-tech handgun, puts himself in God's guiding hand and is led toward firing at Nicolae, the political leader who promotes false peace, in the midst of a mass rally.

The authors have shown that there's one Jew whose psychology they can subliminally make sense of—Yigal Amir, the religious extremist who gunned down Yitzhak Rabin for the "sin" of making peace.

The Jews who actually appear in the series exist to serve the needs of the apocalypse. In his rise, Nicolae gets essential help from an Israeli scientist named Chaim Rosenzweig, who is not evil but misled: The archetypical Jew of the intolerant imagination, he inexplicably scores high in everything but theological truth. "The Messiah had come," Buck muses during a conversation with Chaim in book number two, *Tribulation Force,* "and the Jews left behind had missed him."

Another key to the Antichrist's rise is that he signs a seven-year peace treaty with Israel—which includes rebuilding the Temple. Jews, it appears, unanimously support the project; Muslims agree in the space of a sentence to move the Dome of the Rock to New Babylon. Both assertions are believable—if and only if you accept, with the authors, that scripture requires the reestablishment of the Temple so that the Antichrist can desecrate it halfway through the Tribulation. And it makes sense to hope for both the reestablishment and the desecration, along with the war, earthquake, and locusts, if they're essential preliminaries to establishment of a perfect era of divine rule on earth.

The apocalyptic screenplay demands something else of Jews: to convert in droves. Following the seventh chapter of Revelation, Jenkins and LaHaye speak of countless people accepting Jesus, but the Jews matter most. From among them, 144,000—representing 12,000 from each of the ancient twelve tribes—must become "witnesses," prime movers in conversion of gentiles. In the Left Behind books, the Jewish witnesses are personified by Tsion Ben-Judah, an Israeli rabbi who announces that a three-year study has led him to recognize Jesus as messiah. Ben-Judah's family is murdered by Jewish zealots. Smuggled out of Israel by Buck Williams, hidden in a survivalist shelter outside Chicago, Ben-Judah uses the Internet to preach to all of Planet Earth. His electronic sermons are all the more penetrating because he knows the Bible's original languages. Christianity's ancient, anxious amazement that the people who know the Old Testament best don't accept that it leads to Jesus (don't, in fact, accept that it is *Old* Testament) is at last disarmed. And another crucial problem is resolved: Darby's legacy insists that God's promises to the people of Israel must be read literally, as applying to the actual Jews; yet only those who accept Jesus can enter the Kingdom. Ergo, the Jews will convert. Again, the vision of the future drives present-day activism: It makes sense to proclaim love of Israel and the falseness of its faith, or to support both rebuilding the Temple and spreading the gospel among Jews.

"THE FUTURE IS CLEAR," proclaims the logo at www.leftbehind.com, and the books' success points to the growing breadth of premillennial belief. Those millions of readers are far from alone. Though it does not have a theological monopoly, premillennialism pervades American-style evangelical Christianity—the type of conservative Protestantism that stresses Bible study, publicly testifying to faith, and the personal, adult experience of accepting Jesus, or being "born again."

Between a fifth and a quarter of all Americans are evangelicals, scholars of religion say on the basis of consistent survey data. And that side of Protestantism is flourishing, while liberal denominations shrink. The average age of evangelicals, notes Brenda Brasher, a leading analyst of fundamentalism, is much lower than that of other Protestants—meaning that "in another generation, these people *will be* American Christianity."

Elsewhere in the world, the trend is even more striking. In Latin America, British writer Damian Thomas noted in his 1996 book, *The End of Time: Faith and Fear in the Shadow of the Millennium,* the number of Protestants climbed from 5 million in the late sixties to 40 million in the mid-nineties. Most are evangelicals. Guatemala had become 30 percent Protestant, Brazil 20 percent. One reason for the rise, Brasher argues, is the campaign of Pope John Paul II against the leftist faith of liberation theology. Denied a tie between religion and hope for a better world, Latin American Catholics have been more open to the catastrophic hopes of premillennialism. Across the Pacific, South Korea's Protestants—again, with a heavily apocalyptic orientation—went from 15 percent of the country to 40 percent during the seventies and eighties.

The names used for such believers are slippery. "Fundamentalist" usually refers to those who stress the literal truth of the Bible and Christian doctrine. Most evangelicals don't call themselves fundamentalists, even if they share the same literalism in their belief—and often the same premillennialism.

Of course, no religious group is monolithic; while one pastor may speak constantly of Rapture and prophecy, another may hardly mention it. But believers today can channel-surf for messages: If their own pastor isn't improvising riffs on the End, they might be hearing the message on Christian radio—or finding it in Left Behind books. People who don't use the term "dispensational premillennialist" to describe themselves may still be captivated by the vision of the Rapture and what is supposed to follow.

The breadth of such faith undermines comfortable stereotypes. The image of apocalyptic believers—as "weirdoes," men in ratty clothes on streetcorners with signs reading "The End is Nigh," or as restricted to the American South, or the uneducated, or some other slice of humanity sufficiently Other to be dismissed—will not stand. Today's premillennialists carry on the long tradition in Western history of belief in the End of Days. Rather than dismissing that tradition, we should ask where it comes from, and why it is seeing such a resurgence.

In the Christian world, the standard term for belief that history as we know it will end, to be followed by a divine kingdom, is millennialism. It implies a public salvation, beyond any private salvation of the individual believer. It does not have any necessary connection to the turn of the millennium on the Christian calendar—though the year 2000 provided a lightning rod for millennial belief. In Judaism, the same belief in history's transformation is called messianism, which refers to the expectation of a righteous king, descended from David, who will both restore the Jews' fortune and bring an era of peace for the entire world. The Jewish messiah is expected to be human, not divine, and in the Jewish context the word makes no reference to Jesus.

If the Left Behind books raise questions, they also provide a clue for understanding millennialism. The medium fits the message, for the first, unstated principle of millennialism is that history is the model for all novels. It's written by the Divine Author. It has a beginning; the characters are introduced for good reason; and as a well-formed story, it is built around a central conflict. Most important, it moves toward its inevitable dénouement, known to the Author if not the characters, when the plot will be resolved, the antagonist will get his comeuppance, and the heroes their deserved recognition.

In a master's story, every gun the reader sees hanging on the wall in an early scene will be taken down and fired by a later scene; in the Divine novel, seemingly random events of life also point to the true plot and its outcome—for those who have eyes to see. In his or her own conception, the millennial believer is the Sherlock Holmes of this story, aware of what is happening. Others, blind to crucial evidence, are at best Dr. Watsons.

But this detective story is the length of a grand family epic. A person naturally prefers to live near the end and to see the climax, rather than to be one of the forgotten generations in the middle. "What's left to happen?" a born-again Texas oilman named Hayseed Stephens once said to me. Between Adam and Eve and the year 1900, he said, 5,900 years passed, in which humanity progressed only as far as using horses and a few steam engines. Then the oil industry was born, he said, and "look what's happened in ninety-eight years. We've gone to the moon . . . I preached a sermon three months ago on 'What if the messiah doesn't come soon?' We'll self-destruct. They say knowledge doubles every eighteen months. If this isn't the last day, what'll the last day be like?" With a crescendo like what we're living through, the next page surely must read, "The End."

The risks of reading life this way are many. It leads easily to conspiratorial thinking, for it suggests that all evils are the machinations of a hidden antagonist. It interprets the actions of real people—your neighbor, Russians, people who disagree with your theology, Jews—as fitting that of characters in the story. It constantly needs rewriting, as life fails to fit the believer's detective work about what happens next.

Yet the divine novel is not so easily dismissed. It says that this world is a story that matters, is worth a commitment. It expresses what most of all makes us human—the determination to find meaning and order in what appears disparate and disconnected. It reflects the same desire that draws people to find laws in nature—which partly explains why so many of the millennial believers I've met are people spending their lives in science or technology.

Dispense with the Divine novel, and the world can look random. That can push people to despair or self-centeredness, or to the kind of religion that speaks only of a personal, spiritual salvation, scanting the importance of worldly injustice and suffering. Commitment to history as novel has drawn even those who erase the Author from the title page. Marxism, too, asserted that it had discovered the real story—and that we are on the cusp of the last, decisive battle. The old order of capitalism, Mao assured his disciples, "resembles 'a dying person who is sinking fast, like the sun setting beyond the Western hills,' " while communism alone "is full of youth and vitality, sweeping the world." As usual, the expected dénouement failed to arrive. But the power of the millennial story remains undiminished.

AS CHARACTERS IN THE STORY, we never see the full text. What we have is a long tradition of human attempts to write down fragments of what the Author has in mind. That tradition begins someplace. It often determines the story's setting—*Hamlet* needs its Denmark, *A Farewell to Arms* requires Italy, the Divine drama must also have a scene for its actions. The tradition of history's End is woven into the fabric of our society and our morning news in more ways than we notice.

For practical purposes, the idea of the End begins in ancient Israel, with people like Isaiah, the recklessly pessimistic pundit who refused to recognize that the Kingdom of Judea was enjoying a balance-of-trade surplus and a mostly safe strategic position. Isaiah disloyally called the national leaders "rulers of Sodom," which in the lexicon of the time meant that they'd ignored the underclass, and he warned the country of coming collapse. But he also held out a vision of "the end of days": a world transformed, done with what we call history—which means who fought whom—a time when army-surplus swords would serve as plowshares. It's still a bright vision today. One thread of our intellectual tradition tells us we can get there by human effort, treaty by treaty, one tank refurbished as a tractor at a time. Isaiah thereby becomes the father of evolutionary politics.

Except that in a separate prophecy, Isaiah warns of "a day of the Lord" in which He will "make the earth a desolation, and . . . destroy the sinners thereof out of it." Several centuries later, the prophet Zechariah detailed the cataclysm: All the nations gather to fight

against Jerusalem, they conquer it, ravish the women, take captives—
and then God enters the battle. He stands on the Mount of Olives, east
of Jerusalem, and He scourges the nations with plague, and afterward
they finally recognize Him. This telling of the future says that humanity's house is rotten: It can't be repaired, but must be razed to build a
new one.

Here begins the tradition of "catastrophic millennialism," to use
scholar Catherine Wessinger's phrase: The worse things get, the better they really are, and disaster will destroy the old order to make room
for the new. Human beings can only stand by and watch—unless, in
another variation, they should hurry the cleansing catastrophe along.
A quietism that urges believers to withdraw from an evil society and
wait for God to act is born of the same ovum as the impulse for revolutionary destruction. Politically, both Jacobins and survivalists retreating to Idaho have their roots in the dream of the last days.

In the second century B.C.E., Judea was ruled by the Seleucids of
Syria, one of the Greek-speaking kingdoms carved out of the empire of
Alexander the Great. The king, Antiochus Epiphanes, sought to Hell-
enize the Jews—forbidding circumcision, installing an idol of Zeus in
the Temple. One Jewish response was the successful revolt led by
Judah Maccabee and his family, which resulted in the cleansing of the
Temple celebrated in the Jewish holiday of Hanukkah, and in the brief
flowering of an independent Judea. The First Book of Maccabees, a
royal history, describes the new rulers as enabling every man "to sit
under his vine"—an image of end-of-days peace taken from Isaiah.
The new Hasmonean dynasty, as historian Albert Baumgarten argues,
had at least some pretense of setting up God's promised kingdom
through human force of arms.

A radically different response is the Book of Daniel, the first work
of the genre that came to be known as apocalypse. Daniel is described
as living during the Judean exile to Babylon, but historians mostly
place the book as being written just after Antiochus desecrated the
Temple. The book is packed with bizarre dreams. In one, a figure with
a golden head, silver chest, brass belly, and iron legs is destroyed by a
stone. Through divine help, Daniel decodes the visions, though his interpretations are nearly as cryptic. The golden-headed figure, Daniel
explains, represents four successive kingdoms, beginning with the

Babylonians, each worse than the one before, until God destroys the last and establishes His eternal reign. Further dreams teach that the future will last seventy "weeks" of years; in the last seven-year period an evil prince will stop the sacrifices in the Temple and set up an "abomination" that "causes desolation." Daniel also predicts "a time of trouble, such as never was," after which "many of them that sleep in the dust shall awake" for final judgment.

Historians say the book's images line up with events under the Seleucids, including the king who desecrated the sanctuary. Behind the catastrophe, the book says, is a hidden plan: God is about to intervene, save His people, even raise the dead, and judge everyone. One message is that God's redemption will break the bounds of nature; it will be cosmic, not political. Another is that there's no reason to take up arms against the oppressor. Persecution bears the promise that the world is about to end.

Only it didn't; the Maccabees' answer had worked better. But in time the Hasmonean kingdom collapsed in civil war; Rome conquered Judea. The Jews were "whipsawed" by events, as Baumgarten puts it, and the result was three centuries of the most fevered messianic expectations in Jewish history. Daniel was still construed as predicting the future, and was followed by a slew of new apocalyptic works. Other Jews took the Maccabees' path; messianic hopes fed the Great Revolt against Rome—which ended with destruction of the Temple. Six decades later Rabbi Akiba, the greatest sage of his time, threw his support behind a new revolt and regarded its leader, Shimon bar Kokhba, as messiah. Another sage, speaking for anti-millennialists in all times, told him, "Akiba, grass will grow in your cheeks and he will not have come." This time the defeat was even worse. By some accounts, nine-tenths of Judea's Jews died in battle or from starvation and disease. "Except for the Holocaust, it appears that there has never been another disaster in which so many Jews died at one time as in the disaster of Bar Kokhba," writes Israeli military scholar Yehoshafat Harkabi. Messianism had proved again that it could bring catastrophe, but not redemption.

Jesus appeared during those centuries of ferment. Christianity was the daughter not simply of Judaism, but of a Judaism burning with expectation, standing on tiptoes and ready to leap into the End. In the

Gospel of Mark, Jesus' first words are, "The kingdom of God is at hand." The new faith asserted that the messiah had actually arrived, making the time that follows into a pause before he completes his task. "If we're wondering why so many Christians obsess about last things, we have Jesus to blame," the editor of the journal *Christian History* pungently commented on late-twentieth-century millennialism. Asked by his disciples to tell what would be a "sign of thy coming, and of the end of the world," Jesus told them to look for when "the abomination of desolation, spoken of by Daniel the prophet," stood in the Temple.

Christianity's own great apocalypse, Revelation, was written at the end of the first century C.E. The book's poetic power is undeniable; so is the violence of its vision. Divine judgments come in sevens—seven seals are opened on a book, seven trumpets sound, seven vials are poured out—and each is catastrophic: After war and plague, the seas die, rivers turn to blood, the sun scorches men with fire. At the climax, all the kings of the earth gather at Armageddon to be defeated by Jesus as warrior. The devil is bound for a thousand years while Jesus reigns on earth—hence the concept of millennium, which refers to the length of the divine kingdom, not the date it begins—and at last this world comes to its end.

The place of Revelation in the Christian canon was a matter of controversy, but at last it was accepted—and placed as the final book of scripture. The Christian Bible thereby opened with Creation and ended with the world's end: the Divine novel.

At the same historical moment, Judaism was experiencing a messianic hangover, brought on by Bar Kokhba and perhaps also the rise of the daughter religion. In its final form, the Hebrew Bible ends not with Daniel but Chronicles, a history of normal time—and the book itself ends in mid-sentence, as if asking to be punctuated with an ellipsis: Life goes on. Daniel remained in scripture, but as historian Baumgarten comments, it was put in "the national attic," available but rarely used. Rather than an integrated story of the End, rabbinic Judaism presented a debate, something that can sound to our ears like a postmodernist narrative in multiple voices.

In a passage of the Talmud's Tractate Sanhedrin, for instance, sages suggest calculations of when the messiah will come—capped by a curse: "Rabbi Yonatan said, 'May those who calculate the End have their bones swell.' " For when the redemption fails to come on their date, they lose hope and say it will never come. In other words, the price of acute expectation is despair. Without reaching consensus, the sages turn to more immediate questions. The tension is clear: Judaism could not drop the idea of a messiah; the energy would burst out again. But no agreement was needed on the end of days. What mattered were the laws of how to live today.

Christianity also had to cap the volcano, especially after it became Rome's state religion in the fourth century. The Book of Revelation listed all kings in the devil's column, and demanded King Jesus as earthly ruler instead. Reading it literally was dangerous once the kings were Christians. The best answer was provided by Augustine, the fourth-century theologian who turned apocalypse into allegory. The Kingdom of God was already here; one entered it through true faith. Salvation was to be personal and spiritual, not public and political—except when the subversive energy of millennialism exploded, time and again.

There's a third version of the Divine novel: Islam's. The new religion was born in the seventh century C.E. with its own urgent certainty that the Hour, the time of God's judgment, was near. In fact, argues American scholar David Cook, Muslims rode into holy war and conquered everything from Spain to Central Asia because they felt the End dawning—and God had commanded them to conquer the world in the brief moment that was left. Islamic tradition quotes Muhammad as saying: "Behold! God sent me with a sword, just before the Hour, and placed my daily sustenance beneath the shadow of my spear, and humiliation and contempt upon those who oppose me." As Cook succinctly puts it: "In Islam we have the first example of what an apocalyptic group can achieve when given a limited time to accomplish an impossible task: world conquest. They almost made it."

Islam produced its own versions of future history, in traditions attributed to Muhammad. As both Jesus and the rabbis had done, they asserted that wars and moral corruption will herald the End. Murder and adultery will increase, beauty contests will be held in mosques. The sun—so says a central tradition—will rise in the west. In the world's final days a false messiah, *al-masih al-dajjal*, will conquer the world. He will be a Jew, leading an army of Jews from the east. At last Jesus will return to defeat the deceiver in a battle near Jerusalem. Afterward he will kill all pigs, break all crosses, and leave Islam as the world's sole faith. In many versions, he shares his role as redeemer with a figure called the *mahdi*. All this is the preface for when the dead rise and every man and woman who ever was faces judgment at the valley of Jehosafat next to Jerusalem's walls.

The vision startles because we know these characters, yet they are transformed. At the world's end, the believers of three faiths will watch the same drama, but with different programs in their hands. In one Jesus is Son of God; in another he is Muslim prophet. The Jews' messiah is cast in the Muslim script as the *dajjal*—another name for the Antichrist, the deceiver predicted by Christian tradition. The infidels in one script are the true believers of another. If your neighbor announces that the End has come, you can believe him, even if he utterly misunderstands what is happening.

It makes sense: Christianity's scriptwriters reworked Judaism, and Islam rewrote both. David Cook notes that from the start, apocalyptic ideas moved back and forth between the faiths; the global village is older than we realize. Some of the early spokesmen of Islamic apocalyptic thinking were converted Jews and Christians; they arrived with histories of the future in their saddlebags.

What's more, a story's end is when the truth comes out, the deceived realize their mistake. The deep grievance at the start of both Christianity and Islam is that the Jews refused the new faith—so the Jews must appear in both religions' drama of the End, to be punished or recognize their error.

And the setting of the End is also shared. The crucial events take place in or near Jerusalem. After all, the script began with the Hebrew prophets, for whom Jerusalem was the center not only of their world but of God's, and everyone else worked from their material. Isaiah's announcement of the End of Days comes directly after he laments that "the faithful city [has] become a harlot." That sets up the contrast: In the perfected age, "the mountain of the Lord's house shall be established as the top of the mountains" and "out of Zion shall go forth the law." The messiah's task is to end the Jews' exile and reestablish David's kingdom—in his capital.

Christianity reworked that vision. Jesus, says the New Testament, was not only crucified and resurrected in the city, he ascended to heaven from the Mount of Olives—and promised to return there. Without the Jews' national tie to the actual Jerusalem, Christians could allegorize such verses. The Jerusalem of the End could be built on other shores, and countless millennial movements have arisen elsewhere. But the literal meaning is there to be reclaimed, particularly in a time of literalism, such as our own.

Most striking of all is Islam's adoption of the same setting. For Muslim apocalyptic believers, Jerusalem is the capital in the messianic age. At the end of time, say Muslim traditions, the Ka'ba—Islam's central shrine in Mecca—will come to Jerusalem. The implication is that in Islam, speaking of the apocalypse at least hints at Jerusalem—and a struggle over Jerusalem alludes to the last battle.

Curiously, academic experts often say that Islam assigns scant space to apocalypse. Cook suggests a reason: In the religion's early centuries, believers attributed a vast body of contradictory traditions to the Prophet. Early Islamic scholars winnowed the sayings, establishing which were most reliable. Meanwhile, Islam became the faith of an empire, and it was time to talk softly of overthrowing the given order. So the authors of books containing the "most accurate" traditions, the pinnacle of the canon, said little of the End. "High" Islam appears unapocalyptic. But there are other books, well known to the faithful. On the desk of Sheikh Ismail Jamal, the man appointed by Yasser Arafat's Palestinian Authority as chief religious authority in the city of Jericho, I found a well-worn volume entitled *A Note on the Status of the Dead and Final Matters*. Written in the thirteenth century, widely available today, it's a compendium of apocalyptic visions. The idea of the Hour did not die in Islam.

SO THE QUESTION REMAINS: Why does faith look for a finale? If expecting the millennium leads people to gamble with despair, if—as the nonbeliever and half-believer immediately want to shout—it's downright crazy to think that the world is going to end, especially when we know it never does, then what's the power of this idea? Why can't people put it in the museum of religious concepts, next to Zeus and witchcraft?

Here's a piece of an answer: A believing person knows that God exists and is good. For some, that's only catechism, but for many it's an experienced fact, like the sun's warmth or your mother's love. But another fact is that things happen in this world that simply don't fit with a good God. Babies die. The man next door beats his wife, yet he's rich and respected. Your neighbor dies at war, your children in earthquakes. To believe is to live with dissonance.

People try to give themselves answers, to make the broken pieces of experience fit together. One answer is to tell yourself and others that God's justice and mercy in this world are obvious. A clergyman I know gives sermons about men whose lives were saved because they gave to charity; his own daughter died of cancer in her twenties. His insistence, I suspect, is in proportion to his pain. Or you can believe, like Job's friends, that those who suffer must have sinned. You can create theodicy, defense briefs for God. An old one says that the righteous will be rewarded after death, the wicked punished. This answer helped earn religion the sobriquet "opiate of the masses." Another view suggests that our physical existence misleads us; what matters is spiritual salvation, or enlightenment that allows one to rise above the illusion of suffering.

The most daring theodicy—so argues USC professor Stephen O'Leary, a scholar of millennialism—is to acknowledge that our world is broken. Then you assert that God Himself knows it, and that one day he will fix it, establishing his just rule on earth in place of the injustice that reigns now. That's the answer of millennialism. It is a desperately honest answer because it says there's something wrong with God's creation, and in the same moment it rejects despair.

Naturally, your vision of the repair will depend on what you think is broken. It can be that a beggar stands on the onramp of your freeway in the morning, a bag lady lives on your office steps, and your taxes pay for nuclear bombs. It can be that the president is an adulterer, the newsstand sells porn, and, astoundingly, most of the world has yet to accept Jesus. For my great-grandfather in Russia, it was that he lived in exile from his country under a Christian king who kidnapped Jewish sons for his army, with neighbors who irregularly became a mob hunting "Christkillers." For people living within a kilometer or two of my house, it is that the Jews rule Jerusalem and squabbling Arab juntas have replaced the empire of the caliph. The picture of God's kingdom follows accordingly, but there is also the matter of how badly broken things are, of whether God acting through men and women is already fixing the world, or whether there is no choice but to wait for the Repairman to come to smash and break down and rebuild the world the way He always meant it to be.

Yet in every case, to insist on a messiah yet to come, a kingdom yet to be established, is a principled rejection of business as usual right now. Religions do not excise millennialism because the apparent alternatives are either accepting the world as it is, or abandoning it completely, and either would morally bankrupt faith. The millennial kingdom is required as a standard by which today's kingdom can be "weighed in the balance and found wanting"—a phrase that enters our language from the handwriting on the wall in the Book of Daniel.

That cultural tradition is also at the foundation of secular millennialism, which is driven by the dissonance between what humanity is capable of and what it has become. It, too, provides varied visions of what demands repair, though it must assert that salvation will come by human action.

The power of millennialism is immense. The problem of established religions is how to keep hope smoldering without letting it burst into flames. Because when people give signs to know when the Time has come, and others discover that signs have been fulfilled and that the day is near, and others say the day is here, the irresistible force of enthusiasm inevitably smashes into immovable reality: The world doesn't end. The person who began with a gap between faith and unfair reality now faces the far greater dissonance between certainty of a new dawn and the facts. Almost anything is possible next. Going back to normal life can be the most difficult choice.

As happened in the time of Shabtai Tzvi, an archetypical case of millennial fervor. A Jewish mystic from the city of Izmir, in what is today Turkey, Shabtai proclaimed himself the long-awaited messiah in May 1665, in Gaza on the coast of the Holy Land. There'd been pretenders to the throne of David before, as historian Gershom Scholem writes—but none received more than local support. This time faith in the new redeemer swept up Jews from Morocco to Poland, from Yemen to Amsterdam. Letters from the Holy Land announced that the ashes of the red heifer had been found, or were about to be, that churches had sunk into the ground, that stones had fallen from the sky and destroyed a great gentile sanctuary, either the Church of the Holy Sepulcher or the Dome of the Rock.

Meanwhile, the "messiah" placed himself beyond religious law: He ate foods that scripture prohibited, and sanctified the act by reciting as grace, "Blessed are You, O Lord, who permits the forbidden." By one report, he encouraged his wife's seduction of another man; by another, he had sex with a boy while wearing phylacteries. The reports make sense: There's no better way to show you've entered a new age than to go to sexual extremes, whether celibacy or free love. With the former, you declare that the life of the flesh is over; with the latter, you declare that all bonds belong to the past and have evaporated.

Shabtai Tzvi was just under forty at the time, tall and "corpulent," according to contemporary accounts, which considered that trait handsome. In Scholem's view, he was also a manic-depressive, and when the mania had him he glowed with charisma. A prophet, Nathan of Gaza, told of visions in which divine voices confirmed that Shabtai was the redeemer. But all of this mattered only because Jews were expecting someone to knock on the door of their world just when Shabtai Tzvi knocked.

As Scholem writes, a radical new theology had spread among Jews in the preceding century, a reinterpretation of Kabbalah, or Jewish mysticism. The source was the city of Safed in the Galilee (yes, there is a Galilee); the teacher was Rabbi Yitzhak Luria, known in Jewish tradition as "the Sacred Lion." Luria taught that Creation had included a catastrophe—the forms God created could not hold the divine light He poured into his universe. It was as if boiling oil had been poured into glass. So the world was fragmented from the start, with sparks of holiness mixed with dross. The job of human beings, and Jews in particular, is to repair the world through performing God's commandments. Each religious act lifts a spark, returns it to its proper place—and when people complete the process, the world will be redeemed. Luria created what can be imagined as a cosmic machine: By saying grace or lighting Sabbath candles, a person pulls the levers of the unseen mechanism that brings the messiah. Lurianic Kabbalah can sound like ancient myth—but it also promotes the intensely modern idea of a world progressing toward perfection, powered by human action. And the motivation is overwhelming: Say morning prayers, and you hurry salvation for all humanity.

So Jews expected a messiah. Shabtai Tzvi was all the more convincing because the tidings came from the Holy Land. Nor was it mad to believe. If your neighbors, your clergyman, and your wife know the messiah has come, you'd feel crazy to think otherwise. To believe in Amsterdam in the spring of 1666 that Shabtai Tzvi was the redeemer was as sane—no, it was more sane than thinking in 1917 that the trench warfare in France would end all war, or believing in the summer of 1967 that the Age of Aquarius was dawning over San Francisco.

For the Ottoman sultan, Shabtai Tzvi was simply a rebel. He was brought before the Turkish ruler and offered a choice: Accept Islam or die. The messiah chose apostasy. Martyrdom would have been easier for the believers to explain.

Yet the movement didn't die. If many Jews faced the betrayal of "the redeemer" and returned sadly to normal life, others could not. They'd already entered redemption, and caught between faith and external facts, they chose faith. Condemned by religious authorities, belief in Shabtai Tzvi as messiah survived underground among Jews for generations. Some of the more radical believers engaged in ritual adultery, as a way to affirm they'd entered the redeemed world. In Salonika, in today's Greece, hundreds of families followed Shabtai's example by converting to Islam—an act on the edge of symbolic suicide. Another group, in Poland, converted to Catholicism.

In all of its apparent strangeness, the fever that hit Judaism shows many of millennialism's standard symptoms: First came a claim that new spiritual knowledge was freely available—in this case, kabbalistic secrets—because the End was near. So prepared, a community of faith was ready for good tidings, and the more people who believed, the more sense the message made. The arrival of redemption confirmed faith—but for some, it also erased old rules and authority. When the messiah failed, some believers preferred their new inner certainty over any outside reality. And some responded to disappointment with nihilism—in this case, through apostasy.

Scholem also notes that among Christians, reports of Shabtai Tzvi were read most avidly in London. England of the time, as Barbara Tuchman has put it, "was in a fanatical mood, perhaps the only fanatical period in her history." The name of that fanaticism was Puritanism, which stood on the two legs of millennialism and passionate attention to the Old Testament. Among the radical groups that flourished in the years of Oliver Cromwell's rule were the Fifth Monarchy men: Their name declared that Daniel's four kingdoms had fallen and it was time for the fifth, millennial kingdom, to be ruled by the saints.

Cromwell's Commonwealth permitted Jews to reenter England, which had been the first country in Europe to expel them, back in 1290. Proponents gave two reasons for the move: The Second Coming could not occur until Deuteronomy 28:64 was fulfilled, with the Jews scattered "from one end of the earth even unto the other." England, they believed, was the last corner of the globe without Jews. Bringing some in would pull the levers of another cosmic mechanism. Besides, the Puritans would finally succeed in converting them. Day-and-night reading of the Old Testament had brought recognition that God seemed very concerned with the Jews. The Puritans responded by acting for the Jews' benefit—letting them into England—though the point was not the Jews but the millennium.

Eventually, the Puritan passion cooled. Before it did, some of the most passionate had gone off to colonize a new continent. America was to become the counterlife of England: the way it might have been if the English had continued creating a Puritan society. Millennialism came over with the *Mayflower* and was to be a mark of American religion from then on.

THE LEAD ARTICLE of a Boston newspaper on June 1, 1842, was devoted to a burning question: Must the Jews return to Palestine before the Second Coming? The writer, one G. F. Cox, answered in the negative. As a follower of William Miller, he knew Jesus would return in 1843, and clearly the Jews would not to be back in their homeland by then.

Cox offered several arguments. For one, biblical prophecies of the Jews' restoration referred to the return from Babylon in ancient times, and had already been fulfilled. For another, if they returned again, it would be to build a "wonderful temple, in its structure, gold and other appendages," whose purpose could only be to worship the true God—"the meek and lowly Jesus." What was a Quaker,

Methodist, or any other Christian committed to simplicity of worship to think of such ostentatiousness? The idea, said Cox, appears "absolutely *absurd.*" Still, the newspaper—*The Signs of the Times*—addressed the issue repeatedly. The debate shows the Millerites had a problem: Belief in "restoration of the Jews" as a condition for the millennium was clearly widespread in America.

Neither William Miller nor his followers saw anything absurd in calculating the date of the End, nor in using the Jewish liturgical calendar to do it. Miller, a Baptist farmer from upstate New York, had worked out the date of 1843 at least two decades earlier. He deduced that the world would be six thousand years old on that date. According to an ancient idea, history will last for a cosmic week of seven millennia; the seventh, or Sabbath, will be *the* millennium, of God's rule. He also used Daniel 8:14, which says the "sanctuary will be cleansed" after 2,300 days, which he took to mean that the earth would be burned by fire 2,300 years after the date of the prophecy. That also led him to 1843. When two methods just happen to name the same date, the proof can seem overwhelming. For the same reason, more recent mathematicians of the last days presented multiple calculations to show that the End would come in 2000, or close to it.

Miller, a square-jawed, stern-looking man, published his conclusions in the 1830s, began preaching at churches and camp meetings, and rapidly acquired a following. His chief handler bought the biggest tent in America for his meetings. Besides the Boston paper pumping his message, there was another in New York, *The Midnight Cry.* An estimated fifty thousand Americans were fully committed; an estimated million more expected *something* to happen. Pressed for a specific date, Miller said that by "1843" he really meant the overlapping Jewish year, which he somehow defined as running from one spring equinox to the next, so that the Advent had to occur by March 21, 1844. When that date passed, some followers settled on a new one: October 22, 1844, which they mistakenly believed was the tenth day of the seventh month of the Jewish year, the Day of Atonement. On the chosen night, Millerites gathered to greet Jesus—and met despair. "Such a spirit of weeping came over us as I never experienced before," one said. "It seemed that the loss of all earthly friends could have been no comparison."

The Great Disappointment of the Millerites should have given a bad name to premillennialism—the view that Jesus would return, amid catastrophes, before the millennium. But events a generation later did similar damage to the progressive approach of postmillennialism—the belief that Christians were creating the Godly kingdom of the last days through their own efforts and that Jesus would come only at the end of the one thousand years. The Civil War, the grimy industrialization of America, heresies like Darwinism, all brought pessimism. The field was open to John Darby—whose new theology, in sharp contrast to the Millerites, put the Jews at center stage, in their land.

Darby sought to square more than one circle: to read the Bible literally, yet make its varied voices speak in unison about the End; to preserve Daniel while freeing believers from the book's chronology; to predict a catastrophic end to the present age, while freeing true believers from the travail.

Darby explained that history was divided into periods he called dispensations; in each, God had a distinct way of dealing with humanity. Hence the name dispensational premillennialism. The precise divisions of time would be a matter of debate, but the key point was this: God had been busy with the Jews, and through Daniel, had revealed that seventy weeks of years would pass between their return from Babylon and the reign of the messiah. At the end of the sixty-ninth week, Jesus arrived—and the Jews rejected him. That disrupted the prophetic plan. So God began a new dispensation, in which he built a new, heavenly people: the Church, Christianity. We live in the Church Age, said Darby—and everything between Jesus' first coming and the second was actually a parenthetical clause between Daniel's sixty-ninth and seventieth weeks.

At any moment the Church Age could be completed, and the hiatus would end with the Rapture: Jesus would remove the true believers from earth, and the final seven years of history would begin. In that brief period, the Tribulation, all the furies of Revelation would be loosed. None were allegories; all would be fulfilled literally. And finally, Jesus would return to earth with his saints and establish the long-delayed messianic kingdom. In that time, God's promises to the Jews and the gentiles would fit together: The remnant of Jews who'd accepted Jesus would enter the kingdom together with the returning Christians.

Oh, yes: Midway in the Tribulation, the Antichrist would desecrate the Temple with Daniel's "abomination of desolation." A rebuilt
Temple became essential to the Last Days.

In Darby's new history of the future, the Jews became central actors. God's promise of their return to their land would yet be fulfilled—and once it was, the End was at hand. Yet at the same time, it
was the Jews' fault that the End had been delayed: They'd failed to accept the messiah. Only those who corrected the mistake could merit
salvation. Jews needed to be watched with breathless anticipation, for
if they returned to Zion it would reveal God's plans—and the same
Jews were all terribly mistaken, and would face harsh judgment.

It took a long march for premillennialism, particularly of the dispensationalist variety, to gain its current strength among conservative
Protestants. But it had the advantage of its biblical literalism, and the
promise both of catastrophe and of safety for the believers. It promoted withdrawal from political activism; this world was headed inevitably for disaster. Yet dispensationalists were interested in the Jews
returning to their land even before the idea gained popularity among
the Jews themselves. When the Zionist movement was born at the end
of the nineteenth century, that showed prophecy was coming true.
Squint a little bit to avoid details that don't fit, and the Jews have been
playing their part in the Divine novel ever since.

But it's not enough for them to return to their land, or create a
state. For the stage of the End to be ready, there has to be a Temple.
How else could it be desecrated? That's why, in Tim LaHaye's writing
of the future, Israel leaps at the chance to build the sanctuary. That's
why it's also crucial to know just where the Temple once stood, so it
can be put up in the precise spot it belongs.

"WHEN WE WATCH THE TEMPLE being planned for and getting ready
to be built, we have very mixed feelings, because on the one hand
we're excited because we see the very specifics of God's scenario unfolding before our very eyes. That's exciting. Praise God!"

The voice on the cassette is that of Chuck Missler, former chairman of Western Digital Corporation, ex-expert on getting high-tech
firms out of bankruptcy, a nerd's nerd and proud of it, and today a full-
time teacher of Bible prophecy, a man whose monthly newsletter on

"the biblical significance of current events" goes to 100,000 sub-scribers and whose daily radio show airs on one hundred stations, from New Zealand to Finland. This is one of the "briefing packages" he pro-duces monthly, a pair of audiocassette tapes and a set of notes.

This set is called *The Coming Temple Update:* It brings together lectures from a mid-nineties conference that Missler held in Jerusalem for an evangelical tour group he brought from the United States and any Israelis interested, though not many were. The speak-ers have been talking about that irksome question, just where the Temple stood, which is the same as asking where it will be built, and Missler in his own talk puts it all in context, reminding listeners of the tie between the Temple and the Antichrist. Missler sounds out of breath, as if he can't pause long enough to inhale before rushing to the next idea. He holds the crowd; when he repeats the old line about two Jews having three opinions, you can hear the roar of laughter. Then he says:

"On the other hand we also remember Christ's words that . . . this guy"—the Antichrist—"is going to *betray* Israel in mid-career, and he'll issue in a time of trouble for Israel the likes of which have never occurred at that time, nor ever would happen again. And those words echo in our ears as we think of Auschwitz, Dachau, the horrors of Europe in the thirties and forties, and realize that what Jesus is say-ing is it's going to be worse next time around, that that was just a pre-lude, and it's hard for us to imagine. . . . But it's coming. . . .

"So if we watch the Temple being positioned, on the one hand we're excited because God's plans are unfolding as he said they would. On the other hand if you have friends, if you have a heart for Israel, you can't help but feel pain for them because they have no idea what's coming. . . .

"It's all happening as we speak."

THREE

ThE GATE OF hEAVEN

The past is never dead. It's not even past.

—WILLIAM FAULKNER,
Requiem for a Nun

HAL LINDSEY STANDS a couple hundred feet from the Dome of the Rock and lectures in a quiet Texas drawl to the three-score born-again American pilgrims he's brought to Israel. Lindsey, a short, solid man, is wearing a black print shirt and has a visor cap pulled over his silver hair. His mustache is brown, his eyes silver-gray; thin red capillaries stand out on his pudgy face, the calligraphy inscribed by years of sun on parchment-pale skin. You could take him for an aging biker or, say, a New Orleans tugboat captain—the latter in fact his profession until he found Jesus over four decades ago and studied at the fundamentalist Dallas Theological Seminary, and went on to become the world's single most successful populizer of dispensational premillennialism, the author of what may be the best-selling book of the late twentieth century, *The Late Great Planet Earth*. On his wrist he's wearing a heavy gold watch, given to him by his German-language publisher in gratitude for saving the publishing house.

Lindsey has led his group to a corner of the stone-paved platform several meters above the rest of the wide plaza of the Temple Mount, and is deciphering for them what scripture predicts for history's approaching climax. He doesn't want to shout because he could upset the Muslim guards. Before the mostly fiftysomething pilgrims from California and Washington and Kansas left their bus and walked up the ramp, through the metal detector and into Al-Haram al-Sharif, Lindsey reminded them to leave their Bibles behind because "the Muslims don't allow Bibles up there. They're getting very impudent lately. Luckily I've got it all in my head," which allowed one woman to answer, "God has blessed you in that." But he doesn't need to shout: What you notice entering the Haram is quiet, and open, ordered space. The rest of the Old City is narrow alleys crowded most hours of daylight, a confusion of voices, costumes, bumping bodies. It demands an urban tensing of the muscles, a looking over your shoulder. The sacred square says: exhale. And look at the Dome of the Rock. The building is the statement here.

The base is a perfect octagon. The walls are white marble at the bottom. Above that is shining tile—diamonds of orange and white set in overwhelming azure and green. It is a fountain, the kind that rulers from the desert like to build when they enter lands with water, a fountain frozen forever in a single moment, and the frieze of Arabic lettering on dark blue tile that runs along the top of the octagon is the sparkling foam. And above that is the smaller drum, also tiled, on which sits the golden dome itself, as if the sun were forever rising from precisely behind the fountain. It is a building meant to rule over space, not just the plaza of the Mount but the whole walled city and the roads leading to it and the hilltops beyond. So it is as rich from without as it is from within, where long inscriptions from the Koran proclaim that God is One and has never fathered a child, and where, under the dome's canopy, is *the rock:* the rock on which Jewish tradition says either the altar or the Ark of the Covenant originally stood in the Temple, the same rock from which Muslim tradition says Muhammad ascended to visit heaven.

Archeologists overwhelmingly agree that the Dome marks the location of the ancient Jewish sanctuary. Lindsey once thought so too, and suggested that a new Temple would soon occupy the spot. He has since changed his mind.

"I believe the Temple stood here," he says, pointing to a gazebo known as the Dome of the Spirits, at the platform's northwest corner, a hundred meters from the rock beneath *the* Dome. That theory, he explains, comes from one Dr. Asher Kaufman; he doesn't mention that the maverick Israeli researcher is a physicist, not an archeologist. Lindsey presents some of Kaufman's evidence—under the gazebo, for instance, is the only other bit of bedrock that pokes above the surface of the platform, which could be the real stone that ancient sources speak of. And in Jesus' time, he claims, the Mount's eastern gate faced the Temple. Today the sealed Golden Gate on the east of the Mount lines up with the Dome of the Spirits, not the Dome of the Rock; and even if today's gate is much more recent, he keeps going, it's right above the original.

Lindsey has another, crucial bit of proof. In 1983, he recounts, he was on the Mount with Kaufman, taking pictures for a book and pacing off the dimensions of the Temple, "And as I was measuring those things, I believe the Holy Spirit just thundered in my ear Revelation chapter 11, verses 1 and 2 . . . talking about the angel commanding that they measure out the Temple and the inner court, and then saying, 'Do not measure the outer court, for it is given to the Gentiles.' " With no outer court, he explains, you could build the Third Temple at Kaufman's location, and have enough room to leave the Dome of the Rock in place. So in the Last Days, "they both could stand here at the same time."

Lindsey's implication is clear: If you want to decide what happened on the Temple Mount in the past, first decide what will happen here in the future. Start at the story's end—which for Lindsey is the End of Days—and work back. At the Temple Mount, he has plenty of company in that method. Obviously, if you read history to find out what actually happened in a place—why Caliph Abd al-Malik built the Dome of the Rock, say, or where the Temple stood—this isn't a scientific approach. An archeologist or old-fashioned historian would go ballistic. Yet there's an implied lesson in what Lindsey says. The stories people tell about the past reveal, most of all, what matters to them today. What matters at the Temple Mount are visions of the future, and the irreconcilable demands they make on sacred soil.

Kaufman's theory suggests a compromise, but Lindsey knows that Muslims aren't exactly ready to give up half the Haram for the Temple to be built: "Certainly there has to be a vast political change before anything like that could happen." But the Bible covers that: "Remember in Daniel 9, verse 27, it talks about the coming prince of Rome"—the Antichrist, as Lindsey reads scripture—"and this prince, just seven years before the messiah comes, will make a covenant guaranteeing security for Israel. . . . He's also going to be able to do the impossible, to negotiate a peace with the Muslims so that the Temple can be rebuilt." Lindsey's listeners won't be around for this demonic achievement, because "according to our faith, Jesus Christ is going to take out the true believers before the Antichrist is revealed." Which is good for them, because the peace won't last: "The last war of the world is going to start because of the dispute between the Muslims and the Jews about who owns this area. Many have died in the past over this ground, and many will die in the future. Not that we want to see it, but it's something the prophets predicted." Lindsey sighs slightly over Armageddon, with about as much energy as you'd give the illness of a half-forgotten former officemate.

"Will the Jews have to find the Ark of the Covenant?" a woman earnestly asks him. "They don't have to," Lindsey answers, but he thinks they will, and "that will *propel* them" to start building the Temple. Where did Abraham seek to sacrifice Isaac, a man queries. Right here, Lindsey assures him, though God provided a lamb to prevent the human sacrifice. To tie it all up, he adds that Golgotha is an extension of the same ridge, and "God spared Abraham's son, but he didn't spare His own."

A few moments later, when Lindsey starts talking into a video camera for an audience back home, a Muslim guard rushes over. "You need permission from the Waqf," the Muslim religious trust that controls the Mount, he says. It's a reminder of the present, of how precarious the Muslims feel their hold is, how easy it would be to spark a confrontation. Lindsey argues half a moment, then gives up and drifts off.

As he leaves the Mount, Lindsey banters with his Israeli tour guide, who has his own stories of close calls: "I had this lady say once, 'Why don't the Jews tear this place down and build the Temple?' And that crazy guard was standing right next to us."

Lindsey laughs, and says, "That could start a holocaust."

■

THE TEMPLE MOUNT, at first glance, is one place where facts fit sacred history. Compare it to the Tomb of the Patriarchs in Hebron, the next most sacred spot nearby for Muslims and Jews. That structure also dates to Herod's time—perhaps 1,500 years after the death of Abraham, Isaac, and Jacob, whose resting place it supposedly marks, raising reasonable doubt of whether this is the grave, even before you ask whether the patriarchs were real people or the stuff of stories. Archaeologists have been pricking the Holy Land with shovels since the nineteenth century. Here and there, a find fits a biblical text: Silver weights are inscribed with the price Israelites paid Philistines to sharpen swords in King Saul's time; a recently found inscription mentions "the dynasty of David." Where legend leaves off and history begins is unclear: Yes, the Assyrian king Sennacherib overran the land when Hezekiah ruled Judea in the eighth century B.C.E.; but centuries earlier, was there really a united kingdom of Israel and Judea, which scripture says David ruled? Archeologists known as "biblical minimalists" proclaim there's no evidence that most of the history recorded in the Hebrew Bible ever happened. Critics accuse them of rewriting the past to fit a twentieth-century animus to faith, of creating their own, antireligious myth.

The Mount, on the other hand, is *there,* too large to be forgotten in nineteen centuries since Herod's Temple was destroyed. It takes up nearly a sixth of Jerusalem's walled Old City. The historical record is clear that Herod built a Temple, replacing the earlier version erected on the spot in the fifth century B.C.E. by Judeans returning from exile in Babylon. They, in turn, had built their sanctuary just where the First Temple—Solomon's Temple—stood before the exile. Herod's Temple is described not only by rabbinic texts and the New Testament, but in the detailed works of historian Josephus Flavius. In excavations south of the Mount, archeologists have found steps that led to the Temple gates, stones that fell from above during the destruction. On one stone, from a corner, an inscription reads, "To the trumpeting house . . ." which fits Josephus's account of a priest mounting the tower on the Temple's corner and blasting a trumpet to begin the Sabbath. The dig and the documents line up. The Mount is a landmark, not a myth.

And yet, even the most basic matter is hazy: No one knows precisely where the Temple stood on the Mount. Given today's politics, trying to dig there would be like trying to figure out how a hand grenade works by pulling the pin and peering inside. Even digging *near* the Mount has sometimes ignited riots. The scholarly consensus that the Temple stood where the Dome does, give or take ten meters, allows for countless theories. Then there are mavericks like Kaufman, whose work is cited mostly by people who want to know where the next Temple will be built. Nothing is solid.

The Temple Mount that matters is built out of stories, not stones. Some say the world began here; more say this is where it will end. A Talmudic legend asserts that inside the Holy of Holies—where the Ark containing the Ten Commandments originally stood—was a rock known as the Foundation Stone because the creation of the world began there. Another legend moves the stress to the altar, a short distance away: Adam was formed from the dust here, so that "he was created at the place of his atonement." The Israelites didn't pick this place to worship God; they recognized its primordial holiness. Or so literalists would read that text. An allegorist would say that "created at the place of his atonement" means people are made with both the potential to err and the promise to be forgiven. The Temple's meaning refuses to be tied down.

In his code of Jewish law, medieval philosopher-rabbi Moses Maimonides adds: Not only was Adam born where the altar stood, but Cain and Abel made their sacrifices there; so did Noah after the flood; so did Abraham. The last point seems to have a biblical foothold: In Genesis 22, Abraham is told to take Isaac "and get thee into the land of Moriah, and offer him there for a burnt-offering." "Mount Moriah," the Second Book of Chronicles informs us, is where "Solomon began to build the House of the Lord." Fast-forward several millennia: I tag along when my son's fourth-grade class visits the Old City. "There," says the guide, pointing to the Mount, "is where Abraham bound Isaac." Except that Chronicles is a late rewrite of Israelite royal history. The author could have taken the name "Moriah" from Genesis and assigned it to where the Temple stood to magnify the location's sanctity.

Ironically, while the word "Jerusalem" occurs hundreds of times in the Bible, it's not in the Torah—scripture's first five books, to which Judaism accords the highest authority. The closest is "Salem," probably an early name for the city. In Abraham's time, Genesis says, Salem was ruled by Melchizedek, "priest of God the most high." In fact, archeologists conjecture that Jerusalem was a sacred center long before David conquered it. There's a cave in the rock under the Dome. One theory says it's a Bronze Age burial cave, from 2300–2100 B.C.E. The cult of the dead was strong then; perhaps that's how Salem became sacred.

David conquered the city around 1000 B.C.E. from the Jebusites. Later, the Bible says, he bought a threshing floor from a Jebusite named Araunah and built an altar. There Solomon built his Temple. "Many scholars say this may have already been a holy place," says Israeli archeologist Aren Maeir. "Some point out that a threshing floor could be a focus for fecundity rites."

If Jerusalem wasn't already holy, it's hard to understand why a city stood there. It's on the edge of a desert; the soil is rocky; the sole spring is grade C; the trade routes cross to the north. You wouldn't come here for gold, wheat, or spices. Only to stand at the gate of heaven.

If so, David did what so many conquerers do: Take the holy place of the vanquished, and give it to his triumphant God. Closer to our time, the Christian Spaniards who conquered Cordoba turned its Great Mosque into a cathedral; the Ottoman sultan who took Constantinople in 1453 marched to the city's great church, the Hagia Sophia, and converted it to a mosque. In the oasis city of Bukhara, north of Afghanistan, I was once taken to Central Asia's oldest standing mosque, a sanctuary of ornate brickwork and hexagonal domes. Beneath it archeologists have found a Zoroastrian temple, and a Buddhist one.

Solomon's Temple lasted until 586 B.C.E., when Babylonian emperor Nebuchadnezzar burned the Lord's house and carried the Judeans off to "the rivers of Babylon," thereby providing an archetype for an evil empire. Seventy years later, returning exiles built the Second Temple. At some point, the crowds grew too big for the natural mountaintop that served Solomon. Earthworks turned the top of the Lord's mountain into a human-built platform five hundred cubits square—about 250 meters by 250.

In 63 B.C.E., the Roman general Pompey conquered Judea, and

in 37 Herod was appointed the principality's vassal ruler. The man was, in Josephus's words, "brutish and a stranger to all humanity." To cement his rule, he married the last princess of the Hasmonean dynasty—and murdered her sons, and her, and another of his sons by a different wife, and uncounted commoners. And, yes, he built the most magnificent sanctuary Jerusalem had ever seen, a landmark of the ancient world, the Temple that remains in history's memory.

Standard telling: Herod's Temple was self-aggrandizement, and an unsuccessful bid to buy religious legitimacy from his subjects. An alternative reading: Archeologist Meir Ben-Dov says Roman imperialism brought a Green Revolution to Judea; aqueducts and better-forged plows boosted farm yields—and unemployment. Herod took control of spice-caravan routes, and cash poured into the treasury. Meanwhile, the Temple was strained by 100,000 pilgrims at festivals. The building project sopped up labor and, Ben-Dov might have added, made room for even more pilgrims—customers for faith, the only product Jerusalem has ever had to sell. Put together the images of the age—a global market, economic growth, and dislocation, "a few aristocrats, landowners, and capitalists [who] had almost all the country's wealth," a regime that seemed both to support faith and mock it in the name of "universal" culture—and the desperation for a new, messianic order seems natural. When Jesus said "a rich man shall hardly enter into the kingdom of heaven," he had an audience. In 64 C.E., Temple construction wound up, and thousands were left jobless. The Great Revolt against Rome began two years later.

Herod couldn't change the Temple's size; that was set by religious law. Instead, he built a huge court around it. A ridge continued north from the Temple Mount; Herod's builders sliced into it. On the south and west, they dug to the bedrock, and laid down retaining walls of stone blocks, some weighing fifty tons. Within the walls, arched vaults held up the wide esplanade of the new sanctuary. The new Mount was a giant box plunked down over the original peak. On the esplanade was a set-off square, the original sacred area. Within that was the Temple, a rectangle running east to west and divided into two courts. In the western one, the altar stood before a high structure, which contained the sacred hall where the priests lit the menorah and burned incense, and the Holy of Holies, which would have held the

Ark of the Covenant had it not gone missing centuries earlier. In reconstructions drawn in our day, the complex seems more overwhelming than inviting: massive, angular, a place for a person to feel small, the house of God, yes, but built to a tyrant's vision.

Herod's monument didn't last long. In the summer of 70, Titus's troops razed the Temple, and Jerusalem's walls, and the rest of one of the world's great metropolises.

Sixty years later, the emperor Hadrian decided to rebuild the city—as Aelia Capitolina, dedicated to Jupiter, Juno, and Minerva. That plan apparently sparked the revolt of Bar Kokhba, Rabbi Akiba's failed messiah. Hadrian crushed the rebellion and built his city. A temple to Jupiter apparently stood at the Mount's center. Once again, a conqueror moved his god into the vacant holy place. A fourth-century traveler from Bordeaux recorded that Jews came each year on the anniversary of the destruction, the ninth day of the Hebrew month of Av, to clean the Foundation Stone, while statues of emperors looked over them. The traveler, a Christian, may have wanted to make a point of the Jews' humiliation. But they knew where the stone was.

ASHER KAUFMAN says he knows, too.

On a summer evening, I go to visit him. The Jerusalem neighborhood is *solid*, the streets tree-lined, the middle-class apartment blocks devoid of any desire to attract the eye, their stone walls gray from years of exhaust. Kaufman, in his seventies, has lived here for most of the forty years since he came to Israel. He is wearing gray slacks and a shirt with thin gray stripes, and leads me into a comfortable sitting room with a straightbacked piano and an armchair he offers me and straightbacked chair in which he sits himself, hands folded on his lap. Over his gray hair he wears a crocheted skullcap. He has a Scots accent, melodious; I imagine him playing this accent on the piano, measuredly, with his long fingers. He earned his Ph.D. in physics from the University of Edinburgh. He grew up in an Orthodox family of the religious Zionist variety, which, though he doesn't say so, meant moderation in those days, faith alongside a solid respect for modern education. "You have to be very, very careful when you define who is religious," he says. He prefers to define matters to the millimeter. Actually, in his years as a professor at the Hebrew University, researching fusion and the spectroscopy of ionized gases, he would have regarded a millimeter as a blunt instrument. In 1967, he was called up for reserve duty before the Six-Day War, but sent home because of illness. "On Wednesday, Jerusalem was delivered," he says. "We sat down to eat supper at six o'clock. We began singing *shir hama'alot* before grace with tears in our eyes." The detail means this: *Shir hama'alot,* Psalm 126, "When the Lord brought back those that returned to Zion, we were like unto them that dream," is sung by Orthodox Jews before grace on holidays. Quite a statement, you see. It's not *done* on weekdays.

On the wall is a print of a sixth-century mosaic map of Jerusalem, and a drawing of the Old City from the east, with a flood of light on the Muslim shrines. When did he first visit the Mount? I ask. "That's catalogued, now. Being a physicist, I have to keep a logbook," he says. Or perhaps to catalogue matters, he became a physicist. The logbook says January 15, 1975. He smiles measuredly.

He'd been on sabbatical. He'd thought of using chemical analysis to find the spot in the Kidron Valley, between the Mount of Olives and the Temple Mount, where a drain bearing blood from sacrifices is said to have emptied. He'd been studying Tractate Midot, a treatise on the Temple's measurements from the Mishnah, the second-century compilation of Jewish law. "For some inward reason," he wondered where the Temple stood, "and I had the idea, maybe as a physicist I could contribute something." Of his feeling, he does not offer a precise measure; he doesn't seem to have one. "I think it was a scientist's curiosity, drawn by an invisible hand to investigate the matter."

But as he worked, spectroscopy fell to the side. If he located landmarks listed in Midot, he reasoned, they'd point to his treasure. The way to read the clues, he decided, was to remember that in ancient times east was the cardinal direction, and the Temple was aligned on an east-west axis. Sacrifices of the red heifer, he learned, took place at a point high on the Mount of Olives, from which the priest could see over the walls and into the Temple. From the only spot high enough, Kaufman found that looking due west he saw the Golden Gate and the northern part of the Temple Mount, including the Dome of the Spirits. On Saturday night, December 28, 1974, he recorded: "I have established the approximate site of the Temple, north of the Dome of the Rock."

By the time he visited the Mount, he had a thesis in hand, and a justification for entering holy space: helping to rebuilding the Temple. "Not necessarily that I myself am going to build it," he explains, "but the research could make . . . the rebuilding feasible." Scientific curiosity had gained a meaning. With the details he carefully logs, the stones he measures, he could be mapping redemption. The scientist, too, can be called, according to his craft. He will respond not with ecstasy but with a small smile.

He studied Josephus, Talmudic literature, archeology, "had to delve into Greek," examined aerial photos. And he walked the area. He discovered a piece of Herodian pavement here, a bit of an ancient wall there. At the northwest corner of that raised platform around the Dome, he found a flat-topped rock with remains of a mosaic. Below, the stone showed signs of masonry work. The top, he concluded, was the floor of the inner court of the Second Temple; the lower part was where the wall stood. The distance between two holes reamed in the stone he measured at 43.7 centimeters which, he argued in the *Biblical Archaeology Review* in 1983, was the length of the cubit used in the Second Temple. By the time the article was finished, he'd identified traces of First Temple stonework in the same rock—though by that time the Waqf authorities had covered the spot in dirt and planted a rose garden. His findings—tied together with a few assumptions, he admitted—led him to map both the First and Second temples, with the rock under the Dome of the Spirits marking the Holy of Holies.

The article followed an earlier report in the *Jerusalem Post* on Kaufman's work. Together they brought a burst of interest from a direction Kaufman never expected: American evangelical Christians.

David Lewis, a prominent Pentecostal minister and prophecy writer from Missouri, called the archeology magazine to order a load of extra copies of the issue with Kaufman's article. Lewis—founder of Christians United for Israel and cofounder of the National Christian Leadership Conference for Israel—also contacted Kaufman directly. The physicist's careful log of lectures shows him speaking to a group the minister brought to Israel in the early eighties. Lewis, like Lindsey, cites Revelation 11, reading the verse to me over the phone: "Rise, and measure the temple of God. . . . But the court which is without the temple leave out . . . for it is given to the Gentiles." His explanation puts an edge on Lindsey's: "The importance could be—this is just a possibility—that the Dome of the Rock might not be destroyed when the Temple is built." Listen to that carefully: Building the Temple is as sure as tomorrow's sunrise; the Dome might just be able to stay, in what Lewis calls "a compromise measure that would allow some tranquility for a number of years."

Lewis was hardly alone in his interest. Lindsey got in touch with the physicist. Kaufman spoke to other groups in Israel. He flew to California, where he spoke at Calvary Chapel of Costa Mesa, mother church of a fundamentalist movement that leapt out of the sixties counterculture, which is a story we'll get back to. The church's main sanctuary seats 2,500 and couldn't hold everyone who came for Kaufman's talk, so the overflow sat in a second hall and watched by closed-circuit TV. Later Chuck Missler would invite Kaufman to speak at his Temple conferences. Having a place in prophecy has been helpful; Kaufman puts the honoraria into research expenses. Occasionally he must field bewildering questions. "Some of these Christians say, 'We've heard the building materials are already assembled for the Temple.' Where they got the information from, I didn't know." Perhaps from a novel, supposedly written by God, in which Kaufman is a character, which they've read and he hasn't: If he's found the place, then let the building begin. If war follows, well, that's also in Last Days prophecy.

Archeologists are less sympathetic. Kaufman remembers an editor dropping his article from a scholarly collection, saying "the whole volume was in jeopardy if it was included." But the physicist's strange love for the Mount hasn't flagged. He has studied the charts, drawn by nineteenth-century British explorers, of the ancient cisterns on the north side of the Mount; they line up just outside where he says the walls were. Back in *Biblical Archaeological Review*, he quoted the old British report with a wee bitterness: "No obstacle was put in the way of Captain [Charles] Warren's examining the cisterns with which the area is honeycombed in every direction, the Moslems only considering the occasional disappearance of Captain Warren into one of the tanks as a piece of eccentric curiosity." Yet Kaufman they bother! They put a garden over his rock! When he measured a find, "The guards weren't happy about it." Again, he has not measured the subjective: In the 1860s, Muslims ruled Jerusalem; they had no reason to fear that Warren was a surveyor, come to prepare the way for Temple construction at Al-Haram al-Sharif. Under Israeli rule, a Jew—even a quiet physicist—looking for the Temple's location represents not a quest for history but a potential demand for sacred real estate, a premonition of a *casus belli.*

In Maimonides' list of the Torah's 613 divine commandments, Kaufman reminds me, number 20 is to build a Temple. "In my own humble way, I'm contributing to that," he says. Of course, he came to his research with an open mind, but his theory means that "the Dome of the Rock, this beautiful building, stands where it is. . . . Free access to the Dome can be maintained even within future Temple precincts." The Mount would be divided in two in cooperation with the Muslim religious authorities, north for the Jews, south for Muslims. Science doesn't see any obstacles: "Anything can happen, anything which is physically possible."

(A few days before I first met Kaufman, I'd sat in Ahmad Agbariya's office in the Al-Aqsa Association in Umm al-Fahm. Agbariya stood like a schoolteacher next to an aerial photo of the Haram, and ran his finger around the whole plaza and said, "The entire area is Al-Aqsa." And like the rose garden, I suspect, a bit of that claim reflects a Heisenberg Uncertainty Principle of political archeology: Merely by investigating the place, you risk changing its name and its face.)

But the physicist's Temple is bloodless. "I seem to recall," he says, "that the Temple could be built without sacrifices. There's also an ancient saying that all the sacrifices will be abolished except the thanksgiving offering." He states carefully, as if quoting himself: "A Temple today would be a unifying force for the Jewish people all over the world—a demonstration of the divine presence within the Jewish people. . . . It would replace the Western Wall as a central place in Judaism." It would, I suddenly imagine, be a large synagogue, well-appointed, with a, well, *British* decorum and melodious services.

CURIOUSER AND CURIOUSER: If Kaufman wants no sacrifice—not the lamb burned on the altar morning and evening, or the doves brought by mothers after giving birth—why isn't the Western Wall sufficient as a center for Judaism? Why face off with Islam merely to move prayer services two hundred meters? The Wall already offers evidence that little can disunite the Jews like a central holy place; the Orthodox state rabbinate that controls the spot forbids Conservative and Reform services. Adding a Temple would only add the problem Kaufman suggests dodging: sacrifices.

The Torah devotes immense attention to animal offerings, yet Judaism has managed to live without them for nearly two millennia. It has done so by assigning the Temple to the time of the messiah. The flip side is that when messianism is in the air, both the Temple and sacrifices become practical issues. The calm Professor Kaufman wants a measure of messianism, without getting swept away.

Until 70 C.E., Judaism centered on the Temple and burnt offerings. Strikingly, the two Jews most responsible for post-Temple religion are remembered as predicting the sanctuary's destruction. "There shall not be left here one stone upon another, that shall not be thrown down," the Gospels quote Jesus as declaring. That was about forty years before Titus. "Forty years before the Temple's destruction" says the Talmud, a crimson ribbon that miraculously turned white each Yom Kippur ceased doing so—that is, the ritual inside Herod's edifice had gone hollow—and the doors of the sanctuary opened by themselves, as if to allow enemies to enter. "Sanctuary, sanctuary," said Yohanan ben Zakkai, a leading rabbi of the time, interpreting the signs, "I know that your destiny is to be destroyed." Both the Jewish story and the Christian may have been improved after the fact, but they reflect the troubled mood of the Temple's last years, and the questions about the efficacy of sacrifices.

Sometime during the Roman siege of Jerusalem, Yohanan ben Zakkai escaped the city—by the standard telling, hidden in a coffin that he climbed out of alive, an apt symbol of what happened to Judaism under his direction—and established a new center of Jewish learning in the town of Yavneh. Ben Zakkai was a revolutionary astutely posing as protector of tradition. Before, the ram's horn had been blown on Rosh Hashanah only in the Temple; he ruled that it could be blown elsewhere. He did not say the same of sacrifices. His successors instituted prayers that took the place of burnt offerings, in part by praying for the Temple's restoration. In synagogues, Israeli historian

Elchanan Reiner writes, the front section was divided off; an ark containing Torah scrolls stood in the new "Holy of Holies."

In nostalgia, Jews idealized the Temple; it stood for a lost utopia where God and human beings enjoyed a perfect relationship, a lost childhood. Its destruction symbolized loss of innocence. "The day the Temple was destroyed, prophecy was taken from prophets and given to fools and children," one Talmudic rabbi said. Said another: "From the day the Temple was destroyed, the pleasure of sex was taken [from marriage] and given to sinners." The sanctuary became the symbol of a perfected age. The messiah, repairer of all that is broken, would rebuild it. Yohanan ben Zakkai advised against holding one's breath: "If you have a sapling in your hand and they say to you, 'The messiah has come,' finish planting and then receive him," he said. If the present is a moratorium before the messiah, he was concerned with the moratorium. If the destruction was childhood's end, he was concerned with the religion of adulthood.

Judaism became today's religion of the intellect, with study as the central religious act. It superseded sacrifices by remembering them. The modern denominations of Reform and Conservative Judaism have gone further, altering their liturgy to diminish that memory. Except that sometimes a culture's old memory can come suddenly back to life, like a recessive gene that has waited generations.

For its part, Christianity regarded the razing of the Temple as proof that God had moved his covenant from the old Israel who'd rejected Jesus to the new Israel of the Church. Second-century Christian philosopher Justin Martyr lumped sacrifices together with the Sabbath, circumcision, and all the other commandments that, he said, were irrelevant after Jesus. Besides, Christians argued, Jesus' crucifixion was the last atonement by blood—a thesis that both accepted the idea of sacrifice (even a human sacrifice) and rejected it. Christianity seemed done with the Temple—unless you read verses linking the Temple and the Last Days literally, as today's premillennialists do.

When Constantine made Christianity into Rome's state religion, for once the Mount wasn't refurbished—Jesus had predicted that not one stone would remain on another there. The compromise was to build elsewhere in the Holy City. The Church of the Holy Sepulcher was put up where the crucifixion was said to have taken place; it required tearing down a temple to Aphrodite. The Mount went out of use—except as trash heap—till the next conqueror arrived.

ON THE WALL behind Sheikh Muhammad Hussein's desk is a picture frame. What's inside isn't a picture. On a jet black background, a single word is written in white Arabic letters: "Allah." Darkness, and the white light of God, and nothing else. Hussein is the director of Al-Aqsa Mosque. He has a precisely carved face, a precisely trimmed beard. I've just asked him about charges that renovations at the Haram have harmed archeological remains. "Al-Aqsa is an Islamic holy place. There is no other site that could be affected," he says, leaning forward. The Temple? "This is an Islamic holy site. It never has been related to anything else. It was named Al-Aqsa by God. There is a verse in the Koran."

In a Waqf pamphlet for tourists, the official line is only slightly softened: "The beauty and tranquillity of Al-Aqsa Mosque in Jerusalem attracts thousands of visitors every year. Some believe it was the site of the Temple of Solomon, peace be upon him . . . or the site of the Second Temple . . . although no documented historical or archaeological evidence exists to support this." It's a particularly daring rewrite of the past—as usual with the future in mind: Don't build here. Among the evidence it ignores for the Temple's location is the Dome of the Rock.

As Sheikh Muhammad Hussein says, there is a verse in the Koran that speaks of *al-masjid al-aqsa*, which is to say, "the furthest mosque." That verse is basic to what Muslims today know of the Haram, and especially the rock under the Dome: that the archangel Gabriel met Muhammad at night in Mecca, and led him to a winged steed named Buraq—lightning—on which he flew to Jerusalem, where he met the prophets who preceded him, including Abraham, Moses, and Jesus, and Muhammad led them all in prayer. Then Muhammad ascended to heaven, and the rock tried to follow him and the prophet or Gabriel had to hold it back, leaving hand or foot marks on it, and Muhammad was received by God, who commanded the Muslims to pray fifty times daily, but at Moses' advice, He settled for five.

This is fact, in the same sense that it is fact for Jews that the Temple Mount is Mount Moriah: social fact, as solid and present as the Dome or the Western Wall. But the terse verse in the Koran doesn't say this; it says only, "Glory be to Him, who carried His servant by night from the Holy Mosque to the Furthest Mosque, the precincts of which We have blessed . . ." The rest of the story comes from Islamic tradition. Inscriptions inside the Dome make no mention of the Night Journey—because when the Dome was built, Muslims had not yet agreed on Jerusalem as the site of the Furthest Mosque. The Koran doesn't mention the name Jerusalem, a detail I've heard repeatedly cited by right-wing Jews, and which matters today about as much as the Torah's oversight of the city. Still, it leaves the question of how the Dome got there.

The troops of the caliph Umar (or Omar), second commander of the faithful after the prophet, conquered Aelia Capitolina, which early Muslims also called Madinat Bayt al-Maqdis, meaning "City of the Temple," in 638. Umar, say later Muslim and Christian accounts woven around the event, either accepted the city's surrender himself or came soon after, riding a camel, dressed with supreme simplicity in a camel-hair robe. He asked the city's Christian patriarch, Sophronius, to see where the Temple had stood. A Byzantine account hints that when the patriarch saw Umar there, he knew the world was ending: "Here is that appalling abomination, as prophesied by Daniel, standing on this holy site," we're told that Sophronius said, quoting the sign Jesus had given in Matthew 24:15. Alas, the world didn't end. Instead, Umar ordered the Mount cleared of rubbish and, it's said, had a discussion of where a mosque should be built. A Jewish convert to Islam suggested a spot on the north, so that when the believers turned south to Mecca they'd face the rock as well. But Umar ordered a mosque built at the southern end of the Mount, forerunner of the lead-domed one that stands there today and is called Al-Aqsa: The believers would pray on the platform but with their backs to the Jewish holy place.

That ambivalence wasn't shared by Caliph Abd al-Malik ibn Marwan, who in 691 had the Dome of the Rock built. Historians are frustrated because they don't know quite why. One explanation: Abd al-Malik ruled from Damascus and wanted a holy city nearby, particularly since a rebel leader held Mecca. Problem is, displacing the prophet's city would have been heresy.

The building, though, provides clues to its purpose. Its Byzantine form half-suggests a church, and the Dome overshadows the city's Christian shrines. Inside, mosaic inscriptions from the Koran address "the people of the book," the Islamic name for the religions of the Bible, here clearly the Christians: "Do not say things about God but the truth! The messiah Jesus, son of Mary, is indeed a messenger of God. . . . So believe in God and all the messengers, and stop talking about a trinity. . . . Verily God is the God of unity. Lord Almighty! That God would beget a child? Either in the Heavens or on the Earth?" For the Jews, the message was even simpler: The Dome stands where everyone knew the Temple did. Islam, the building says, is the culmination of Judaism and Christianity.

Some early Muslims may have seen the Dome as the Third Temple. Muslim texts praising Jerusalem link the two buildings, researcher David Cook notes, and apocalyptic works foresee Islam's armies conquering Constantinople and Rome to recover Temple treasures stolen by the Romans. Apparently they'd be put in the Dome of the Rock, the millennial Temple.

Maybe this was a meaning acquired after the Dome was built, like the link to the Night Journey. But the original inscription above the east entrance did speak of Muhammad interceding for his believers on the day of resurrection. Over time, everything on the east side of the Haram was tied to final judgment and mercy, writes another historian: "The Golden Gate is known in Muslim sources as the Gate of Mercy and Repentance; the small Dome of the Chain [east of the Dome of the Rock] is the place where the just and damned will be separated . . ." The Temple sets the stage for the apocalypse.

Except that today, Jerusalem is ruled by Jews. In the eyes of Muslims, Islam is embattled here, not triumphant, and its hold on the Haram is threatened by the Jewish messianic vision. Anxious about the future, Muslims seek to erase the Temple from the site's past. In the work of radical rewriting, they are not alone.

TUVIA SAGIV INSISTS he didn't set out to show that the Western Wall was not really the outer wall of the Second Temple. He had no intention, he says, of trying to prove that the stones caressed daily by tourists and yeshivah students alike are actually the wall of the temple of Jupiter built by Hadrian celebrating his victory over Judaism.

"It's an intellectual issue that aroused my curiosity. Like a kid taking apart a watch," says Sagiv. "I'm not compelled by any passion for redemption, any footsteps of the messiah." He appears even more out of place than Asher Kaufman in the Temple business, where the standard Israeli actors are either sun-browned archeologists or bearded men whose oversized skullcaps are the ID badges of the Orthodox far right. Sagiv, clean-shaven, does have a yarmulke tucked above his ring of unkempt curls, but it's in the all-black, crocheted style favored by Orthodox yuppies taking evasive action against any political statement. When he meets me at his door on a frighteningly well-gardened street of castle-sized homes in Ramat Aviv Gimel—a monied neighborhood of Tel Aviv that Israelis regard as synonymous with secularism and dovish politics—he's wearing jeans and a T-shirt. Downstairs in his architectural office, several staffers are quietly working. His executive desk stands behind a glass wall and doors. The place says success, tastefully. He and his partner specialize in multilevel burial projects designed to solve Israel's shortage of cemetery space.

Sagiv, in his fifties, took up iconoclasm during a stint of reserve duty as an Artillery Corps officer in Israeli-occupied Hebron in the mid-eighties. "I started asking all sorts of questions about the Tomb of the Patriarchs," he recalls; architecturally, it didn't seem to line up with ancient texts. Eventually, "I came to the conclusion that the Tomb we know today is really an Edomite sanctuary. It's got nothing to do with the Jews."

He pauses, grabs some breath, lets his voice drop: "And then I got the idea that the Jews fooled the Arabs. There's a Jewish tradition that when the Arabs came, they asked the Jews where the tomb was. The same story's told about the Temple. I said to myself, if they fooled them about the tomb, all the more so they would have about the Temple." So he began looking for where the sanctuary *really* stood.

To the quest, he says, he brought "an interdisciplinary approach—Talmud plus architecture, a three-dimensional way of seeing things." In the accepted wisdom, he decided, altitudes didn't line up. Take the water problem: The Romans brought water to the Temple via an aqueduct that descends at an even, stunningly engineered grade of 0.15 percent from pools twenty miles away. The remains of the aqueduct can still be seen. The Talmud says it provided the water for a ritual bath, at an elevated spot in the Temple compound, that the High Priest used. Sagiv pulls out a diagram and jabs it. The aqueduct is far too low for the purpose. "If I put the Temple at the Dome of the Rock, and here's the pipe, how'd the water go *up?* The only answer is to lower the Temple!"

Studying Jerusalem's original topography—"I stopped working, I ran to libraries . . . I related to this like an architectural project, don't ask me who the client is, I don't know"—he concluded that the Temple actually stood between the Dome of the Rock and Al-Aqsa, at a spot originally lower on the hill.

Sagiv's radical conclusion: Hadrian built the raised plaza of today, and it's both larger and higher than the square where the Temple stood. The Western Wall where Jews pray is actually one side of that pagan construction. That, he insists, provides an answer to another problem: Today's Temple Mount plaza is much larger than the area described by the Mishnah, and much bigger than anything built anywhere in the Roman Empire in Herod's time. But, he says, it fits the massive scale favored in the time of Hadrian. At the top stood the temple of Jupiter, he says, which would have been in the style of the day: a rectangular building, an octagonal one and, in the open area between, a statue of the emperor on horseback, saluting his god. Deep within were the ruins of the Jewish temple. A fifth-century Bible commentary by Church Father Jerome, he says, places the equestrian statue directly above the site of the Holy of Holies: the emperor declaring his victory over the God of the Jews.

Then the Arabs, Sagiv asserts, built Al-Aqsa and the Dome of the Rock on the ruins of the pagan sanctuary—believing it the "Temple of Solomon." He produces a floor plan of the Muslim shrines and another, on transparency, of a second- to third-century temple to Jupiter at Baalbek, in today's Lebanon. It shows a rectangular hall and a hexagon. Sagiv puts one plan on top of the other: They virtually line up. "That's coincidence?" he says, quietly, amazed. "It's like it's the same architect"—certainly, the same period. I can hear the joy, as if the boy dissecting the clock has just reached the shimmering mainspring.

Wanting more evidence, Sagiv says, "I looked for nonintrusive methods" of examining the Temple Mount. "Infrared gives amazing results." He linked up with an Israeli firm that does aerial infrared survey work "and for the last five years, every plane that goes up with the equipment, every copter, material reaches me." He shows me pictures of the Mount that have the fuzzy look of fetal ultrasounds. In one, four thick subterranean lines can be seen between the Dome of the Rock and the mosque to its south. "It could be that down there—it's wishful thinking, but maybe those are the remains of the Temple. You're looking, for the first time in two thousand years, at the Temple."

Each time he mentions one of the activists interested in building the Third Temple, he says, "I don't agree with his politics." But he's spoken to enough of them to say, "There are people who want to do what the [1980s] underground tried"—blow up the Dome. "It could start World War III . . . I don't know how much the intelligence people know, but the ground's on fire. They shouldn't say afterward that they didn't know." Sagiv knows the clock he has opened has wires leading out of the back, leading to a bomb.

But he'd like to think that he has helped defuse it. He says he has convinced Israeli militants not to attack the Dome to make room for the Temple, because "it would be like when spies shoot the wrong guy."

And, he says, he has a way Jews and Muslims could settle their claims to the site. "Each side says, 'It's all mine.' If I'm right, there's a solution." Another sketch emerges, of a multilevel peace plan: "We'll break through the Western Wall and be able to look at the remains of the Temple. They'll be above, and we'll be below, until the coming of the messiah . . . I have problems with sacrifices. . . . Just looking could be more spiritual."

The Muslims? "Everything needs to be done in coordination with them," Sagiv responds. Muslims have an interest in dispensing with the idea that the Dome sits where the Temple did. "There has to be cooperation, international efforts," he says. Tuvia Sagiv, it turns out, also has a utopian vision, though visions aren't his shtick. It's a subtle dream: driven by fascination with the lost sanctuary, yet recognizing that the Temple can't be had. Jews will contemplate the physical symbol of innocence, yet won't try to rebuild it. The faiths will live in peace—explicitly because of an architect's design, implicitly because of an agreement it would take nothing short of divine intervention to work out. The dream accepts that redemption isn't at hand, and also hints that it is.

There are people who swear by Sagiv's "southern theory." But for them, he's talking about where the Temple should be built. To spread his ideas, Sagiv lectures in homes, West Bank settlements—and for Chuck Missler's Christian tour groups. Missler was introduced to him by an octogenarian Jewish Temple activist named Stanley Goldfoot. In the 1980s, Goldfoot distributed maps showing Kaufman's "northern theory." He stopped after meeting Sagiv. At first Missler had Sagiv lecture at his Temple conferences; eventually he dropped the other speakers and just brought the architect.

"The infrared information I've seen is not conclusive, but tends to support Tuvia Sagiv," says Missler. For him, Sagiv is another proof that prophecy is coming true. "What interests us," Missler says, "is not the specifics, but the fact that the [research] is being pursued . . . that somewhere along the way the Temple will be rebuilt." A website presenting Sagiv's theories was set up by other born-again Americans. Missler's comments about a coming time worse than the Holocaust don't worry Sagiv. "For now, they're helping me. If that's what he believes, what do I care? . . . Just because of their beliefs, something's going to happen here?" It's a surprising comment, because Sagiv says he's met Jews who "just because of their beliefs," could indeed make something happen here.

ON A WARM SUMMER DAY, I find Dan Bahat sitting under a grape arbor and sorting ancient pottery shards in the Arab neighborhood of Silwan, just outside the Old City walls, almost in the shadow of Al-Aqsa. Muscular, bald, tanned, with a huge gray mustache, dressed in faded shirt and shorts, deep-voiced, speaking Arabic, German, English, and Hebrew in rapid succession, Bahat would be Central Casting's choice for an archeologist. The potshards come in tagged plastic bags from this year's dig, where he's looking for the northern wall of pre-Solomon Jerusalem. If you don't wish you could join him after ten minutes of conversation, you were born without the gene for adventure. The shovel he puts in the ground is a time machine.

Sagiv's location for the Temple? "It's a cute theory," says Bahat, who served for years as Jerusalem district archeologist for the state's Israel Antiquities Authority. "I don't agree with any of it." The Mishnah's description of the Mount, 500 cubits by 500, refers to how it looked before Herod, he says, and the only spot topographically large enough is at the top, where the Dome stands. As for Sagiv's view that Hadrian built the Temple Mount, "there's absolutely no source for that—a huge construction project like that, perhaps the most immense building of the classic age. On the other hand, the best visitors to the Temple . . . give an exact description of what we see today." Neither is there any evidence, he adds, that the Muslim shrines stand on Roman foundations.

Other archeologists are equally unimpressed. Ya'akov Billig helped direct the 1994–97 excavations south of the Temple Mount, and has studied the aqueduct central to Sagiv's theory. The ancient water line, he says, arrived at the Temple at just the altitude of the Mount today, which is no problem. For the Talmud's statement that the aqueduct served the High Priest's elevated ritual bath comes from the fourth-century Babylonian sage Abaye, and "I dare to assert that Abaye's conclusion was wrong," Billig, an Orthodox Jew, says dryly. "Not everything a rabbi said in Babylon is Torah from Sinai." The past will have to be written according to the evidence written in rock, after all.

Besides, Billig has proof the Western Wall existed at the time of the Temple. On the Roman street that runs along the Wall, "we found 350 coins on the paving stones. Not one was dated later than the end of the Great Revolt." And everything was covered by stones that fell from above when the Temple was destroyed. An archelogist couldn't ask for more. It's precise evidence that the street was used until the date of the Temple's destruction—and that the Temple wall stood next to it at the time. "It was a time tunnel," Billig says. "We uncovered finds from the last moments of the Jewish people as a free nation in its land." Sagiv's claim that Hadrian built the Mount collapses.

When archeologists speak today of solid scientific research on the Temple's location, they're most likely to refer to Leen Ritmeyer. The Dutch-born Ritmeyer came to Israel as a kibbutz volunteer after the Six-Day War in 1967, "got interested in Israel and the Bible," and settled in the country two years later. In 1973, he got work at the excavations next to the Mount's southern wall under Hebrew University professor Benjamin Mazar, training on the job as an archeological surveyor and architect—drawing and interpreting finds, working from what's left of ancient buildings to describe what once was there. Eventually, he became an expert at reconstructing archeological sites. Today he lives in England, where he earned a Ph.D. at the University of Manchester in the development of the Temple.

To locate the Temple, Ritmeyer used Mazar's work, and the explorations of Captain Warren, and more evidence he found himself. A key clue: On the northwest corner of the platform where the Dome of the Rock stands, there's a set of stairs. The stairs are at an odd angle to the platform—because the bottom step, Ritmeyer discovered, is really a building stone marking a pre-Herodian wall. The wall, he found, was precisely parallel to the eastern wall of the Mount, and by one standard measure of a cubit, the two walls are five hundred cubits apart. Ritmeyer was beginning to map out the original Temple Mount, from before the time of Herod. Another clue: In the eastern wall, Warren had found just the slightest bend, marking the point where the wall once ended. That was the southeastern corner of the original Mount.

Detail by detail, he marked out the sacred 500-by-500-cubit square. Inside, at the right place, is the peak of the original mountain: the rock under the Dome, known in Arabic as Al-Sakhra. On it, he says, he found evidence of the walls of the Holy of Holies, and a rectangle where he believes the Ark of the Covenant stood. To measure it, he used a method called archeometry: "You give a computer several photos taken from different angles. It analyzes them . . . and creates a plan. I couldn't walk on the Sakhra, so I got a set of photos taken at beginning of the century and fed it into the computer." The rectangle is precisely two and a half cubits long, the length of the Ark. It's a bit wider than the one and a half cubits that the Bible specifies. Ritmeyer says that left room to place the Book of Deuteronomy next to it, in line with a biblical command.

"Until my research," he says, "archeologists ignored the Mishnah," the source for the 500-cubit-square sanctuary. "I showed that it referred to an earlier Temple. . . . Even in Herod's time, only that was considered holy." And not only that, one of the Dead Sea Scrolls gives the same measurements, and so does the biblical prophet Ezekiel in his vision of the Temple-to-be, he says, "So you wonder if the future Temple will be on the same area. And so you get a future dimension, a prophetic dimension to an archeological find," he goes on, and it hits me that the phone must be quivering in my hand, because the conversation has just morphed, the exacting Leen Ritmeyer is not talking about archeology any more, but eschatology, the science of the future, unless when you talk about the Temple Mount there is no way to divide the two, though he reassures me, "This is only my personal view, it doesn't affect my work, which is purely archeological and architectural."

He was raised Dutch Reformed. "They say when you die you go to heaven. I believe in the establishment of the kingdom of God on earth with its capital in Jerusalem. The physical factor of Jerusalem and the Temple Mount became very important in my life," he says. Because of archeology, "the Bible came to life. . . . It gave me an idea of why the State of Israel was established. I started reading prophecies on Israel and the Temple Mount, Isaiah and Amos. . . . You have to understand the past to understand the future."

In England, he says, he has joined the Christadelphians, a small Christian denomination founded in the mid-nineteenth century and pro-Zionist from the start. "The greatest thing that's happened in this century is creation of Israel, not just for Jews but as a fulfillment of prophecy." The peace process, he suggests, also fits prophecy. "After a short period of peace will come a time that's not so pleasant for Israel," that is, he says, "the time of Jacob's trouble," which is another name for the Tribulation, and "then the Messiah's kingdom."

A LOT OF RITMEYER is rooted in nineteenth-century England. In an article on his research, he describes Captain Charles Warren as "a brilliant engineer" whose work, "carried out while he was still in his twenties, stands as a landmark of systematic investigation . . ." In the name of science, Ritmeyer writes, Warren was willing, for instance, to lower himself forty-two feet into a Temple Mount cistern, then spend hours slipping in the three feet of water at the bottom in winter weather in order to measure the subterranean chamber—with the result that "he returned to England in ill-health, suffering from fever and exhaustion." In short, the man any archeologist would wish to be.

Ritmeyer does not mention that after his expedition Warren wrote *The Land of Promise,* a book arguing that Britain's East India Company should colonize Palestine with Jews. The idea was popular in England at the time, as historian Barbara Tuchman has written, both because it promoted British imperial interests and because it fit the Bible's prophecy. Those two motivations would lead England to the Balfour Declaration of 1917 in favor of a Jewish homeland in Palestine, and from there to ruling over Palestine. Once there, the British would find themselves unsuccessfully adjudicating the irreconcilable demands of Jewish nationalists and Arab nationalists. The struggle would burst into flames at a predictable spot.

FOUR

FOR GOD
AND COUNTRY

Praise the Lord and pass the ammunition.

—Title and chorus of 1942 hit song,
words and music by Frank Loesser

F OR MUSLIMS, that Friday was Muhammad's birthday. For Jews, it
was the tenth of Av, one day after the fast that commemorates the destruction of the First and Second temples. For the British, Friday, August 16, 1929, was the day that the Palestine Mandate began to come
undone.

The major prayers of the Muslim week are on Friday. When they
ended that day at Al-Aqsa, some of the worshipers burst into a stone
courtyard nearby, perhaps ten feet wide, stretching for a little more
than seventy feet along the Western Wall. Since the late Middle Ages,
that narrow space had served as the most sacred spot for Jewish
prayers, the place where a man or woman could touch stones that remained from the edge of the Temple. The day before, on the anniversary of the destruction, several hundred Jews had demonstrated at the
Wall to emphasize Jewish rights to the spot. A photo of a few of them
shows a line of young men and women, some in shorts, some apparently in regular shoes. The dress matters: As a sign of mourning, religious Jews do not wear leather shoes on the fast day. The protesters

were nationalists; they came because the Wall was sacred to the Jewish nation, not necessarily to the Jews' God. At the end of the demonstration, they broke the terms of their official permit to protest: They raised the blue-and-white Zionist flag and sang the Zionist anthem, "Hatikvah," before leaving the Wall to the pious. For Muslim protesters who came the next day, the wall was part of Al-Aqsa, the spot where Muhammad had hitched his supernatural steed Buraq—and the beachhead from which the Jews threatened the Muslim shrines. They expressed their views by beating Jewish worshipers.

The following Friday, August 23, thousands of Muslims crowded the Haram. An Arab eyewitness would recall years later that when the crowd burst into the Old City streets, the poor Arab youths who worked as porters in the markets screamed, "O Jews, the faith of Muhammad is fulfilled with the sword." Armed with clubs and knives, Arabs assaulted Jews in the Old City, and by an hour later were attacking other Jewish areas of Jerusalem, especially outlying, isolated ones. The attacks were nearly all in one direction, but not entirely: In one recorded case that day, Jews killed several Arab bystanders. The British police were horribly undermanned, and the Jewish self-defense group, the Haganah, was half-organized and quarter-effective.

Violence spread through the country. On the second day it reached Hebron, where several hundred Orthodox Jews lived among twenty-thousand Muslims. Rioters moved from Jewish house to house, murdering and looting. Sixty-seven Jews were killed, including a dozen women and three children. Most of the town's Jews, on the other hand, were saved by Arab neighbors. A girl named Rivka Slonim would recall that her family's Arab landlord galloped in from his vineyards, "stood at the door of the house, and announced that over his dead body would anyone enter this house. And so he drove off the mob . . . and we were saved." The marauders slaughtered her brother and sister-in-law, who lived elsewhere; their thirteen-month-old son survived because he was covered in his parents' blood and taken for dead. Outnumbered, British police shot at rioters to kill.

In a week and a half of terror in Palestine, 133 Jews and 116 Arabs were killed. A few Jews returned to Hebron, only to leave in later disturbances. In a new account of the period, Tom Segev is unusual among Israeli historians in citing a Jewish official who wrote that "in isolated cases" Jews "went shamefully beyond the framework of self-defense." In one instance, they broke into a mosque and destroyed holy books. But those were the exceptions: As a British commission of inquiry concluded, the "disturbances . . . took the form, for the most part, of a vicious attack by Arabs on Jews." A pro-Arab account in the 1973 book *The Politics of Palestinian Nationalism* mentions "attacks on Jewish communities in Jerusalem, Hebron and Safad"—and refrains from supplying a single detail that might trouble the conscience. A 1998 report published on the website of the Palestinian Authority is even more evasive: It explains that "in 1929, in response to provocations staged by Jewish religious extremists on the Jerusalem holy sites, riots erupted and violence took to the streets." It's "violence" that took to the streets, not Arab rioters.

For all three sides, the "events" of 1929 were a turning point in the struggle for control of Palestine. Jews spoke of "pogroms"—a term that alleged British complicity, just as the czarist regime was complicit in Russian pogroms, and that fit Arab hostility into the long experience of anti-Semitism. Pro-Israeli histories often describe Hajj Amin al-Husseini, an Arab nationalist who held the top Muslim religious post in Palestine, as exploiting tension over the Wall to ignite violence. But Zionists could no longer ignore Arab opposition to creating a Jewish state in Palestine, and had learned that British support was unreliable. Pro-Arab accounts, when they don't skim past the riots, stress that they galvanized Arab nationalism in Palestine. The British commission stressed as the explosion's underlying cause "the disappointment of [the Arabs'] political and national aspirations" in Palestine. In British policy debates, August 1929 became Exhibit A for officials who argued that the Balfour Declaration's promise of a "national home" for the Jews had been a mistake.

The accounts share this much: Two national groups were wrestling for one piece of land. Unable to settle that conflict, the British would stumble out of Palestine in 1948, and Arab and Jew would continue fighting until, in the last quarter of the century, they began giving up some pieces of their dreams in return for some measure of peace, despite its fragility. Nineteen twenty-nine is a reasonable point for marking when a dispute turned into a war.

Yet the overlapping accounts also share a failure to focus on where the bleeding began. At most, they describe the Western Wall as an instrument used by one side or the other to rally its forces. For, they say, this battle is about nationalism, a secular view born in the nineteenth and twentieth centuries that puts aside religion as the source of identity and values, and says instead that the ultimate value is your nation—the people who share a language, a territory, a culture, a political history. The peasant from the village outside Jerusalem was therefore an Arab, not a Muslim. To clarify matters, the Jews often called themselves Hebrews: They'd pensioned off God, they were returning to their land as a nation. The nation of Arabic-speakers and the nation of Hebrew-speakers had gone to war over a piece of territory ruled at the time by the empire of English-speakers.

Which is true, but is not the whole matter: It ignores the role that faith and millennial visions played in the Arab-Jewish conflict from the start and still play. It ignores how nationalism, as the sorcerer's apprentice, appropriates the apparently extinguished symbols of faith, only to see them burst back into flames in his hands. Jerusalem and the Temple Mount are not incidental, in 1929 or at crucial moments that have followed in the Arab-Israeli conflict, right up to the present day. They are where God and country meet, where nationalism is rewritten as millennialism.

Start with the British: The logic of national interest, surely, brought them to Palestine. The territory was on the road to India, and on the flank of the Suez Canal. In the Great War, it was the entryway to the Ottoman Empire; after the war it would serve as the bridge between Britain's African empire and and its sphere of influence in the Middle East. Imperial logic said Britain must take Palestine and rule it, directly or by proxy. Yet on November 2, 1917, two days after General Edmund Allenby's Egyptian Expeditionary Force took Beersheba from the Ottoman Turks and prepared to march north toward Jerusalem, the British government announced an entirely different rationale for the campaign: Foreign Secretary Arthur Balfour sent a letter to British Zionist leader Lord Rothschild, informing him that the cabinet had approved "a declaration of sympathy with Jewish Zionist aspirations": "His Majesty's Government view with favour the establishment in Palestine of a national home for the Jewish people . . ."

Five weeks later, Allenby's army took Jerusalem. For two days after the actual conquest, the general's arrival was meticulously planned. As Allenby's biographer noted, making sense of the concern with the ceremony, Christian armies were returning to the city for the first time since the Crusades. Allenby arrived at Jaffa Gate riding a white horse, with the pomp of a king. Then, before he entered the Old City, he dismounted and walked forward. A standard account of the general's reason: His Savior had entered this city on foot, and so would he.

Allenby's humility is the footnote that makes sense of the Balfour Declaration: Conquering the Holy Land requires more than strategic logic; it has to fit religiously. Despite what prime minister David Lloyd George wrote in his memoirs, Britain did not promise the Jews a "national home" in gratitude for Zionist leader Chaim Weizmann's invention of a method for synthesizing acetone for the British war effort. Neither, argues Barbara Tuchman, was the Balfour Declaration aimed at garnering support from American Jewish bankers or Russian Jewish Bolsheviks, though Lloyd George also made that claim; both groups were anti-Zionist. The declaration was a statement by the British to themselves, a way of giving meaning to the conquest that *they* understood.

That logic was rooted in the fervor for the Old Testament and the hope for the millennium, which together had led Cromwell's England to reaccept the Jews, and which saw a resurgence in nineteenth-century Britain—not just among groups such as the Christadelphians or John Darby's premillennialist Plymouth Brethren, but also among mainstream Anglicans. The twin results were the desire to convert the Jews and the desire to return them to their land. Tuchman writes of the exemplar of these passions, the influential philanthropist Anthony Ashley Cooper, Earl of Shaftesbury, that "despite all his zeal on the Jews' behalf, it is doubtful if Lord Shaftesbury ever thought of them as a people with their own language and traditions. . . . To him, as to all the Israel-for-prophecy's sake school, the Jews were simply the instrument through which Biblical prophecy could be fulfilled. They were not a people, but a mass Error that must be brought to Christ in order that the whole chain reaction leading to the Second Coming . . . could be set in motion." His pet causes included the massive, thoroughly unsuccessful London Society for Promoting Christianity Among the

Jews. He was the chief actor behind England's 1838 decision to appoint a vice-consul in Jerusalem, delegated to offer protection to local Jews as if they were Englishmen. As the first Western diplomatic representative in the city, the vice-consul was an imperial fingerhold, but in Shaftesbury's mind he was also a step toward the prophesied restoration of the Jews. Shaftesbury combined the two interests by pushing through the establishment, by parliamentary act, of a Church of England bishopric in Jerusalem, expecting somehow to bring Jews, once restored to the land, to Anglican truth.

Neither Balfour nor Lloyd George was a millennialist, but they were products of an England suffused with such belief, and of the ardor it produced for the Old Testament. Balfour defended his declaration to Parliament by arguing that Christendom must not be "unmindful of the service [the Jews] have rendered to the great religions of the world." Lloyd George commented that when he discussed Palestine with Weizmann, Zionism's apostle to the British government, Weizmann "kept bringing up place names that were more familiar to me than those of the Western front." The two statesmen could regard restoring the Jews to their land as a British task because English millennialism had made this a reasonable project, even for those who weren't thinking about the millennium. The theological purpose had become a political "sympathy with Jewish Zionist aspirations"—which also relieved it of the irksome expectation that the Jews were about to measure up and become Christians. Except that once England actually ruled Palestine, the simple commitment of the Balfour Declaration slammed into the real world.

IF BRITAIN'S POLICY in Palestine began as half-secularized, half-conscious Christian millennialism, Zionism was a far more self-aware transformation of Jewish messianism into a secular political project.

The harnessing of religious energies is clear in popular depictions of Theodor Herzl, the Viennese Jewish journalist whose *Der Judenstaat (The Jewish State)* became Zionism's manifesto and who founded the organized Zionist movement in 1897. Herzl was utterly nonreligious. But as a correspondent in Paris, he covered the framing of French army captain Alfred Dreyfus for treason, and the wave of anti-Semitism it set off in France. The affair convinced him Jews would be safe only if they had a state—"the house which is to shelter the Jewish nation." The phrase is packed: It defines the Jews not as a faith community but as a secular nationality. And it argues for a state as "shelter"—in Herzl's view, an answer to immediate dangers, not the ideal kingdom of the Last Days.

Yet Jews found it easy to portray him in the traditional vocabulary of messianism. A 1901 book cover shows Moses leaning out of clouds to pass Herzl his staff: the former redeemer in robes, the latter redeemer somehow managing to look prophetic even in fin de siècle formal dress. The classic photo of Herzl, shot by Zionist artist Ephraim Moshe Lilien, shows him on a hotel balcony gazing into the distance. The image was recycled in a drawing; Herzl looks out from a balcony at a line of people marching uphill toward Jerusalem's walls, while an oversized sun rises behind the city—the dawn of redemption. A postcard printed in Cairo after his death bears a Hebrew elegy that begins, "Where are you, Herzl? Where are you, God's messiah?" Lilien outdid them all in a drawing of Adam and Eve's expulsion from Eden: The winged, naked angel guarding Eden's gate wears the Zionist leader's face, as if Herzl had it in his power to reopen the way to paradise lost.

Zionism offered Jews more than "shelter." If modernity had cost you your faith, Zionism allowed you to remain a Jew, by reframing the Jews as a nation. The Bible became national literature; Hebrew would be the nation's vernacular, not the sacral tongue. From the start, Zionists claimed to be better Jews than the Orthodox: The Orthodox only prayed for redemption; Zionists were making it happen.

Juggle both pieces of the idea: Zionism was messianism, but it was also something transformed. Its relation to the traditional vision of the future was uncertain, shimmering, constantly shifting. It aimed literally at ending the exile. Describing Herzl as messiah was an exuberant metaphor, but the exuberance came from a place in the gut that half-wanted to believe literally. Hovering in the air was the idea that Zionism would renew an ideal Jewish past—an adaptation of Judaism's hope that redemption will "renew our days as of old." Lilien's imagined biblical scenes show lush women draped in flowing dresses and headscarves. A 1912 photo from Palestine shows a real-life Jewish woman caught by the camera while harvesting wheat: Her white dress reaches the ground, her sleeves are long swathes; a white scarf hangs from her head over her back; she could have walked out of Lilien's dreams. Kibbutzim, the Zionist communes, created ceremonies to present their fields' first fruits on the spring holiday of Shavuot, restoring its agricultural roots—but not the actual ancient procession of farmers bearing first fruits to the Temple. The question was which parts of redemption should be read as metaphor, and when to demand literalism. A British offer to establish a Jewish colony in East Africa flopped because Zionists wanted the actual Land of Israel.

Precisely because Zionism offered only pieces of redemption, brought by human efforts, much of Orthodox Judaism in Europe opposed it. For religious Jews who did join the movement there were two options. One was to stress the practical—a state as shelter against physical attack and assimilation. The alternative was developed most clearly by Avraham Yitzhak Kook, a Lithuanian rabbi who moved to the Holy Land in 1904. The fact that Jews were returning to their homeland, he said, was proof that the divine redemption had actually begun. Secular Zionists pioneers who farmed the land and built new towns, he said, were carrying out God's will—unknowingly, despite themselves—and would eventually return to religion. Kook's ideas draw on classic Jewish mysticism, particularly the teachings of Rabbi Yitzhak Luria, the sixteenth-century Sacred Lion of Safed. Yet they also affirm a nineteenth-century faith in human progress and reflect the confident reading of "inevitable processes of history" popular among left-wing radicals of the time. Zionism had made messianism secular; Kook made Zionism part of God's plan.

At a holiday table in 1980, a bent-backed neighbor with a cracked voice told me what happened after Britain appointed Herbert Samuel, a Jewish politician, as the first high commissioner for Palestine. Arriving in Jerusalem in 1920, Samuel was invited on the Sabbath to the main synagogue in the Old City to chant the weekly passage from the biblical prophets. The hall was packed, my neighbor remembered; he'd walked from the ultra-Orthodox, anti-Zionist neighborhood of Me'ah She'arim to see the great man. Samuel finished the text and chanted the standard prayer that follows, a request that God send the messiah "speedily, so our hearts will be glad; a stranger will not sit on [David's] throne, and others will not be given the honor due to him."

And then, the old man told me, still stunned by it all six decades later, the crowd burst into ecstatic tears. Without intending to, Samuel had just lit the cold words of liturgy on fire: For the first time in nearly two thousand years, a gentile was not ruling Jerusalem. Not that you could think Samuel was the messiah, not that he was anything but a servant of the British crown. But he was really standing there. It's unlikely that the congregants were followers of Kook. But in the real world, people don't live by consistent ideologies; we're moved by conflicting, mismatched pieces of ideas, symbols, words buried in the memory waiting to be resurrected.

In this case, the words included *messiah, redemption*—and, inevitably, *Temple*. A 1904 Zionist calendar published in czarist St. Petersburg shows the figure of a prophet or priest; behind him is the walled city of Jerusalem, taken up mostly by an oversized, rebuilt sanctuary, lit by a burst of sun from dark clouds. The legend is from Psalms: "Oh that the salvation of Israel were to come out of Zion!" That's likely to have been symbolism—but persuasive symbolism. In the spring of 1928, Zionist leader Menachem Ussishkin gave a fiery speech in a central Jerusalem synagogue. Ussishkin was a Zionist maximalist, known for waving aside Arab demands as irrelevant. In his speech, he insisted on the Jews' right to a state in all of Palestine, and concluded by declaring, "Let us swear that the Jewish people will not rest or be silent until our national home is built on our Mt. Moriah." Ussishkin's "Temple" was political independence, but his declaration could conjure up other associations, in the minds of Jews and Arabs alike.

And the issue of the Western Wall was no metaphor. In the last years of Turkish rule, wealthy Jews had tried to purchase the prayer area, which belonged to an Islamic trust, to no avail. By Turkish regulations, Jews did have the right to pray there. By the strict letter of the law, they didn't have the right to bring benches, or Torah scrolls, or the divider between the sexes required by Orthodox law—though they often did so, without official objections. The British, unwilling to touch the unstable structure of religious claims they inherited in Old Jerusalem, took the de jure position: no benches, no accoutrements. So on Yom Kippur 1928, when a British police officer saw that the ultra-Orthodox Jews had put up a cloth-and-wood divider, he ordered his men to remove it—which they did, in the midst of the most sacred day of the Jewish year, while women worshipers screamed, and one male worshiper held desperately to the divider until he was thrown with it outside the Old City walls.

There's an irony here: Secular Zionists had a bitter ideological battle with the ultra-Orthodox. Praying at the edge of the ruined Temple, secularists felt, represented the old way of seeking redemption. But once Jewish rights there were assaulted by the British for the sake of the Arabs, the Wall had to matter. If mainstream leaders didn't protest strongly enough, the way was open for opponents on the right to show they were more patriotic. Young rightists who marched to the Wall on the ninth of Av were appropriating one more piece of religious tradition for Jewish nationalism.

Not that the line between religion and nation is so sharp. On the Arab side at the time, the distinction may have been meaningless.

HAJJ AMIN AL-HUSSEINI was appointed Jerusalem's mufti, the highest authority in questions of Muslim law, by Herbert Samuel's administration. The job was an Ottoman post, but the British made Husseini the official head of Islam in all Palestine. Again, the ironies are wondrous: Palestine was carved out of the Ottoman lands after the Great War as a political entity in order to realize Balfour's promise to the Jews. Samuel, a Jew, chose Husseini under pressure from local Muslims—who mobilized because they saw the opposing candidate (so historian Yehoshua Porath writes) as someone who "was prepared to hand the Al-Aqsa mosque" to the Jews. In short, Husseini owed his realm, his job, and his issue to Zionism.

From Yom Kippur 1928, Husseini spearheaded a public campaign to protect Al-Buraq al-Sharif, that is, the Western Wall, from the Jews. Meeting British officials, the Supreme Muslim Council argued that the Jews aimed at taking over Al-Aqsa. A convention led by Husseini established a public committee to defend Al-Buraq; pamphlets flooded the country. Looking back, those months appear as a long fuse leading to August 1929 and the corpses in Hebron.

In Israeli accounts, Husseini often appears coldly Machiavellian in his use of Al-Aqsa. That makes sense if you regard Arab nationalism as a secular cause, if you presume religious language can't possibly be serious and must be a cover for something else. It makes sense, as well, if you presume Jews aren't interested in building the Temple—if it's obvious to you that this particular piece of redemption is purely a symbol, as it was for almost all secularists, or dependent on divine action, as it was for almost all the Orthodox. Even Kook, testifying before the British commission, drew a sharp distinction between the pieces of redemption in human hands and those in God's hands. The Temple, he said, belonged in the second category, so "until the day of redemption, we are not even allowed to enter the area surrounding the Holy Temple"—that is, the Mount.

But Husseini could exploit Al-Aqsa because it resonated for him, as it did for his audience. In the twenties he raised money throughout the Muslim world for renovations of Al-Aqsa and the Dome. In the process, he focused Islamic attention on Jerusalem. Muslims could believe that a divider at the Wall would be followed by a roof, to be followed by a gradual takeover of the Haram: Gradualism was in fact the Zionist strategy for settling Palestine. The Jewish slogan was "one more goat, one more acre." And Judaism, Muslims knew, did expect a Third Temple. The Muslims' fears *were* exaggerated, but they had a bit of truth to work from. They misread Zionism as religious messianism, just as secularist Zionists misread Husseini as secular nationalist. And that misreading also holds a piece of truth. The events of August 1929 did galvanize the political struggle against the Jews and British; it was a step toward Palestinians regarding themselves as a nation. Husseini's Al-Aqsa evangelism among the Muslims provided a symbol for the Palestine cause that would become central among Arab nationalists.

AVRAHAM STERN was a rebel even among rebels, too extreme for the average extremist. A Polish-born Jew who admired Mussolini, he'd been a member of the Irgun Tzva'i Le'umi (National Military Organization), the right-wing Jewish underground in Palestine. In the late '30s, Palestine's Arabs revolted against British rule; attacks on Jews were common. The Irgun rejected the mainstream Haganah policy of restraint and launched revenge attacks on Arabs: gunfire at a bus here, a bomb in a market there, the murder of innocents as payment for the murder of innocents. From there it went on to battling the British, who sought to satisfy the Arabs by restricting immigration even as desperate Jews were trying to get out of Europe. But when World War II broke out, the Irgun declared a truce: Fighting Germany was more important than driving out the British. Such zigzagging wasn't for Stern: In spring 1940, he and his followers left the Irgun to create a more radical group that would keep fighting the British. They robbed banks, tried to assassinate mandatory officials. In Hebrew the group was called Lehi, an acronym for Fighters for Israel's Freedom. The English called it the Stern Gang, even after police ferreted Stern out in a Tel Aviv apartment in 1942 and shot him dead. The group's new leaders included Yitzhak Yezernitzky, who later changed his name to Yitzhak Shamir and decades later became Israel's prime minister. Lehi's ideologue was Yisrael Scheib, who eventually took the Hebrew last name Eldad, after the biblical figure of a common man seized by the spirit of prophecy.

In a newspaper called *The Underground,* Lehi published its eighteen principles of Jewish national renaissance. Number 18 read: "Building the Third Temple, as symbol of the era of the Third Kingdom." After Israeli independence, the group's veterans republished the principles, with an emendation. Now number 18 said: "Building the Third Temple, as symbol of the era of total redemption." Historian Joseph Heller explains that "Third Kingdom" sounded too close to "Third Reich"—a sensitive point, especially since Lehi was stained by having unsuccessfully offered its services to the Axis against Britain in 1941.

The emendation makes the point clearer: "They were a messianic movement, especially under Stern," says Heller. Lehi was an exhibit of where blind, unbending consistency can lead human beings. Zionism appropriated messianism selectively, half-metaphorically. Lehi rejected selectivity: A political rebellion would bring redemption; and "Temple" really meant a temple, as the nation's sanctuary.

But then, strong enough circumstances could make even someone less extreme feel the literal force surging out of the symbol. Someone like David Shaltiel, commander of the Haganah, the Jewish militia-turned-army, in Jerusalem during Israel's War of Independence. Shaltiel was forty-five, which made him an old man among the Jewish fighters. Shaltiel's military training was also unusual: He'd spent five years in the French Foreign Legion. Later he became an arms buyer for the Haganah in Europe; in 1936 the Gestapo arrested him in Aachen. "He was in Dachau and Buchenwald and another sixteen prisons," says his widow, Yehudit Shaltiel. In Dachau, she says, he was put in charge of burying the corpses. He gave the harrowing task a measure of meaning. "They'd toss the dead in a room. He made sure they had a religious burial." Somehow, he was released before World War II began, and got back to Palestine, where he became a Haganah officer.

One piece of Shaltiel's biography wasn't at all unusual among the intensely secular men and women of the Haganah and its Palmah strike force: He came from an Orthodox home—in his case, in Hamburg. "They were super-religious," his widow says. "He rebelled. The way he told it, when he was thirteen, he walked out of the synagogue on Yom Kippur and ate pork, and waited for God to strike him down." When He didn't, young Shaltiel was done with religion. The story may be a self-written myth—"I don't think it's true. Where would he get pork on Yom Kippur?" says Yehudit. But eating pork on Yom Kippur was considered the epitome of blasphemy, a ceremony for rejecting religion based entirely on the forms of tradition. Even if Shaltiel made up the incident, it demonstrates the appeal that ritual still had for him.

For a person can't completely erase his past; the shadow of the old writing remains on the page. In the midst of his Haganah work, even when the militia had joined the rebellion against the British after World War II and Shaltiel had gone underground, "Once a week he had this Polish Jew over so they could sing Sabbath hymns together," his widow says. He loved reading the Bible; he loved religious ceremonies.

Shaltiel's command was one of the toughest in the War of Independence, which began after the United Nations voted in November 1947 to partition Palestine between a Jewish and an Arab state. Arab forces opposed to partition battled Jews even as the British pulled out, leaving a shambles in place of the bright dream of empire and fulfilled prophecy. With Jewish Jerusalem under siege, Shaltiel's soldiers sometimes fainted from hunger at their posts. On May 28, 1948, two weeks after the Zionist leadership proclaimed the establishment of the State of Israel, the Jewish quarter of the Old City fell to Jordanian troops. Strategically, the Old City wasn't crucial. Symbolically, though, it stood for the Jewish past and hopes for the future.

At dawn on July 17, a U.N. ceasefire was due to take effect in

Jerusalem. By now, the siege had been broken; Shaltiel's troops had food, ammunition, reinforcements. He decided on a last bid to take the Old City. Haganah troops would attack where the walls ran across Mt. Zion, on the southwest of the Old City. Irgun and Lehi fighters, now operating under the Haganah command, were assigned to attack at New Gate, on the northwest. Shaltiel was confident of victory; he had a special explosive charge designed by a physicist that would blow a hole in the stone wall on Mt. Zion. So confident, in fact, that he prepared his victory speech in advance—and had a lamb ready to sacrifice on the Temple Mount.

As his widow tells it, Shaltiel simply believed that was the proper way to mark the Jews' return to the Old City as its rulers. Shaltiel died in 1969; no one knows whether he expected more sacrifices, whether he was thinking about that sheep as an offering to God or a mark of sheer wonder, a sign perhaps that the people driven from the Mount by Titus had come back. I suspect Shaltiel did not really know himself. As a stickler for discipline, he certainly would not have crossed the orders from David Ben-Gurion, leader of the new state, not to damage the Muslim shrines. But Shaltiel was an avatar of Zionism; he'd learned his symbolic language from religion even if God had not done him the simple favor of punishing him for eating pork. When all the allegories for salvation seemed ready to turn solid, he prepared a lamb for the altar.

The commander of the Lehi forces in Jerusalem, Yehoshua Zetler, was less impressed with Ben-Gurion's orders. If the attack succeeded, he planned to raze the Muslim shrines on the Mount, and he equipped three of his men with cannisters of TNT.

Shaltiel's offensive failed; his physicist's bomb made a black mark on the four-hundred-year-old Ottoman walls but didn't create the slightest opening. The commander told his troops to honor the 5:00 A.M. ceasefire.

Even then, hope flickered in Lehi. In a memoir, Yisrael Eldad wrote of his feelings a month later, on the night of the Ninth of Av, in the Lehi base in Jerusalem.

    And the heart imagines: Perhaps it will break out tonight. . . .

If only they had a sense for history. Oh, if only! And precisely on this night, the night of the first destruction, the night of the second destruction, precisely on this night if only they burst through and got there—for they are capable of bursting through and getting there. . . . There are enough arms, and there are young men, and there is Jerusalem, all of her desiring it, ready for a dread night like this, if only they would burst through, if only they would get there.

To the Wall, to the mourning, to what has been abandoned.

To break through and set it all aflame. In fire it fell and in fire it will rise again. To raze it all there, all the sanctified lies and hypocrisy. To purify, purify, purify.

It didn't happen. The Jewish state was born without the Old City. Reading Eldad's erotic-apocalyptic fantasy, I have to wonder if it was just as well. Ben-Gurion *didn't* have control of Lehi: In September, its men would assassinate U.N. emissary Count Folke Bernadotte in Jerusalem. And even as matters stood, the new state aroused messianic hopes. The official Chief Rabbinate, acting in the spirit of Kook's theology, instituted a Sabbath prayer for the welfare of the state that referred to it as the "first flowering of our redemption." Perhaps the fact that you couldn't get to the Old City served to say: Calm down. The messiah isn't here yet.

Jews weren't alone in feeling that the new state was pregnant with biblical meaning. In his 1996 book, *Beginning of the End: The Assassination of Yitzhak Rabin and the Coming Antichrist,* Texas pastor John Hagee recalls sitting with his father when news came over the radio of Israel's establishment. His father, Hagee says, told him, "We have just heard the most important prophetic message that will ever be delivered until Jesus Christ returns to earth." For dispensationalists, the Balfour Declaration had been exciting, but Israel's birth was absolute proof: The Bible's prophecies of the Last Days were coming true. As time passed, premillennialist writers would regularly link May 1948 with Jesus' answer when his disciples asked for a sign of the end: "Learn a parable of the fig tree; When his branch . . . putteth forth leaves, ye know that the summer is nigh: So likewise, when ye shall see all these things, know that it is near. . . . This generation shall not pass, till all these things be fulfilled." Israel's creation was interpreted to be "these things"—so the Second Coming was near.

And yet, Israel's independence was just the start. Events in Jerusalem nineteen years later would amplify expectations into ecstasy.

"WHERE IS OUR HEBRON—will we forget it? . . . And our Shechem, and our Jericho, where—will we forget them?. . . . every bit of earth belonging to the Lord's land—is it in our hands to give up even one millimeter?"

The speaker was Rabbi Tzvi Yehudah Kook. The occasion was an Israeli Independence Day celebration on May 14, 1967, at Merkaz Harav, the yeshivah his father Avraham Yitzhak Kook had founded and which he now headed. When he spoke at the religious academy that night about Hebron, Jericho, and Shechem (the biblical name of Nablus), Tzvi Yehudah Kook was describing how he'd felt twenty years before, when he'd heard of the U.N.'s decision to partition Palestine. But he was also conveying the longing he still felt for the pieces of biblical Israel that had fallen under Jordanian rule.

Kook's disciples would soon regard his speech as prophecy. May 14 was the day Egyptian President Gamel Abdel Nasser put his army on full alert. The next day Nasser sent two divisions of infantry into the Sinai Peninsula. The Middle East was sliding toward war.

Kook wasn't alone in longing for what lay beyond the ceasefire lines. At an Independence Day music festival held in Jerusalem, popular song writer Naomi Shemer presented a new work: "Jerusalem of Gold." It was a dirge for the divided city. The second stanza said:

> *. . . The market square is empty*
> *no one visits the Temple Mount*
> *in the Old City . . .*

The song sounded like a pop lament for a lost lover, and like a medieval hymn mourning the Temple's ruins—except that the hymn would have mentioned God. In part, Shemer's song worked because it conveyed the strange illusion that the Old City and all the land beyond it had remained empty since 1948, waiting for the beloved to return. There was no conflict with a rival for the city's favors; romantic fulfillment required only that the lovers, nation and city, be rejoined. The third, and originally the last, stanza said: "Your name burns the lips/ like an angel's kiss"—a touch of eroticism deepened, for those who knew, by the fact that a "Jerusalem of gold" was a 2,000-year-old term for a woman's tiara, the kind a wealthy man would give his bride.

The song was an immediate hit. Later it would be said that the military chief of staff, Yitzhak Rabin, left the festival when he received word that Egypt had closed the Straits of Tiran, imposing a blockade on Israel's southern port of Eilat. In fact, the straits were closed a week later, but the story puts everything in one place: The hero, the casus belli, and the song that became the war's anthem. And if the conflict began with real-world strategic issues of navigation rights and national survival, the anthem expressed the mythic meaning that the war would take on.

For Israelis, the three weeks after Independence Day seemed like the countdown to the end of *their* world. Jordan and Iraq joined the Egyptian-Syrian defense pact; Nasser spoke of exterminating Israel; Iraq's president promised that the Arab forces would "meet in Tel Aviv and Haifa." Within Israel, men were called up to their reserve units, and parks were prepared to serve as graveyards. If the Arab countries were slouching toward a war they weren't prepared for, the civilian on the street in West Jerusalem didn't know that.

Under public pressure, Prime Minister Levi Eshkol brought his political rivals into government: Menachem Begin, ex-head of the underground Irgun, as a minister without portfolio; Moshe Dayan, a former chief of staff, as defense minister.

As a military hero, Dayan boosted public confidence. He was an aristocrat of secular Zionism—born on the first kibbutz, a second-generation member of parliament in a country not yet twenty years old in 1967. But he also had a personal reputation for philandery, and a fascination with archeology that paid no attention to laws against unauthorized exploration. He loved the Bible, but read it the way he read the country's soil, as history book.

Dayan would become the patch-eyed poster boy of victory in '67, yet he actually inherited a military prepared by Rabin and others. The move for which he does deserve hero status took place halfway into the realm of religion. Rather than a conquest, it was a concession—at the Temple Mount. If God does stick his finger in history, He has a sense of humor in His choice of saints.

By the first days of June, diplomatic efforts to solve the crisis were stalled. Israel's government feared giving the Arab states more time to organize a war effort, and decided on a preemptive strike. The offensive was aimed at Egypt, at the threat from the Sinai, not at the Old City and Jordan. Early on the morning of Monday, June 5, waves of Israeli warplanes bombed Egypt's air bases, destroying its air force on the ground. It was a ruthless gamble—only a dozen planes were left behind above Israel to defend against possible attack—but it worked. (Miracle: a gamble that works.) The battle was lopsided from then on. Eshkol, meanwhile, sent a message to Jordan's King Hussein via a U.N. peacekeeping officer: We don't want war. The message arrived after Jordanian shells had begun falling on West Jerusalem.

When Colonel Mordechai Gur arrived in West Jerusalem on May 30 as part of the war preparations, "Mt. Scopus served as the axis of thinking and planning. The possibility of an all-out offensive against Jordan seemed distant"—so Gur would write in his memoirs of the war. Mt. Scopus was the original campus of the Hebrew University, a hilltop north of the Old City. Since 1948, it had been an Israeli enclave surrounded by Jordan, guarded by a few dozen Israeli troops. Israeli military planners feared that Jordan could easily grab it, and so prepared to push out of West Jerusalem and connect with the enclave. When the fighting began in the city, a brigade of young reservists from the paratroops was assigned the job.

At noon on Tuesday, June 6, Dayan arrived by helicopter in West Jerusalem. Major General Uzi Narkiss, head of the army's Central Command, met him. In a jeep, they drove through a swath of land taken before dawn that morning to Mt. Scopus. There they climbed to the roof of the old university library and looked out over the Old City. The view from the spot is superb; the Dome of the Rock seems near enough to reach out and grab. Narkiss said, "Moshe, we have to go into the Old City."

Dayan's reply: "Absolutely not." Surround the walled city from the east, he told Narkiss, but keep clear of "all that Vatican."

Fact is, Dayan also wanted to conquer the Old City, but without damaging the holy places there, without risking diplomatic fallout. At a cabinet meeting that day in Tel Aviv, Dayan explained that once besieged, old Jerusalem would soon surrender. But at 4:00 A.M., a sleepless Menachem Begin heard on the BBC that the Security Council had called for a ceasefire. A ceasefire had cost Israel the city in 1948. Hurried phone calls to Dayan and Eshkol followed. By eight on Wednesday morning, Gur and the paratroop brigade had orders to attack.

THEY ENTERED on the northeast, through the gate (known as St. Stephen's in English, Lions' Gate in Hebrew), Colonel Gur riding at the front of the column in a half-track that jerked through smoke and ash and gunfire from Jordanian Legionaires on the walls, past a burning bus that half-blocked the gate, Gur wondering if his own fuel tank would burst into flames, the half-track rumbling down the narrow street, and then turning off at the spot Gur remembered from a photo, his men firing in all directions; moments later they burst through another gate onto a path between trees and into a plaza with a shining octagonal building and a dome in front of them, and the men were off the vehicle and running toward it. And Gur was on the radio to Narkiss, who was himself racing toward the city gate in a jeep, he'd left his own half-track behind because it was too slow, and Gur told him: "The Temple Mount is in our hands."

In Hebrew, that took just three words, which would be the symbol for the country that everything had turned out impossibly better than expected, assuming you or your husband or your son weren't dead, or that you weren't one of the paratroopers who stood at Lions' Gate that day and watched three Arab men and a woman carry a dead girl to the cemetery just outside and dig her grave, that you didn't have to stare into the eyeless face of grief. On the Mount, some of Gur's men flew an Israeli flag on the Dome of the Rock.

Roaring up the road up to the gate, Narkiss passed a startling figure at the head of a line of paratroopers: Shlomo Goren, the army's chief rabbi, was running uphill, a Torah scroll under his right arm, a ram's horn in his other hand, his beard thrust forward. Soaked with sweat, the fifty-year-old chaplain refused a ride, insisting he'd reach the Mount on foot. From the top of the walls, Jordanian soldiers continued to fire. Goren was roaring out song.

Goren had been the head of the military rabbinate since the state was founded. Before that he'd been close to Lehi. Supremely self-confident, a passionate believer in the sanctity of the land and the state, Goren was a man swept away that day, the herald of the Lord. Blasting his shofar, he arrived on the Mount moments after Narkiss, bowed toward where the Holy of Holies had stood, which is to say the Dome, and shouted biblical verses. As Narkiss tried to speak into a microphone that a Voice of Israel reporter handed him, Goren again blew his horn, the wild wail drowning out the general's voice. Hundreds of soldiers, Narkiss wrote afterward, began singing, "Jerusalem of gold, of copper, and of light . . ."

There was one incident on the Mount later that day that Narkiss left out of his memoirs. Thirty years later, terminally ill, he told it to Israeli journalist Nadav Shragai, on condition that it be published only after his death. While soldiers still "wandered about the plaza as if they were dreaming," the rabbi walked up to the general. " 'Uzi,' Rabbi Goren said to me, 'Now's the time to put one hundred kilos of explosives in the Mosque of Omar [the Dome], and that's it, once and for all we'll be done with it.'

"I said to him, 'Rabbi, stop.'

"Goren said, 'Uzi, you will go down in history for this.'

"I answered, 'I've already put my name in Jerusalem's history.'

"But Rabbi Goren kept going, 'You don't grasp the immense meaning of this. This is an opportunity that can be exploited now, this minute. Tomorrow it will be impossible.'

"I said to him, 'Rabbi, if you don't stop now, I'm taking you from here to jail.' " According to Narkiss, Goren turned and left without another word.

Goren wasn't alone: A young chaplain named Yisrael Stieglitz—who in his later rabbinic career would be known as Yisrael Ariel—was assigned to guard the entrance to the Dome. Ariel would later be quoted as saying that he thought he was just keeping the spot clear until army engineers arrived to raze the shrine.

Yet for most, the Mount wasn't the real destination. A group of soldiers ran on, found the gate and the steps that led down into the alleyways and to the courtyard of the Western Wall. Narkiss and Goren arrived soon after, Goren again blasting on his ram's horn, while the soldiers hugged and stared upward and tried to make sense of what they were feeling.

Someone thought to send a captured Jordanian jeep into West Jerusalem to bring Tzvi Yehudah Kook and David Cohen, another leading spiritual figure among religious Zionists, an ascetic who, among other things, let his hair grow long. By one account, the idea was that of an Orthodox paratrooper who'd attended Cohen's lectures; by another, it came from Goren, the ascetic's son-in-law, who sent an aide for the sages. Cohen lived in a mostly non-Orthodox neighborhood but rarely left his house. A woman who looked out her window and spotted a big, bearded, long-haired man in a long coat sitting in a jeep dashed to one of her Orthodox neighbors to announce: "The messiah has come!" That day in Jewish Jerusalem, you didn't have to believe in God to be swept up in the feeling that redemption was at hand.

Kook told a rabbinic colleague afterward that he asked what gate they'd use, and Goren's man told him, "We've taken all the gates," to avoid telling him they'd cross the Temple Mount. If Goren was trying to win on points that day, to show that it was permitted to tread on the sacred ground, he was disappointed again: Kook crossed the plaza, but as radical as he was in his messianism, he—like his father—placed Temple-building at the end of the process, and would join a rabbinic ruling against setting foot on the Mount.

Religious Affairs Minister Zorach Warhaftig heard of the Old City's conquest on the radio that morning in Tel Aviv. His National Religious Party was known then for moderation on foreign and military policy. At a wartime cabinet meeting, he and Dayan were the minority that opposed opening a third front against Syria and taking the Golan Heights. When he heard the news from Jerusalem, Warhaftig immediately summoned his driver and headed for the city. Three decades later, a shrunken, impatiently incisive man in his nineties, one of the last two living signators of Israel's declaration of independence, he would still proudly point out that he was the first cabinet minister to reach the Wall. Like others, Warhaftig accidently crossed the Mount, where Goren was already busy surveying the area. The chaplain wanted to determine where the Temple had stood.

Defense Minister Dayan arrived on the Mount at two in the afternoon. With him were Narkiss and Meir Shamgar, head of the army's legal corps. Dayan, the amateur archeologist, had to be impressed with the shrines, and to feel the history of place. He was less impressed by the Israeli flag on the Dome, which Shamgar pointed out to him; the defense minister gave orders to take it down.

Visiting soldiers in the Sinai, Naomi Shemer added a new verse to her song.

> We've come back to the cisterns
> to the market and the square
> a shofar calls on the Temple Mount . . .

As in the original verses, the new one didn't hint at the presence of Arabs. The cry of love consummated was Goren's shofar blast on the Mount. Secular lament became sigh of exultation.

The war ended on Saturday, June 10. That night the bulldozers of the combat engineers entered the Old City. Twenty trucks waited outside Dung Gate to evacuate the Arab families of the Mughrabi quarter, a warren of tumbledown buildings that surrounded the Western Wall courtyard. An Israeli officer, the deputy military governor of East Jerusalem, told the mukhtar, the neighborhood leader, that the residents had to leave their homes—they'd be given the houses of other East Jerusalemites who'd fled. When the residents refused, the officer ordered a driver to start demolishing the first house. Minutes later, medics were treating the wounded, and the other residents were packing bundles to go. The bulldozers worked all night. By morning, they'd carved a wide field in front of the Wall and lengthened the exposed stretch of Herodian stones to 200 feet. Three days later was the holiday of Shavuot—in ancient times, one of the three annual pilgrimages to the Temple. On Shavuot 1967, an estimated 200,000 Israelis came to the Wall, in a festival of longing realized and amazed victory. This time there were no British soldiers to remove the divider between men and women.

Who gave the orders to raze the Mughrabi neighborhood? The mayor of Jewish Jerusalem, Teddy Kollek—a political ally of Dayan— has claimed he thought of it. Warhaftig switches the emphasis— Dayan initiated the operation, in coordination with Kollek—and criticizes them for acting too quickly, "without any consideration for the residents." There were legal means to reach the same goal, with proper compensation, even if it would have taken longer, he argues.

On the Saturday morning after the war, Dayan returned to Al-Haram al-Sharif with a set of staff officers. At the door to the mosque building, a group of Muslim leaders met him. The Israelis took off their guns and their shoes and entered, crossing the prayer carpets in the wide hall. Maybe you'd like to talk, Dayan said. But where, one of the Muslims answered. Here, Dayan said. There are no chairs in the mosque, the hosts pointed out. The defense minister sat down, crosslegged, on one of the rugs. The Israeli brass and the Muslim clerics followed suit. What's on your mind? Dayan asked. His hosts complained that their water and electricity had been cut off; Dayan ordered a staffer to get it straightened out, fast. And then he explained why he'd come: Israeli troops would leave the Haram, he said. Israel would be responsible for overall security, but would maintain it from without. The Muslim authorities would guard the area of the Haram and set the rules in the Dome and the Mosque. The old ban on Jews visiting was over; they would have free access, as long as they respected the customs of the site.

Dayan had decreed the new status quo: Under Israeli rule, the Haram remained a Muslim religious site, to be run by Muslims. For the sake of historical ties, Jews could now enter the Temple Mount— but de facto, Israeli policy was that they wouldn't pray there, wouldn't turn it into a Jewish place of worship. For that, there was the new square at the Wall.

Dayan's ersatz solution left much open to later conflict: How far religious autonomy went, for instance, and whether Jews had the right to pray within what was both Al-Haram al-Sharif and the Temple Mount. Those questions wouldn't really be settled by the Protection of Holy Places Law that Warhaftig presented to the Knesset, in a speech that still infuriates rightists because he spoke of the sanctity of the Western Wall instead of the Mount—because, he explains, "the Temple Mount belongs to us but isn't in our hands. It's in the hands of millions of Muslims," and he saw no reason to turn a conflict with the Arabs into a battle with all Muslims, "all the way to Indonesia."

The arrangement left Muslims angry and frustrated with the Israeli hand wrapped around Al-Aqsa. It left the possession of the

Mount as the most difficult question inside the dilemma of Jerusalem within the riddle of making peace between Jew and Arab.

Yet if you step back, what Dayan said sitting crosslegged in Al-Aqsa was a victory over history: The war didn't need to be the triumph of one religion over another. Unlike the Spaniards at Cordoba or the Turks at Constantinople or countless conquerers of Jerusalem in the past, Israel wouldn't evict the old faith and install its own. The two religions would live next to each other.

To try to make that work, Israel needed the Wall. It was territorial compromise—a separate holy place for each faith. The Muslims would have no veto over Al-Buraq. Warhaftig's criticism of Dayan was right: Razing the Mughrabi quarter, as it was done, defied decency, law, and human rights. Dayan may have done things that way because he didn't care about law. Or he might have acted quickly because he wanted it done before that crowd arrived on Shavuot and the old courtyard overflowed and people started thinking about the wide esplanade of the Mount and perhaps claimed that space for Jewish prayer—which even in retrospect presents a moral dilemma that should make your mouth twitch: driving people from their homes to prevent a holy war. To keep the state neutral between religions.

The astonished joy Israelis felt at "the Temple Mount is in our hands" made sense. In three days, they went from fear of annihiliation to victory: the experience of apocalypse. And the victory brought a return to a place to which you go when the messiah comes. To hear the messiah's footsteps was mistaking the symbol for the reality, but people navigate life by symbols. In the words "a shofar blows on the Temple Mount," it was easy to hear a whisper of redemption.

What do you think of the messianic fervor that followed 1967, I ask the wizened Warhaftig. "Messianic fervor does not surrender to reason, to *ratio*. Responsible people have to maintain reason," he answers, and then adds: "Messianic fervor is the secret of existence, it's true. Without it, the fire goes out. But reason has to control it. I tried to channel the fervor to the Western Wall."

"If Zorach Warhaftig hadn't given the Temple Mount back," a Jerusalem rabbi told historian Joseph Heller in synagogue, "the messiah would have come in 1967."

FIVE

A TASTE
OF PARADISE

An' even the Jordan river has bodies floatin'.
But you tell me, over and over and over again, my friend,
Ah, you don't believe we're on the eve of destruction.

— "Eve of Destruction," words by P. F. Sloan,
recorded by Barry McGuire, 1965

REVEREND IRVIN BAXTER is a big beefy casual man with a size XXL smile and a penchant for deciphering prophecy. He does it on his daily radio show, in his *Endtime* magazine, and at prophecy conferences where he regularly speaks. In the summer of 1999, he expected a final-status agreement on Israeli-Palestinian peace in the year 2000 that would lead to building the Temple. And "when the decision is made to rebuild the Temple," he said, "we'll have evangelists filling whole stadiums. Most people believe that when that agreement is signed, it will trigger the final seven years" of history.

Baxter knows how news can sock people in the soul. In June 1967, as an itinerant evangelist is his early twenties, still learning the trade, he was leading a three-week revival in a Pentecostal church in Ypsilanti, Michigan. It was a simple brick place with a dais in front and room for two hundred people—well-paid workers from the GM factory, schoolteachers, middle-class folk. The local pastor, he says, "was quite a preacher on biblical prophecy." And for a long time, he'd been teaching "that when Israel crossed the fence into East Jerusalem, the prophesied Rapture of the Church would occur."

The reasoning, Baxter explains, was that in Luke 21, when Jesus tells his disciples how to know the End has come, he says, "Jerusalem will be trodden down of the Gentiles, until the time of the Gentiles be fulfilled." For dispensationalists, it's been "the time of the gentiles" since, as Baxter puts it, "the Jewish people rejected Jesus," and "brought on the two-thousand-year exile." If the Jews retook Jerusalem, the pastor believed, the "treading down" was over, and so was the world as we know it.

So it had "an electrifying effect," Baxter says, when the pastor announced in church on June 5, 1967, that war had broken out in the Middle East—and that if Israel crossed the line in Jerusalem, the Rapture would follow. When young Baxter gave the invitation to be saved, "We had an extraordinary response," with people coming forward and lining up across the whole front of the church to accept Jesus while there was time, and be baptized, and be swept away by the spirit and speak in tongues.

When "the fence came down and the Temple Mount was captured," Baxter says, for a couple of nights the old pastor wouldn't come up on the platform; he felt perhaps he'd been a false prophet, "he was recovering his equilibrium, asking, 'What happened, where did I go wrong?' " The third night, "he got up, and said that the time of the gentiles is over, and if you're gonna get saved now, your gonna have to squeak in the door," which turned the excitement up even higher. It was a fantastic revival.

Except that the pastor was wrong the second time as well: No Rapture. But he was seventy-five, and much loved, so "one misunderstanding wasn't going to capsize him."

The pastor wasn't unique, though. "There were a number of ministers around the country who made predictions like this. There were large meetings, people were very concerned," Baxter says. Israel, it seemed, had fulfilled the final prophecy. Baxter allows that even then, he didn't agree. "I think Jerusalem is still trodden down as long as mosques are there" on the Temple Mount. But as a guest speaker, he didn't voice that view in the Michigan church.

Baxter says he's been back to Ypsilanti often; he never brings up what happened. But many of the people who were saved in June '67 are still in the congregation. The hopes weren't dashed, only delayed. And the congregants were solid people: Like their pastor, they didn't capsize.

DENNIS MICHAEL ROHAN arrived at St. Stephen's Gate early on August 21, 1969. A few moments later, Muhammad Hilwani ran up to meet him. Hilwani worked as a guard for the Waqf, the Islamic trust, at Al-Haram al-Sharif. Rohan, a twenty-eight-year-old Australian tourist, had promised a solid payment for the chance to enter Al-Aqsa mosque before visiting hours to take photos.

Rohan had come to Israel months before to learn Hebrew and work as a volunteer at Kibbutz Mishmar Hasharon, between Haifa and Tel Aviv. The young people from around the world who drifted through kibbutzim at the tail end of the sixties were "pretty wild," remembers Avinoam Brog, who was the kibbutz's counselor for volunteers. Rohan stood out: serious, short-haired, a hard worker in the kibbutz vineyard. "He talked about religion and Jesus and messiah. No one realized just how serious he'd turn out to be," says Brog, who later became a psychologist (and whose older brother, Ehud Barak, was later elected prime minister). One day Brog came to Rohan's room to remind him of a volunteers' meeting. "He said, 'I'm not coming. I only take orders from God.' I said, 'So maybe you should go to Jerusalem. You'll be close to Him.' " The next day, Rohan left the kibbutz. Thinking back, knowing better now how the mind works, Brog says, "That could have been the trigger."

In Jerusalem, Rohan spent two two weeks at Temple Mount, wandering about, lying on the carpets inside Al-Aqsa, and picking up a reputation as a good tipper. Once he got in an argument with Israeli police at a gate, and had to take a cop to his hotel room to show his passport. For several days he hired as his guide Munir, an eighteen-year-old Muslim. Rohan gabbed with him, hinting but not really saying what his interest was in the place—and one day offered three hundred dollars if Munir could guess why he was in Jerusalem. The guide, a good listener, jotted down what he'd heard from Rohan. He added bits from a letter he'd received from an American missionary he'd guided; he guessed this was Rohan's melody. One such sentence: "The knowledge you have of the Temple site should make you a candidate . . . to be protected by the true God through the forthcoming destruction." Rohan was thrilled by that line.

From St. Stephen's Gate, Rohan and Hilwani entered the Haram and walked to the mosque, where the guard let Rohan go in by himself. On either side of the wide center hall, rows of marble columns set off narrower aisles and support wooden rafters. Rohan strode to the inlaid cedar pulpit, brought by Saladin eight hundred years before to celebrate driving the Crusaders from the Holy Land. From his knapsack, he took a couple of containers of kerosene, soaked a scarf, laid it across one of the pulpit's wooden stairs, and lit it. Leaving the mosque, he thanked Hilwani, walked off—and began running when he heard a scream of pure agony behind him. Inside the building, flames spread to the carpets and rafters. Black smoke rose from Islam's third-holiest mosque. Rohan caught a cab to the bus station, and rode back to Mishmar Hasharon.

Sixteen fire trucks battled the blaze for hours. The firefighters also had to struggle with an angry mob of Muslims, some of whom were convinced the Jews were spraying gasoline to feed the flames. Even as the mosque burned, the city's Muslim leaders met, and accused Jewish-run City Hall of cutting off water to the Haram to keep the fire going. When Prime Minister Golda Meir and Defense Minister Dayan visited Al-Aqsa in the afternoon, they found pools of water and burnt beams on the floor, and open sky above the hall.

In 1967, Israel had annexed East Jerusalem, drawing a map of a unified city. The flames at Al-Aqsa scorched that map, exposing the border drawn in invisible ink between the Arab city and the Jewish. With angry demonstrations spreading, Israel's government imposed a then-unprecedented curfew on East Jerusalem. The fire also scorched one of Israel's most cherished claims since reunification: that it was protecting the holy places of all three faiths. Trying to shift the blame, one cabinet minister suggested on the radio that Arab provocateurs lit the blaze.

The police reached a different conclusion. Eyewitness descriptions reminded a policeman of the Australian who'd caused trouble at the gate. A squad headed for his hotel room—where they found a bottle of gasoline and a piece of paper with the handwritten words "Mishmar Hasharon." The next morning, police arrested Rohan. In questioning, he boasted of the crime. "God wanted me to build this Temple," he said. "Therefore if I am the chosen one to do this, then I [would] have to prove this by destroying the mosque."

The arrest of a foreign Christian didn't end the furor against Israel. A general strike was held in the territories under Israeli occupation since 1967. Mosque loudspeakers in Cairo blared accusations of Israeli arson; Egyptian President Nasser declared that it was the sacred duty of all Arab nations to go to war. King Faisal of Saudi Arabia put his military on alert for a holy war to "liberate Jerusalem."

Rohan's biography made some sense of his confession. In 1965, his wife left him, taking their two-month-old baby. Soon after, he began hearing voices from heaven; his behavior led to four months in a mental hospital. After his release, while working as a sheepshearer, he joined the Worldwide Church of God, a California-based movement on the fringes of fundamentalism. From Australia, he wandered to England, then to the kibbutz, where he again heard voices: He would marry his Hebrew teacher; he would build the Temple and rule over Jerusalem. His Israeli judges ruled that he was paranoid schizophrenic and had acted "under a pathological impulse he could not control." Rather than convict him, they committed him to a mental institution.

The insanity verdict made it easy to regard Rohan's crime as a freak accident. His religious beliefs were also offbeat. The Worldwide Church of God's leader, Herbert Armstrong, emphasized Bible prophecy, but rejected the doctrine of the Trinity. And he taught that the British were descended from the Ten Lost Tribes of Israel. Fundamentalists saw Armstrong's church as heretical; typically, premillennialist writer Randall Price describes Rohan in a recent book as a "cult member." Like "crazy," "cult member" is a way of saying: Not our problem.

That response is too pat. Even if Rohan was insane, the way he expressed that madness was shaped by beliefs with a much wider context than the Church of God. Armstrong repeatedly warned that the Tribulation was about to begin. The repeated predictions may have made him unusual—but not his certainty that the Second Coming was near.

Rohan's one friend on the kibbutz was a young American student for the ministry. Rohan told him he expected the End to begin "at the end of this year or next year" with the building of the Temple. As Rohan saw matters, two years had passed since "the time of the gentiles" ended in the Six-Day War. How much longer could there be?

Rohan wasn't unique in expecting the End in 1967, or in seeing the Muslim shrines on the Mount as the last obstacle. (Why he decided to attack Al-Aqsa, instead of the Dome, remains a mystery.) He is unique only because he did capsize. Others waited patiently for God to act. Rohan decided that God was acting through him.

Are preachers who tied the Rapture to Israel's birth or conquest of Jerusalem, who spoke of the Temple as a prerequisite for the Second Coming, responsible for Rohan standing in a dawn-lit mosque with a flaming scarf? The question has no simple answer. It could be asked of leaders of any political or religious movement when their rhetoric is taken with deadly seriousness by the insane or extreme. Perhaps no one can be expected to plan for the craziest of listeners. Then again, if you happily predict apocalypse, explain how and where it will begin, can you avoid all blame when someone goes to the spot you've marked and acts?

Israel weathered the incident relatively easily. After occupying the West Bank, it had deported or jailed much of the local leadership; two decades would pass before Palestinians were ready for revolt. Despite his vocal response to the arson, Egypt's Nasser was a secular nationalist who'd driven Islamic fundamentalism underground. Had the arson occurred in a time when Islam was more powerful in the Arab world—say, three decades later—the consequences could have been much worse.

Still, even after the cinders were cleared away, the mosque repaired, Muslim anxiety remained. For many Muslims, Israel was responsible for the fire, even if it wasn't clear how. Such is the progress from anxiety to conspiracy theory: If the link between the evil and the enemy isn't obvious, it must be covert, and all the more nefarious. In fact, Israel's only role in Rohan's crime was that it had been cast, through no choice of its own, in a starring role in a Christian Endtime drama. But Muslim fears had this much basis: After 1967, Rohan wasn't the only one who expected the building of the Temple.

■

THE SIX-DAY WAR did more than create a new political and military map in the Middle East. It also changed the mythic map, in a piece of the world where myths have always bent reality.

For Israelis, even those furthest from faith, it was easy to regard the victory as a kind of redemption. Jews, inscribed in history as victims, were now victors. The homeland, partitioned in 1948, was all in Israeli hands. For some Israelis, especially Orthodox Zionists, the exultation coalesced into religious and political doctrine. The conquest of "our Hebron and our Shechem," the Old City and the Temple Mount, showed that God was leading His people to final redemption. As never before, messianism became a respected ideology, powering the movement that settled Jews across the West Bank. The settlements changed the map of the land even more, and would vastly complicate any effort to divide it between Israelis and Arabs.

But Jerusalem is the capital of other myths as well. And so Israel's victory became part of a second story, taking place far from the Holy Land: the resurgence of Christian fundamentalism in the last third of the twentieth century. In the sixties and after, a generation already rife with apocalyptic hopes, the Jewish conquest of Jerusalem provided "proof" of premillennial doctrine. It amplified hopes for the Second Coming; it spurred some people to predict just when the great event would take place.

The developments among Christian and Jewish believers weren't separate tales. In unnnoticed ways, ideas born in one faith influenced individuals in the other. Christian millennialists eagerly watched the Middle East for more signs. In time, some moved from being onlookers to being participants, offering support to Israel—or to the Israelis deemed most likely to make prophecy come true.

And inevitably, the Temple Mount captured the imagination of Jewish messianists and Christians expecting the End. Under Israeli rule but not really under Jewish control, the ancient threshing floor was a physical representation of believers' reality: Salvation was almost within grasp, but not quite. The temptation was to try to change the reality at the Mount, by subtle means or explosive ones.

■

THE PHOTO WAS TAKEN from the east. You looked at today's Jerusalem as if you were standing on the Mount of Olives: the Old City in the foreground, the New City behind. Except that the golden Dome of the Rock and the gray dome of Al-Aqsa were gone. In their place stood the Temple, rectangular and massive. This isn't the long-ago past, the picture said; it's tomorrow, or later on today.

The first time I saw it was in 1978, when my yeshivah took a field trip to the West Bank. The picture took up a piece of the wall in the communal dining hall at Ofrah, an early outpost established by the Orthodox settler movement called Gush Emunim, the Believers' Bloc. Years later, Ofrah founder Yehudah Etzion told me that he made the montage and hung it on the wall. The picture was black and white, shadow and light. I remember my shock at the urgency it spoke: Raze now, build now. The picture shouted the messianism that brought Gush Emunim's members to settle in occupied territory. With hindsight, it also hinted at the violent plans taking shape in a few people's minds.

Gush Emunim was born out of Israel's ecstasy in 1967, as given form by Rabbi Tzvi Yehudah Kook. Following his father, Kook explained twentieth-century events as steps toward Israel's redemption. Now came a victory that anyone with eyes in his head could see was pure miracle. For religious Zionists, Kook's messianism was a ready-to-wear concept to dress the naked feelings of wonder.

Kook and his disciples saw no line between theology and day-to-day politics. At a meeting with Orthodox cabinet members soon after the war, one rabbi explained that "the Holy One gave us the land through obvious miracles" and therefore, "He'll never take it from us." The government wouldn't be able to give up occupied territory even it wanted to; Israel was ruled from on high. At an Independence Day celebration, Kook told followers, "There are people who speak of the beginning of redemption in our day. Open your eyes and see that we are now in the middle of redemption. We are in the parlor, not the entry hall." The scent of paradise was in the air.

Unlike Christian premillennialists, Kook and his followers didn't set a date for the messiah to come. They didn't presume the need for an apocalypse; they described redemption as a gradual process, like the sunrise. They did, however, share the millennialist's certainty that current events were part of the drama of the End. And while God was directing history, His believers could help it in the right direction. Since the Jewish conquest of the Land of Israel was a step toward redemption, the believers' task was to take possession of the newly conquered land by settling it.

Kook's followers weren't alone in wanting Israel to maintain permanent rule of the West Bank, Golan Heights, and Sinai Peninsula. Secular politicans and intellectuals took the same position. Under Prime Minister Golda Meir and her successor in the mid-seventies, Yitzhak Rabin, official policy was ill-defined—caught between historic ties to the land, desire to hold territory for defensive reasons, and apprehension about ruling hostile Palestinians. Kook's disciples suffered no uncertainty, and they had the immense motivation of people bringing salvation. Foot soldiers of the political right, they were ready to outmaneuver the government to plant new communities in the territories.

The first Orthodox group settled in the hills between Bethlehem and Hebron just three months after the war, led by Hanan Porat, a student of Tzvi Yehudah Kook. Another Kook disciple, Rabbi Moshe Levinger, brought sixty people to spend the Passover holiday in a Hebron hotel in the spring of 1968. Then they refused to leave. Eventually, the government let them establish Kiryat Arba, a Jewish town on the edge of Hebron. It became the hotbed of settler extremism. Hebron's appeal included the little sister of the Temple Mount—the Tomb of the Patriarchs, also holy to both Muslims and Jews. A daily struggle ensued between settlers and local Arabs over use of the shared site.

In 1974, Kook's followers organized themselves as Gush Emunim and faced off with Yitzhak Rabin. The new prime minister wanted to keep the mountain ridge that ran through the northern West Bank free of Jewish settlements, so that its Palestinian population could be returned to Arab rule. Yehudah Etzion and a few other young Gush Emunim activists quietly punched the first hole in that policy. The Israeli army was building a base on a mountain called Ba'al Hatzor. Etzion and his friends got work on the site. One night they camped out at an abandoned Jordanian army base nearby. Rabin's defense minister and chief rival, Shimon Peres, allowed them to stay. The rough camp became Ofrah. Once again, messianism defeated realism.

Success and burning enthusiasm made the Gush the leading force in religious Zionism. The victory of Menachem Begin's Likud party in the 1977 election looked like one more proof that God was directing history as the Gush expected. For the first time, the expansionist right ruled Israel. Thousands of Gush Emunim settlers moved into the occupied territories, to which they referred by the Hebrew acronym Yesha—meaning "salvation." Messianists had become legitimate partners in national policy.

But when Begin met Egyptian leader Anwar al-Sadat at Camp David in 1978, he agreed to trade the entire Sinai for peace with Egypt. The Gush's theology didn't allow for the sacred state giving up land. Redemption was supposed to race forward, not retreat.

Gush activists led the public protests against the withdrawal. When Israel's parliament approved the Camp David accord, settler journalist Hagai Segal recalls, a friend advised against giving up hope, saying, "God hasn't resigned yet, thank God." Like the members of countless other millennial movements, the Gush's "redemptive Zionists" had reached the moment when the world defies prophecy. "From that moment on," Segal writes, "Gush Emunim lived in anticipation of a miracle."

BITTERLY AS ISRAELIS DEBATED the future of the territories acquired in 1967, there was one point of consensus: The conquest of Old Jerusalem was irreversible. Within the Old City, the symbol of everything that the war had changed was the Western Wall. Religious Jews flocked to pray there. For the nonreligious, the Wall was the shrine of national triumph and of restored connection to the ancient past. "In the first days after June 7, 1967," wrote prominent Israeli journalist Uzi Benziman, "the Western Wall was inscribed in national memory as the supreme embodiment of Jewish independence . . . the zenith of Israeli control of Jerusalem, the ultimate expression of national unity." Underlining the point, Benziman portrayed the archeological dig that soon began nearby, along the Temple's southern wall, as staking a secular claim to the area, competing with the Orthodox. (The dig's key funder had a different agenda: The largest donor was Ambassador College in Pasadena, California—part of Herbert Armstrong's Worldwide Church of God.)

Yet the choice of the Wall, rather than the Temple Mount, implicitly meant accepting a limit to victory. Israel was not all-powerful; it still had to live with the Arabs. The government worked to insure that all fervor was "channeled to the Wall." In the summer of 1967, when chief army chaplain Shlomo Goren planned to hold services inside the Haram, the cabinet ordered security forces to direct Jewish worshipers from the Mount to the Western Wall. From then on, that was policy, intended to avoid turning the holy site into the arena of holy war.

The decision stuck because Jewish religious authorities backed it up. Soon after the war, Israel's chief rabbis issued their statement warning Jews not to tread on the Mount. It cautioned against "violating the purity of this holy place" and added that because the Temple's precise location had been forgotten, visitors risked entering the Holy of Holies. The chief rabbis are state officials, not popes. But a whole list of influential rabbis added their signatures, in an unprecedented consensus.

Among them was Tzvi Yehudah Kook. Kook was the high priest of human action to bring redemption, but like his father he set a limit—a stone wall. He opposed setting foot on the Mount. He even rejected the folk custom of writing prayers and slipping them into the Western Wall's cracks. Secular millenarians claim that human beings can fix everything broken in the world. Close as he was to their hubris, Kook held on to some religious humility: The Temple stood for the last stage of perfection that only God could provide. The distinction between the two stages was hard to explain. Kook aroused his followers, encouraged them to court redemption—and told them that the climax, the building of the Temple, remained forbidden.

Just how far the Temple was from mainstream Israeli consciousness, a January 1972 memo by Meir Shamgar testifies. Shamgar was the army legal officer who'd accompanied Moshe Dayan to the Mount in 1967; he had since moved up to become Israel's attorney general. Now he was responding to a request to register a nonprofit organization under the name "Association to Build the Temple in Jerusalem," with the goal of raising funds for construction. He rejected the request, fearing fraud: The founders would "exploit the naivete of people in Israel and abroad to raise funds for a purpose that they are not authorized or capable of carrying out." Shamgar, an avatar of reason and the calm rule of law, apparently did not consider that the applicants could be dead serious. In a common misreading of millennial groups, he treated them as con men.

But on the fringes, some Israelis were afire over the Temple. Mostly, they were veterans of the old far right, prophets of the antidemocratic, irredentist nationalism of the kind that had plagued Europe between the wars. Since 1948, they'd wandered in the political wilderness in Israel. The victory in 1967 gave them new hope for secular messianism, and they were not perturbed by rabbinic strictures against entering the Mount. A Lehi veteran named Shabtai Ben-Dov filed suit demanding that access to the Temple Mount be controlled by people "concerned with protecting it as a Jewish holy place." The Supreme Court rejected his suit. It did the same to a suit by Lehi ideologue Yisrael Eldad and others who demanded the right to hold Jewish prayers on the Mount. The Court said the government had the authority to restrict use of a place sacred to two faiths—especially a place uniquely "known for calamity."

In fact, the word "right" was misleading. Despite the way Temple activists sometimes present the issue to American audiences, this wasn't a struggle over civil liberties. Eldad, Ben-Dov, and others like them were messianists; they regarded the Mount as the steppingstone to redemption; and they wanted to wrest it from the Muslims. The state refused to create an opening for them.

Ben-Dov's form of messianism was particularly striking. In the 1940s, like many members of the Jewish underground movements, he was captured by the British and exiled to East Africa. There he pursued a ferocious program of self-education—philosophy, history, political theory—in pursuit of a unified theory of Jewish redemption. He returned home after Israeli independence, but found the state a painful letdown. Ben-Dov disdained democracy, couldn't bear seeing people put revolution behind them and get a personal life. In economics, he sought "purposeful state planning that would organize the nation as an idealistic army . . . while utterly negating all divisive personal interests." Politically, he wanted a nation mobilized by "pride, power and the uninhibited will to act," ready to wipe out its enemies.

In short, Ben-Dov sought something close to Jewish fascism. But in a 1960 book, *The Redemption of Israel in the Crisis of the State*, Ben-Dov concluded that plain old "Nietzschean-nihilistic desire for power" wouldn't awaken Israelis to their destiny. Alas, the Jews didn't seem cut out for standard fascism. But, he said, a return to ancient forms could do the trick. Ben-Dov argued for establishing a theocracy, ruled by a king and a Sanhedrin—a council of religious sages—and guided by values of "conquest and holy war." This, he said, was "a vision of total redemption."

Ben-Dov reveals a missing link between fascism and political fundamentalism. Like other secular millenarians, from communists to Nazis, he asserts that the perfected world can be reached through political action. However, he takes the form of that perfected world from religion, read with ruthless literalism—"kingdom" really means monarchy. Ben-Dov failed to spread his doctrine. Perhaps Israelis did have strong antibodies to fascism. But he did win one disciple: the son of friends, Yehudah Etzion.

In the days after the Camp David accord, Etzion didn't join the protest movement against withdrawal. Instead, the tall, pale, red-haired man with the gray-blue eyes worked in Ofrah's cherry orchards and studied Ben-Dov's writings. At the moment when Tzvi Yehudah Kook's reading of the future had failed, Ben-Dov provided answers. Kook was wrong to sanctify the existing state, Etzion concluded. What was needed was direct action to bring the redemption.

Etzion's colleague in radical thinking was a career army officer and religious scholar named Yeshua Ben-Shushan. Known for his deep knowledge of mystic doctrines, Captain Ben-Shushan was treated in Gush circles as a saint. He and Etzion studied together once a week. It was Ben-Shushan, apparently, who suggested to Etzion that the Dome of the Rock should be destroyed. He called it the "abomination"—by one account, a word he took from the Book of Daniel's description of the "abomination of desolation" that would desecrate the Temple in the last days. If so, he was the rare Jew who tried to decipher that book of the Bible. The idea grabbed Etzion. Israel's failure to destroy the Dome in 1967, Etzion would say in his confession several years later, proved that "the state does not consciously aspire to redemption" —in his eyes, an indictment for failure.

Etzion asked Ben-Dov, on his deathbed at age fifty-five, whether razing the "abomination" would catalyze redemption. "If you want to do something that will solve all the Jews' problems, do that," the dying Lehi man told him.

So the idea began to take form. Others were recruited—Menahem Livni, a Kiryat Arba settler and deputy battalion commander in the combat engineer reserves; Haim Ben-David, a Golan Heights settler. The plan, Ben-David would tell an investigator after his arrest, "was a stage in the spiritual redemption of the Jewish people. What was new for me was that this was a physical action that would lead to a spiritual action." It was a strange comment, because "physical actions that lead to spiritual actions" were basic to Gush Emunim's messianism. What was new was the shattered patience, the idea of acting on the sacred ground of the Mount, the violence.

The plotters were not alone, though, in seeing the Temple Mount as essential to God's design. Half a world away, Christian millennialists were avidly waiting for the Temple to be built—as a step toward the Second Coming. Some even believed they knew when it would happen.

THE CHURCH PARKING LOT IS wide enough for a mall. Everything here is wide: the streets, the sky over the condo developments and low offices, the vast centerless sprawl of southern California. A schoolbus is parked in front of Calvary Chapel's K-12 Christian school. At the end of the 1990s, the preteen kids who pour into the unadorned sanctuary for a chat with an assistant pastor about love have the tucked-in, angst-free look that my parents and their neighbors dreamed of for their children and didn't get in the same southern California thirty years earlier.

The night before, the hall was nearly full, which meant close to 2,500 people for Pastor Chuck Smith's Bible study—one small portion of the membership of twelve thousand families. Smith, a wide-shouldered man with a ring of gray hair and the big hands of someone who has lived by physical labor, spoke without fire or brimstone—only a slight laugh or stressed syllable moving like a small wave across the smooth surface of his talk—about the Sermon on the Mount. He told of an incident from decades before: He'd been a pastor in Tuscon; he made a house visit to a woman churchgoer who had a crippled daughter; the husband began cursing him violently. "He was angry with God. He said: 'I just brought my second little girl home from the doctor, and she's been diagnosed with polio.' I said: 'Sir, do you serve God? . . . Then why do you think God owes you anything?'" It's an explanation of suffering as simple as the one Job's friends gave him. Smith isn't offering radical insights; he offers certainty.

In the morning, waiting for Smith in the church office, I look at a framed photo of a different Calvary Chapel, nearly three decades before: a circus tent with the sides rolled up, so you can see that it's full, overflowing; young men and women sit on the lawn around it; a long-haired guy walks with his girl; a motorcycle with a high-backed seat is parked next to old station wagons. I can't see Smith, but I know he's inside—Pastor Chuck, father of the Jesus Movement, teaching the fundamentalist Word to the acid-singed and anchorless who washed up each week in greater numbers.

Smith came to Costa Mesa, south of Los Angeles, in 1965. He was sick of denominations, and therefore willing to take a church where twenty-five people attended his first Sunday and to repair mobile homes for a living. When he looked at the hippies who filled the beachtowns, he admits, he thought, "Get a job, get a bath." But his wife wanted to understand them, so they invited one to move in, and he brought friends, who brought more. Smith sat on the floor and taught Bible. He rented a house for a Christian commune, and then needed two houses, seven, a ranch in Oregon where his young followers learned carpentry or plumbing or how to use heavy equipment and then spread out in teams of nine to set up new communes, five to work and four to minister, and he had one hundred houses and more. He baptized in the Pacific, ten thousand people at the water, Pastor Chuck striding into the surf fully dressed to immerse hundreds of converts. He began recording his Bible talks; a cassette duplicator churned out copies by the time people left services. In the aural generation, the cassette defeated Gutenberg; rock worship filled the tent that Smith flung up while building his church. "You can tell a church born in the United States after 1970 by the size of its tweeters," says Chuck Fromm, Smith's nephew and chairman of the Corinthian Group, which produces music for congregations.

Still, one of Smith's followers, a sixties-rock-band-promoter-become-nineties-art-dealer, gives me one printed product of Smith's cultural revolution: a magazine-sized pamphlet of the Gospel of John, rephrased in Smith's stone-simple English, illustrated by Rick Griffin, a legendary sixties artist known for Grateful Dead and Jimi Hendrix album covers. "Incredible message BEAT DEATH live forever," the booklet's cover says. Inside, the woman Jesus met at the well is a sepia-toned ripe-chested sex goddess. Where Jesus promises that the dead will rise, a barefoot man wearing a guitar on his back, a harmonica brace on his chest, and Bob Dylan's face is trucking out of a portal, looking back at skeletal figures imprisoned in black night.

In thirty-five years, starting from his Jesus Movement base and spreading far beyond, Smith has begotten an entire new fundamentalist movement—hundreds of Calvary Chapel churches in the U.S., among them nine of the country's twenty-five largest congregations, not a denomination but an immense chain of franchises of born-again Christianity. Across the country, close to two hundred radio stations broadcast his tapes and live worship and talks by the men he's trained, some of them the lost-and-found kids from the sixties beachtowns. You have to ask how it took fire: how a man preaching determinedly conservative Protestantism—who in a tape on Revelation asks rhetorically why God would "want to leave us here on this rotten earth any longer than necessary"—succeeded in a generation celebrating the gorgeousness of life with sex, drugs, and protest. He was opposed to organized religion, he says, just as they were. "They were searching for peace and love, and to me that's exactly what we have to offer," Smith says. "Why were they taking drugs? They were trying to make a spiritual connection." One could add: Fundamentalism, too, is a radical critique of American society. In a strange sense, Smith and the SDS were in the same business.

And both offered apocalypse. The sixties, as writer John Judis has argued, were another American outburst of millennialism. The hour was at hand, Aquarian or Marxist, to be achieved by spiritual energy, music, and street protest. Those already living in the new age were no longer obligated to the rules of the old, sexual or otherwise. Judis argues that the wave began with an optimistic millennialism, the hope of peaceful transformation, and ended with a dark expectation of apocalypse. But dark dreams were present from the start. In 1965, Barry McGuire's hit song warned that "we're on the eve of destruction." In 1971, McGuire was baptized as a born-again Christian. Aquarius had failed to dawn, and if you still wanted apocalypse, you could go to the source. Says Smith: "Even non-Christian hippies had an apocalyptic thing. [Charles] Manson was looking for the End."

So Smith's premillennialism found a ready audience. "The Book of Revelation was one of their favorites, and Daniel, and Ezekiel 36–40, where he prophesies the rebirth of the nation of Israel, the coming invasion of a confederacy of Muslim nations. All these things began to look like they were shaping up. In 1967 Jerusalem was again under the Israelis." So at a crucial moment of his career, he could point to a stunningly fulfilled prophecy, one that said the moment was urgently near. "It all has apocalyptic significance," he says.

Smith wasn't alone in preaching that message. Through the sixties, ex–tugboat captain Hal Lindsey lectured on campuses about Christianity. Lindsey's Bible was as clean of metaphor and ambiguity as an engineering text. "If you take the Bible literally," he says, "then you come up with the premillennial point of view. I *hate* those who read their ideas into the scripture by using allegory." In April 1967, Lindsey says, he told a university audience that if these were the times he thought they were, the Jews would soon conquer Jerusalem. He spent the Six-Day War glued to the tube, overjoyed by news of Israel's victory "because I loved Israelis personally, and . . . it was a confirmation of what I knew had to happen."

Two years later, Lindsey wrote *The Late Great Planet Earth.* A friend who had gone into religious publishing told him that the manuscript was "a different style than any Christian book that has ever been written," but decided to gamble. "We predict it will sell very well, 35,000 copies at least," he told Lindsey. In thirteen months, the book sold its first million. At the end of the nineties, Lindsey says, 34 million copies were in print in fifty-four languages.

From the title on, Lindsey's book tapped the mood of the time.

Since 1968, bookstores had been hawking *The Last Days of the Late, Great State of California*, based on pop predictions that California would fall into the Pacific. Implicitly, *Planet Earth* was the sequel, a day-glo apocalypse that wrapped up scripture, headlines, and pop-culture puns: A section on Babylon in Revelation is called "Scarlet O'Harlot"; the "now generation" becomes a label for those who will see the End. Lindsey opens by discussing popular interest in astrology, argues that if you want to know the future, you should check out biblical prophets, then turns to Jesus and "the big question": "Why did the majority of the Jewish people . . . reject Jesus of Nazareth as their Messiah when He came?"

Lindsey, premillennialism's greatest populizer, gives Jews two central roles. The first—despite his insistence of love for Jews—is the classic one of Christian anti-Jewish polemic: They are "the Jewish people who crucified Jesus" and the archetype of those who ignore the truth of prophecy. The second role is to fulfill prophecy despite themselves. Two of three crucial prophecies that herald the End have come true, Lindsey says: The Jewish nation has been reborn in Palestine, and has repossessed old Jerusalem. So, "There remains but one more event to completely set the stage for Israel's part in the last great act of her historical drama. That is to rebuild the ancient Temple . . ." Prophecy says it will happen, even if the Dome of the Rock stands in the way: "If it is the time that this writer believes it is, there will soon begin the construction of this Temple." Put yourself in Lindsey's shoes, and the confidence makes sense: Prophecies *had* come true; he'd called the Six-Day War.

Lindsey also presents evidence that Temple-building is near, in the form of quotations from "a famous Israeli historian": Yisrael Eldad. "From the time that King David first conquered Jerusalem until Solomon built the Temple, just one generation passed. So it will be with us," he cites Eldad as saying. Eldad was in fact a history professor; perhaps Lindsey didn't know that his "famous Israeli historian" was also the ideologue of a fanatical fringe. It didn't really matter. Eldad fit his theory. Lindsey's book set a pattern among prophecy writers: the most extreme of Israelis loom largest, because they fit prophetic expectations.

Eldad did a particular favor by speaking of "one generation."

Lindsey explains Jesus' "parable of the fig tree" and asserts: "When the Jewish people . . . became a nation again on 14 May 1948, the 'fig tree' put forth its first leaves." That means the events of the end would take place within a generation, which "in the Bible is something like forty years." Therefore, Lindsey asserts, "If this is a correct deduction, then within forty years or so of 1948, all these things could take place." It was a carefully hedged bet, but he'd still put his money down: The End was likely around 1988.

CHUCK SMITH took this logic a step further: He hoped for history's turning point at the start of the eighties. A longtime associate explains the logic: 1988 was a likely time for the Second Coming. Allowing seven years for the Tribulation, that might just put the Rapture in 1981. "Chuck Smith is very focused on the Rapture," says the associate, and "was really focused on 1981." Nineteen eighty-one passed—and Smith said nothing about the missed date. His flock was left to wonder. Asked years later about the prediction, he shrugs it off as a mere possiblity he raised. The expectation of apocalypse remains valid, he says; he's still part of the generation that saw Israel created. But whatever questions he asked, answers he found for why 1981 went quietly by, he's not discussing—perhaps not even with himself.

Still, it's provocative that Smith took a sudden interest in the Temple in the early eighties—perhaps seeking the missing factor that was needed in order for the End to proceed. Smith invited Asher Kaufman to Calvary Chapel to explain where the Temple would stand. He got another overflow crowd when he invited Stanley Goldfoot, the South African–born Jerusalem businessman who in those years was the contact for Christians eager to see the Temple built. Marginal in Israel, Goldfoot was now treated as a prophet by thousands. For years he listened to the tape of his talk over and over to hear the applause.

Goldfoot's desire for the Temple is ultranationalist; he speaks of "Jewish might emanating to the whole world" from the site. In 1948, Goldfoot was Lehi's intelligence chief. Half a century later, memory fading from his eighty-five-year-old mind, he still recalled in perfect detail how he planned the murder of U.N. negotiator Count Bernadotte. "We decided he was the enemy, and we *executed* him—

on the seventeenth of September, at ten past five." Bernadotte's offense, in the eyes of Goldfoot and his comrades, was reviving a U.N. proposal to internationalize Jerusalem. Goldfoot's face glowed with true love when he described to me the weapon his men used, "a German machine gun . . . a wonderful gun, it never had anything wrong, never a stoppage." Arrested after the murder, he was released several months later without charges.

In the seventies, Goldfoot published a journal called the *The Times of Israel,* which in his words was "extreme right-wing—I'm very proud of it." He was one of the founders of the far-right Temple Mount Faithful. Eventually, he decided to turn to "the *goyim*"—gentiles, setting up the Jerusalem Temple Foundation. Based in Los Angeles, the group's board consisted of Goldfoot and several American evangelicals. Besides arranging for the old Lehi man to speak to born-again Christian groups in the eighties, the foundation's activities remain mysterious. By one report, it raised $10 million, some for construction of the Temple, the rest earmarked to support the settlement movement.

There's no doubt, though, of Goldfoot's role in the radar affair: In the early 80s, he learned that Lambert Dolphin, a physicist at the Stanford Research Institute in Menlo Park, California, had pioneered methods to "X-ray" archeological sites, peering inside without opening them. Working at Egyptian tombs, Dolphin used ground-penetrating radar, along with a form of sonar and a method for tracking how electricity flows through the ground. Goldfoot asked Dolphin if he'd like to try those techniques at the Mount.

He asked the right man. Dolphin describes himself as a seeker from early childhood. "I thought at first science would lead me to ultimate answers. In grad school, I began to see . . . fine Nobel Prize winners, but none had answers. . . . I tried psychoanalysis, then went to Jung and Eastern religion. I took LSD; I thought somehow it would provoke a religious experience, but none was to be found." Dolphin began reading the Bible. Jesus was real, he decided; prophecy was real, for "the Jews were back in their land."

Examining the Mount was an opportunity for science to serve faith. The funding came from Chuck Smith and Western Digital chairman Chuck Missler. Between them, Missler says, they put up "fifty to a hundred grand, out of our own pockets." In April 1983, Dolphin's crew of seven arrived in Israel and began testing their equipment at archeological sites. Dolphin wanted to get the bugs out before approaching the Mount, where he hoped to locate the Temple's foundations and underground cavities—perhaps a secret room where the Ark of the Covenant was hidden. For Smith, too, the lost Ark was the greatest draw: "To think of seeing the two tablets of stone, what that would be!" The discovery, he thought, would inspire Jews to build the Temple.

At ten o'clock on a May night, Dolphin's team arrived at the Western Wall with a van full of equipment. Goldfoot arranged it all with Rabbi Yehudah Getz, the state-appointed rabbi of the Wall. The gates of the plaza were opened and the van rolled across the square to the entrance to a tunnel.

The tunnel had its own peculiar history. After 1967, competing with secular archeologists, the Religious Affairs Ministry began an unlicensed excavation. Starting at the Western Wall plaza, workers dug northward, under the Old City's Muslim Quarter. The horizontal shaft took them through the construction and debris that, over the centuries, had hidden most of the Mount's western side. In 1981, ministry workers found a sealed gate. They broke though, into a chamber beneath the Mount. Getz tried to keep the discovery a secret, as did his ally Shlomo Goren, who'd since been appointed one of Israel's chief rabbis. Like characters in a *Thousand and One Nights* story, the two thought they'd found the lost doorway to underground treasure—or at least, a chance to establish a Jewish presence under the Mount. When news of the discovery broke, Getz said the opening might well lead to the hidden Ark of the Covenant. It was a tunnel to past and future—except that word got out, and young Muslims lowered themselves into the cavity by ropes through openings in the Haram surface above, carrying trowels and cinderblocks to build a wall against the Jewish invaders. By the light of floodlights, yeshivah students and Arab workmen battled with stones and fists in the depths over the forgotten gateway to God's mountain. Police sealed the opening with concrete. The incident was forgotten, or rather left beneath the surface of memory.

So Getz was happy to let Dolphin set up his sonar in the nighttime quiet of the shaft and search for lost treasures. But as the physicist and his crew pulled up, plainclothesmen appeared. Return to your hotel, they told Dolphin, and report to police HQ tomorrow. Dolphin was anxious: "We thought we were in big trouble." In the morning, a police intelligence officer calmly told him and Goldfoot: We know all about you; we were waiting for you; the Waqf has asked that there be no electronic probing beneath the mosques. The physicist was free to leave. His written account of the incident exudes a whiff of rancor at the Muslims who, he complained, had been given "veto power" over the tunnel.

Still, the goal of the mission wasn't pure research. Both Missler and Smith stress that building the Temple isn't a job for Christians—as part of the Endtime drama, it's up to God, who will direct his actors, the Jews. Yet remaining a spectator is difficult. A Christian can try nudging the Jews to begin the final act. Smith hoped finding the Ark would provide that push. Says Missler: "Understanding where the Temple stood is a major prerequisite to any ambition to rebuild." The implicit purpose of probing beneath the Mount, even without moving a single stone, was to hurry the End. That was also the subtext of a burgeoning relationship between conservative Christians and Israeli leaders.

"I WAS TALKING to Menachem Begin," Chuck Smith recounts. "I said, 'We are very close in our beliefs. You believe in the God of Abraham, Isaac, and Jacob; we believe in the God of Abraham, Isaac, and Jacob. You believe the messiah is coming soon; we believe the messiah is coming soon. The difference is that you believe it will be the first coming, and we believe it will be the second coming.'"

Smith was just one of many evangelical leaders who met Begin, Israel's prime minister from 1977 to 1983. The Begin administration, say Israeli political experts, was the first that actively sought to tap evangelical enthusiasm for Israel and turn it into political and economic support.

The reasons for that support aren't restricted to Israel's place in prophecy. In part, it reflects a wider Christian effort to come to terms with the Holocaust. The genocide demanded a moral reckoning with the Christian roots of European anti-Semitism. Supporting Israel is grasped as a concrete way of expressing repentance. It reflects, as well, the Old Testament stress of many fundamentalists, which leads to a search for Christianity's Jewish roots.

The ways of supporting Israel also vary. There are straightforward political efforts, such as lobbying and newspaper ads. There's also philanthropy, such as raising money to help hospitals or buy ambulances. When the exodus of Soviet Jews began in the 1990s, conservative Christians in the U.S. and Europe began contributing to the costs of transporting immigrants to the Jewish state. Israeli Jews regard immigration as a humanitarian cause; the motivation hardly matters. Yet for the Christian donors, part of the attraction was the chance to speed fulfillment of Endtime prophecy by helping with the ingathering of the exiles.

For in fact, premillennialism is the way many evangelicals make sense of supporting the Jewish state. Premillennialists often assert that they're free of theological anti-Semitism—unlike other Christians, they don't believe God has cast off the physical nation of Israel in favor of the spiritual Israel of the Church. Yet they speak of Jews as having rejected Jesus, and as being fated either to accept Jesus or to be destroyed in the End Times. A theology that says that Jews as a community have denied God in the past and are destined to be punished in the future is hardly free of anti-Semitism.

One standard-bearer of Christian backing for Israel is the Missouri pastor David Lewis. Lewis—who stepped beyond evangelical boundaries to found the National Christian Leadership Conference for Israel with mainstream Protestants and Catholics—says "the churches have treated [Jews] very badly through the centuries" and "have a repentance to do." Then he adds, "If we want to be observers of prophecy we can, or we can be participants. We choose to be participants," which means "doing everything we can to insure the survival of Israel . . . and to support the building of the Temple."

Toward the latter goal, Lewis hosted Stanley Goldfoot several times on the program he once had on nationwide Christian TV. Asked about Goldfoot's role in the Bernadotte assassination, Lewis says, "There was a war. . . . He was a soldier in the army. It's comparable to asking me if I'd feel bad if Bin Laden were assassinated. I wouldn't be the one to assasinate him, but I wouldn't feel bad." By that judgment, negotiator Bernadotte becomes the moral equivalent of a terrorist; the Lehi men who murdered him become "soldiers." For Lewis, helping Goldfoot was part and parcel of backing Israel. Support for extremists is built into his support of the country. If the goal was Israel's real-world benefit, the two would hardly be compatible. But both are meant serve a different purpose—being a participant in prophecies of the End.

STILL, GOLDFOOT WAS only talking about the Temple. The real threat to the Temple Mount in the early eighties, so it seemed to any-one reading Israeli newspapers, came from the violent milieu of Rabbi Meir Kahane. Founder of the Jewish Defense League in New York, Kahane moved to Israel to 1971 and made a name for himself on the far fringe of the right. Among the aims of his Kach ("Thus!") party was making sexual relations between a Jew and an Arab a capital crime; the party's eventual goal was the expulsion of all Arabs from Israel and the occupied territories. Kahane's small group of aggressive followers splattered Jerusalem walls with posters demanding that Israel "erase the mosques from the Temple Mount."

Kahane's ideas provided part of the inspiration that brought Alan Goodman to the Temple Mount on April 11, 1982, carrying an M-16 rifle. A Baltimore-born immigrant to Israel, Goodman was a loner in his late thirties. A few weeks before, he'd been drafted into the Israeli army. Entering the sacred plaza, he shot and wounded a Waqf guard, then ran toward the Dome, injuring another man on his way—and then killed a Muslim guard who tried to shut the shrine door. Inside, Goodman kept firing through windows and doors. Forty-five minutes later, he surrendered: He'd run out of bullets. The attack sparked a week of violent protests in the West Bank and Gaza Strip. Goodman insisted he'd acted on his own, in vengeance for Arab terror and "in order to liberate the Temple Mount." But Kahanist leaflets were found in his room, and Kahane paid for his legal defense. Goodman was sentenced to life; fifteen years later, unrepentant, he was sent home to the United States.

The tie between Kahane and Yoel Lerner was stronger. Lerner, who immigrated from the U.S. a decade before Kahane, was one of the JDL leader's early recruits in Israel, and for six years a central member of his organization. "I became convinced that Kahane was philosophically right, that [what he said] was in keeping with Torah, that it *is* Torah," says Lerner. Kahane, he says, united nationalism and Judaism, and kept "the Jewish people in the center." Rephrased in words Lerner wouldn't use: The doctrine made national egotism into the cardinal religious virtue.

Tall, heavy, mountain-shaped, Lerner speaks calmly, with an occasional giggle of pride, about a lifetime of agitation and conspiracy. The first time he went to jail for plotting an attack on the Mount was in 1974. Suspecting he'd been involved in attacks on Christian missionaries, police searched his house—and found a plan to "damage" the Muslim shrines in order to shatter post–Yom Kippur War peace talks. In the early eighties, he and a teenager were convicted of planning to set a bomb next to the Dome. Lerner protests his innocence in both cases—but brags that he had every intent of carrying out a 1978 plot to overthrow Israel's government and establish a theocracy. Bombing the Dome was the last in a series of planned actions to destabilize the country so that his underground group—known as Gal, a Hebrew acronym for "redemption for Israel"—could take over.

Lerner's "master and teacher," Meir Kahane, also spent time in prison for a Temple Mount plot, though the details were never heard in open court. In May 1980, he was jailed for several months by administrative order, under a much-criticized Israeli statute that allows such action to head off security threats. According to Carmi Gillon, ex-head of the Shin Bet internal security agency, Kahane's planned MO "wouldn't have caused a lot of damage. But it would have been a provocation."

Provoking Arabs was a Kahane specialty. His image in Israel was of an Orthodox brownshirt who offered poor Israelis a racist explanation for their troubles: It's all the Arabs' fault. Gush Emunim and secular right-wingers avoided him, in part because of his explicit racism, in greater measure because—as Gush activist Yisrael Harel has written—he "was an outsider, a foreigner." In fact, the line between the Gush and Kahane was not so sharp. In 1981, the No. 2 man on Kahane's ticket for the Knesset was Rabbi Yisrael Ariel, a student of

Tzvi Yehudah Kook. The West Bank settlement of Kiryat Arba, founded by Kook followers, became a center for Kahane supporters.

Yet Harel is right: Kahane was foreign. The cacophonous advocate of Jewish authenticity had learned his style in America. Indeed, he'd once done a reasonable job of passing as a non-Jew. In the mid-sixties, he led a double life: Rabbi Meir Kahane at home, "Michael King" in his work as an anticommunist writer and pro–Vietnam War activist. At a party in the uppercrust Long Island town of East Hampton, he told a woman he met that he was a Presbyterian. And, as *New York Times* journalist Michael Kaufman discovered, "King" had an affair with a twenty-two-year-old gentile model, Gloria Jean D'Argenio, who jumped to her death from the Queensboro Bridge when he said he couldn't marry her.

By 1968, Kahane shed the identity of "King" and adopted a new model: the Black Panthers. His new Jewish Defense League organized community patrols to escort Jews to synagogues in urban neighborhoods. Uninvited, Kahane led followers carrying chains and clubs to "protect" a New York Reform synagogue. "It was the symbolism of 'We too are powerful,' " says Kaufman. "It was fascist imagery, even with the Panthers. The most powerful image of the time was Huey Newton with guns."

With street theater came a theology that stood Judaism on its head. Traditionally, for instance, a Jew who is honest in business, or resists anger, "sanctifies the Divine Name"—that is, shows others the purity of his religion and God. When a Jew is crude, dishonest, cruel, he "desecrates the Name." But for Kahane, God's reputation was purely a function of Jewish might. If Jews were killed, God looked weak; if they were strong, God's power was revealed. The "upturned Jewish fist" sanctified the Divine Name.

Kahane's violent views received ample media attention. But his intense messianism was virtually ignored beyond his circle of followers. In a 1983 book, *Forty Years*, he described an insight that came to him while in prison. The Holocaust, he said, was the worst possible desecration of the Name, because Jews were so weak. God therefore created the State of Israel to prove His might. He gave the Jews forty years, or "a few more, a few less," to prove themselves—to create a theocracy, "drive out the Arab . . . cleanse the Temple Mount"—before the End. If "the Jew" passed the test, redemption would come peacefully. If not, it would be preceded by a "needless holocaust, more horrible than anything we have yet endured."

This is a messianism strikingly different from that of Tzvi Yehudah Kook. Unlike other Israeli messianists, Kahane sets a date for the end—forty years or so from Israel's creation. Unlike other Israeli messianists, he postulates catastrophe—a holocaust worse than the one inflicted by the Nazis—on the way to the redeemed world, unless Jews behave by his definition of righteousness. Like Hal Lindsey, he writes of "the Jew"—turning all Jews into a single, mythic being. Like Lindsey, he reads world politics and describes how Soviet moves will lead to apocalypse.

Certainly, the particular fury of Kahane's work—his personal venom toward most Jews—was his alone. But whether the borrowing was conscious or not, his ideas about apocalypse, like so much else about him, appear drawn from an American milieu: They bear a striking resemblance to the popularized premillennialism of Christian prophecy writers. One premillennialist writer returned the favor. In his popular tract, *88 Reasons Why The Rapture Could Be in 1988*, Edgar C. Whisenant cited Kahane to prove that "the Jewish people recognize the significance of the 40 years from 1948 to 1988." After a long text from Kahane's book, Whisenant summed up: "The 40 years end for the church age on Rosh-Hash-Ana [sic] 1988." The Tribulation would follow.

In Israel's 1984 elections, Kach received 1.3 percent of the vote, enough to win one seat in parliament. Kahane dreamed of being prime minister. "My brother had a secret that he never told his followers," says Rabbi Nachman Kahane. "He brought them to the one-yard line, but he didn't take them over it. If he got to power, he would push the hand of God. He'd make war on all the Arab countries, and say to God: You have two sons, Isaac and Ishmael. Now choose." Israeli politicians didn't know that, but they did see Kahane as a threat to democracy. The Knesset passed a law banning racist parties from elections, and Kahane was barred from running in 1988. Two years later he was shot dead in New York by an Islamic extremist.

In one attempt to blow up the Dome, a suspected link to Kahane evaporated during the investigation. On the night of January 26, 1984, a Waqf guard saw silhouettes crossing the Haram and blew his whistle. Four men turned and escaped over the Mount's eastern wall, which they'd scaled a few minutes before. Behind them they left knapsacks full of explosives. Police picked up a pair of Kahane's followers.

But detective work led to a different destination: the abandoned Arab village of Lifta on the edge of Jerusalem, home to Shlomo Barda, an ex-con turned messianic dreamer. During a stay in the U.S., Barda had taken an interest both in Chabad hasidism, an ultra-Orthodox movement that lived in burning expectation of the messiah—and in Christian fundamentalist hopes that a Third Temple would pave the way for Jesus' return. Back in Israel, he settled with three friends in Lifta, where they patched together their own tiny sect: verses from the Hebrew Bible and New Testament on the walls, belief in the mystic energy of the village spring, and a conviction that blowing up the Dome would bring the messiah. Barda was sentenced to eight years in prison; two comrades were committed to mental institutions. Police never caught the fourth man. Nor did they nail down suspicions that Christian fundamentalists funded the bombing bid, helping Jews to carry out their role in the End.

And as in the Rohan case, the insanity verdicts made it too easy to dismiss messianism. For as the Israeli public learned soon after the Lifta case, people who are quite sane can also decide that God has called on them to hurry redemption.

THEY MET nearly every Thursday night at Yeshua Ben-Shushan's house in Jerusalem. The year was 1979. They discussed the impending withdrawal from the Sinai, and the "abomination" of the Dome of the Rock. Ben-Shushan, mystic and officer, saw the two matters as one: The Temple Mount was the wellspring of spiritual energy, nourishing whoever controlled it, and the Muslims had it. Yehudah Etzion agreed—God's refusal to move forward with redemption could be explained only by Israel's failure to remove the Muslim "desecration."

Without knowing it, they'd fallen into an old trap set for those who figure out God's plans for the future: History stopped following prophecy. They wanted to know why, and they found the human act that could remedy matters. And without realizing it, they'd taken the

Temple—in Jewish tradition, a symbol of the perfected world, a small piece that stands for the whole—and made it everything. They'd stumbled into mysticism, the book of allegory, and they read it as battle orders.

The group grew. One recruit was Gilad Peli, whose father had been Yitzhak Shamir's personal secretary back when Shamir was a leader of Lehi. Another was Dan Be'eri, a Frenchman. Be'eri's father had converted from Catholicism to Protestantism; Be'eri's own search as a French student in the sixties led him to communism, as "a rational system . . . to fulfill Christian ideals," and then to Israel to volunteer on kibbutz (the pinnacle of socialism) and learn Hebrew (the language of the Bible) and finally to convert to Judaism and express his passion for a perfected world through redemptive Zionism. Nearly a score of men eventually took part in the plot.

The most carefully planned, extensive plot to destroy the Dome of the Rock was not dreamed up by Kahane's ruffians. It was concocted, as ex–Shin Bet chief Gillon puts it, by "the Who's Who of Gush Emunim," men who went to meetings with the prime minister. Rabbi Tzvi Yehudah Kook, it's said, stood in respect when Yeshua Ben-Shushan entered the room. They were not mad. The group's leaders, in particular, possessed the seductive brilliance of extremists: clarity and consistency. Their ideology was not a strange aberration; it was a logical conclusion of Gush Emunim's politicized messianism.

Etzion, the prime mover, believed the grand act of "purifying" the Mount would arouse public support for his imagined Redemption Movement. It was the common fantasy of terrorists: Flagrant violence will arouse the masses from their incomprehensible lethargy. Some of his colleagues were uncertain. The Dome had to go, they agreed, but could the Israeli public possibly understand why they'd appointed themselves to act? For reassurance that they were on the right path, they sought approval from religious sages. Yeshua Ben-Shushan went to Tzvi Yehudah Kook. But there were people outside the door; instead of asking out loud, Ben-Shushan took a picture of the Dome and swept his hand across it, as if erasing it. The aging rabbi asked what he meant; Ben-Shushan repeated his pantomine; Kook still didn't give a clear answer.

It's hard to imagine that Kook understood, much less would have approved. A man who regarded putting a note in the cracks of the Western Wall as desecrating it wasn't going to agree to a bombing on the Mount. His responsibility was indirect, half-substantial: From him, the conspirators learned that you could hold meetings, fight a battle, or build a town, and thereby bring history's dénouement closer. Then they stepped beyond the limit he set. Though some were still undecided about carrying out the attack, they agreed to join in preparations. As Hagai Segal writes, "They could not completely reject a proposal, no matter how hopeless, to help rid the Temple Mount of foreign structures." In a dance of doubt and desire, they moved forward with the plot.

What alerted the public and the Shin Bet to the existence of a settler underground was a digression. In May 1980, Palestinian terrorists shot and killed six yeshivah students leaving Hebron's Tomb of the Patriarchs. Menachem Livni wanted revenge, and turned to Etzion for help. For targets, they chose prominent Palestinians whom they blamed for incitement against settlers. For manpower, they began with the Temple Mount group. For a date, they chose thirty days after the attack in Hebron, the end of the Jewish mourning period. Livni was a professional at building bombs: The charges had magnets to stick to a car's undercarriage, and detonators that would go off when the vehicle moved. On the morning of June 2, when Nablus Mayor Bassam Shaka started his car, an explosion shredded his legs. Another blast wounded Ramallah Mayor Karim Khalef. The Israeli army sent a sapper to a third mayor's home—and a bomb attached to the garage door blinded the soldier. The timing proved that Jews had set the charges, but Shin Bet investigators got nowhere. They had no idea that the bombings were only a sideline for people planning an attack that could have sparked far worse bloodshed.

For two years, the conspirators studied the Mount. In the day, some visited as tourists, to check guardposts and learn whether there was an alarm system and what locks they'd have to break. Not everyone was willing to set foot on the Mount—there was the problem of ritual purity, the lack of ashes of a red cow, though Yeshua Ben-Shushan assured them that for this purpose it was OK. Livni pored over aerial photos. He came up with a demolition plan: Twenty-eight specially designed charges would be strapped to pillars in the Dome. He was a careful man, technically precise. He and Etzion went to a metal shop and had containers made for the explosives. They found a young pro-settler army officer who explained where to buy silencers for Uzi submachine guns in case they ran into Muslim guards during the operation. They convinced him to get them Uzi barrels to take to the machine shop, which he did by going to an army dump and saying he wanted to build a Hanukkah menorah out of gun barrels. His imagined menorah provides an apt image for their faith: a ritual object built out of weaponry.

Etzion, Livni, and others stole the explosives they needed on a winter night from an antimine device called a Viper, which they got to at a badly guarded army engineers base in the Golan Heights. Peli brought a jeep and they filled it to the level of the seats. Later Livni packed the charges into the casings. To save Israel, they had resorted to stealing from the Israeli army. "It was a problematic act, on the face of it theft pure and simple," Etzion said in his confession. "But we hoped that if the operation succeeded, and the whole process of redemption resulting from it also succeeded, then this act, ex post facto, would also become legitimate." Inwardly, the messianist already lived after the redemption, the revolution, and judged himself by the standards of the new era.

And then, with the custom-made bombs ready for use, luck finally turned against them. Livni caught hepatitis. Without him, there was no way to act—and while he lay sick, Israel completed its withdrawal from the Sinai in April 1982. They'd missed the moment for preventing the pullback. What's more, the failure of the movement against withdrawal proved to some conspirators that their doubts had a basis: The Israeli public wasn't interested in redemption; it wouldn't rise up, cheering, when the bombs went off. The plan required at least twenty men, and Etzion now had nowhere near that number.

Then again, Etzion stresses that the purpose went far beyond stopping the Sinai withdrawal. And as former Shin Bet chief Carmi Gillon says, the plan didn't die in 1982, "It didn't even go to sleep, it was a bit drowsy." Some members continued with practical preparations, he says—for instance, trying to acquire more sensitive detonators. "In their interrogation," he says, "they didn't bring it up as an idea that had died." As long as the underground remained undetected, the threat still existed.

But in 1983, after the murder of another yeshivah student in Hebron, Livni masterminded a new terror attack: In broad daylight, two men entered Hebron's Islamic College, spraying bullets and tossing a grenade. They murdered three students and wounded thirty-three. Beforehand, one of the gunmen visited Ben-Shushan's house. "Yeshua, give us your blessing," he said. "We're going to take revenge." The "saintly" Ben-Shushan blessed him: "To peace and a good life."

At last the Shin Bet began closing in. One night in 1984, three men entered East Jerusalem with Livni's latest handiwork: powerful bombs that they attached to the bottoms of five buses belonging to an Arab company. They were set to explode in late afternoon, when the buses would be packed. It would have been the worst terror attack ever seen in the land between the sea and the Jordan River. At 4:30 A.M., the men finished their work—and Shin Bet agents grabbed them. The arrests began. When they came for Etzion two days later, he was in the Ofrah synagogue for weekday morning services. The agents let him finish praying, then took him in.

Only when the interrogations began, Gillon says, did the security agency hear about plans to blow away the pillars of the Dome. In the public eye, the group was infamous for its attack on the mayors and the Islamic College. In fact, the Temple Mount plot was the father of the others. It was when they began planning to expedite redemption with explosives that they exempted themselves from the morality that binds ordinary people.

Had they bombed the Dome, says Gillon, citing military intelligence evaluations, they might have created a casus belli uniting the entire Muslim world against Israel. The judges agreed; one wrote that destroying the Dome would have added a religious conflict with hundreds of millions of Muslims to the existing national conflict between Jews and Arabs, and "in the not-too-distant future, the risk of world conflagration."

Given that danger, it's stunning how little time the underground's members spent behind bars. Livni and two others were sentenced to life for the Islamic College attack—but their sentences were commuted three times, so that they left prison in less than seven years. Etzion was out by 1989. Once the initial shock passed, the Israeli justice system dealt with the underground's members as if their crime were a surfeit of patriotism; the subversiveness of their intent was ignored.

The case split Gush Emunim between those who condemned their comrades and those who defended them. But once out of prison, the ex-terrorists were readily accepted back into their communities, sometimes into leadership positions.

Unlike many of his comrades, Yehudah Etzion never expressed regret for his actions. Ten years after his release, sitting in his living room in Ofrah, relaxed, utterly confident, he insisted that the Jewish people must return to the Temple Mount, that "ignoring the Mount is a disaster" because "the Muslims draw their power from holding that place." His mistake, he concluded even before his arrest, was tactical: He'd acted too quickly. He hadn't gotten the message across to a large number of people that the Temple mattered. That's why, he decided, he'd been unable to recruit enough who were willing to act. He had to create the movement first. And he set out to do that.

SIX

CONSTRUCTION WORKERS OF THE LORD

> *The old idea of sacrifice was this:*
> *that blood of the lower life must be shed for the feeding*
> *and strengthening of the handsome, fuller life.*

> —D. H. LAWRENCE,
> "The Old Idea of Sacrifice"

AYOUNG MAN CARRIES A YOUNGER GOAT. He cradles it in his arms—a small, brown, gently bleating, long-faced beast. The goat's got no idea what's coming.

We're standing on a hilltop behind Abu Tor, a Jerusalem neighborhood where artsy couples with comfortable cash flows have moved into sixty-year-old stone houses with arched windows and have redone the insides with lofts and oak bookshelves. The blood-red anemones of spring are sprinkled between weeds and broken hunks of concrete dumped here by a gentrifier's contractor. Look out through the solar panels on the roofs, and on the next hilltop northward the big sunrise-gold Dome shimmers over the Old City wall. A flock of children, the girls in flowered dresses, the boys wearing baggy corduroy pants and checked shirts and wide skullcaps, skims over the weeds and rocks,

138

oblivious to the cameramen shouldering raven-black cameras and the soundmen with boom mikes next to the strange metal structure that looks like a rust-colored water heater on legs and is actually a custom-built oven for roasting an animal sacrifice.

Besides journalists, there are a couple of dozen adults and as many children. It's noonish; the holiday of Passover begins at sunset; and nearly everyone in the country, especially anyone religious, is in the fine-tuned panic that comes before the annual clan feast. To be here you have to believe that when you sit tonight in your living room with once-a-year silver on the table and recite the story of how the Israelites left slavery for freedom, the festival is a broken imitation of what it should be because the blood of your family's lamb or kid wasn't dashed on the altar today.

The goat is on the ground with its legs tied. Yehudah Etzion and another man hold it down. A few children run off, yelling, "I don't want to see." Others push to get a good view. The slaughterer has a two-foot-long knife; he recites a blessing and makes a quick motion and the goat gives one dark low bleat. "May it be Your will that we will one day be privileged to slaughter it in its place, in the sanctuary, next to the altar," Etzion pronounces.

The goat's blood gathers in a burgundy puddle. The slaughterer slits its belly from the gonads up to its head. Boys lean over him, watching. One says, "Dad, is he still alive?" A girl, much smaller, has a quicker grasp. "It's not *nice,* Mommy," she says.

Off to one side stands Gershon Salomon, silver-haired, face shaved glass-smooth except for his full mustache. His hand rests on his cane, reminder of the injury he suffered decades ago in a skirmish with Syrian forces. Salomon, leader of the Temple Mount Faithful, the man best known for publicly demanding that the Muslims be thrown out of the sacred site, isn't looking at the goat. He's here, but the sacrifice doesn't engage him. What drives him is nationalism—the nearly extinct messianic nationalism of the secular far right. "The Supreme Court should be on the Temple Mount," he once told me. "The Israeli army should parade there." The shrine of patriotism and pageantry. When a TV crew turns from the goat to film him, he warns of political dangers in a warm, practiced voice: "The whole world has its eyes on Jerusalem to turn it into an international city or an Arab-Muslim city.

The Land of Israel is being closed off to us, piece by piece." Of altars and offerings he says nothing.

The goat hangs by two hooks from a metal frame as the slaughterer and his assistant strip its skin. Etzion lectures on how it was done once: The whole Temple courtyard was full of small groups, each with an offering. I think of the bleating, the smell. The slaughterer pulls out the pink intestines and drops them on the ground. "The internal organs were burned on the altar, which we can't do today," Etzion says. "We live in a warped reality." Boys try touching the guts with their fingertips. The goat is mounted whole on a spit of pomegranate wood and lifted into the roaring fire in the oven. A settler from Kiryat Arba tells a TV camera that Jews should be doing this on the Mount, that they could remove the Muslim shrines "just like the Arab houses [that stood] next to the Western Wall."

At last, the goat is out on a table, being carved; Etzion hands out foil-wrapped chunks to take home and serve for the holiday. Salomon tells me that his good friend Reverend Irvin Baxter, editor of *Endtime* magazine, will visit Israel soon; Salomon will lecture to Baxter's evangelical tour group and speak on his radio program. "He deals in prophecy. He believes the course of redemption depends on Israel," Salomon says. Christians from all over the world send him letters, he says, basking in the attention.

I walk up a dirt path and out a gate to the street. A teenage girl in jeans rushes by me, carrying two bouquets of flowers for the holiday. If this is distorted reality, let us make the most of it. I suddenly let my breath out, as if I've been holding it for two hours. Twenty minutes' brisk walking and I'm home.

Yehudah Etzion, I assume, will fold his tall body into his car and drive north out of Jerusalem, his gray-blue eyes watching the road that sweeps through the dry slopes. He'll drive into Ofrah, its lush lawns over-irrigated in front of the tile-roofed houses, an artificial Garden of Eden in the midst of a desert. Etzion will enter his house with his chunk of grilled goat. On the wall of his living room hangs a picture of the Temple Mount. If he wishes more people had come to his ceremony, he won't say so. The movement he established after his release from prison is called Hai Vekayam, which means "everlasting"—as in his hopes. He is a revolutionary on a long march, one he sees as lasting a generation or more.

Etzion's house is across the street from the two-story village center where he has his office. In it, countless drawers are packed with acquittals and convictions and appeals on charges of illegal assembly and interfering with a policeman in the line of duty, all from attempts to lead Hai Vekayam activists on to the Temple Mount to hold prayer demonstrations asserting Jewish proprietorship. Somewhere is the letter he got in 1995 from Benjamin Netanyahu, then a candidate for prime minister, promising that once elected he would arrange for Jewish worship on the Mount. It was a campaign promise not kept—but striking because it was made to a man who does not vote on principle, who preaches that the current regime has lost all legitimacy and must be replaced by a king and council of sages and Third Temple.

Etzion still believes the Dome must be removed. But first must come "the lengthy stage of preparing the public." Once there's a wide desire, "a group will arise that will know how to translate the desire into action." Who knows, he once told me, if the support is wide enough, maybe there will be some way other than an explosion to get rid of the Dome. The goal of demonstratively trying to pray on the Mount, of organizing mass meetings—presumably, of anything he does—is to arouse that support.

He knows there are fellow travelers, people who want a Temple even if they think him too radical. And there are even wider circles: people, for instance, who will sit down tonight and use as their Haggadah—the script of the Passover dinner ritual—the book produced by the Temple Institute, with drawings of how a paschal goat or lamb is sacrificed. A bit more of the public will be a bit readier for his ideas.

American political commentator Charles Krauthammer, defending the Netanyahu government against Arab claims that it wanted to destroy Al-Aqsa, once wrote that there are about as many Israelis who want to build the Temple as Americans who believe they've traveled on UFOs. He was right that Netanyahu didn't plan to harm Al-Aqsa. On the other hand, I wonder if anyone has built a flying saucer landing pad as near to Krauthammer's house as Etzion's sacrifice was to mine.

THIS MUCH IS TRUE: A group of people gathered on a Jerusalem hillside to sacrifice a goat is out of sync with Israeli society. They and other

Jews who regard building the Temple as a pressing necessity are on the fringe. But it is a dangerous mistake to dismiss them as harmless kooks.

To start with, the size of that fringe has grown. The goal of Etzion and other activists is to convince Jews that pristine Judaism requires a Temple, and that building one is a practical program. They seek to persuade their coreligionists that leaving the Temple Mount as a Muslim holy place is unnatural and necessarily temporary. They have not turned such ideas into mainstream opinions, but they have won some converts and sympathizers. They have gained enough legitimacy that a major politician could regard it as useful and acceptable to court their support.

They have achieved that measure of success because the divide between them and the mainstream is not absolute. Messianism was one voice of Zionism from its start. In the generation since 1967, the mood of most of Israeli society has swung from messianism to realpolitik, from nationalist fervor to watching NASDAQ prices of Israeli high-tech firms. Abu Tor's gentrified living rooms are closer to today's conventional aspirations than a paschal sacrifice. But the idea that the state of Israel is a step toward redemption hasn't evaporated. It became common wisdom among religious Zionists; it drove the West Bank settlement movement. Those Jews who speak of building the Temple are the people who take the messianic interpretation of Israel's existence most literally. Their appeal is that they reject giving up the dream and going back to normal history. They conjure up symbols that are still potent for many other people.

There are some Temple activists, such as Etzion, who speak explicitly of the need to assert Jewish ownership of the Mount and to remove the Dome. Others insist that God will solve the problem of real estate. Some say their quest is purely spiritual; they speak in the tones of seekers, not political extremists. Yet to fan Jewish aspirations for a Temple is to promote dissatisfaction with the status quo at the Mount; it necessarily deepens conflict over the holy place. Even the most eccentric of the professedly nonpolitical dreamers help cultivate the public support that Yehudah Etzion seeks. However unintentionally, they increase the chance that someone will conclude that the critical mass exists for "translating desire into action" at the Mount.

The goal of would-be Temple-builders is not simply to alter the form of Jewish worship. It is to bring a redeemed era, beyond history as we know it. Their expectation of reaching that era is mistaken, but mistaken is not the same thing as insane. It's worth wandering through the Temple movement, watching how believers think: Precisely because they are extreme, they present a clear picture of the logic of messianism and millennialism.

THE SYNAGOGUE is on a side street in northern Jerusalem, the ultra-Orthodox slice of the city. The main hall could seat a hundred people. In a narrower room to one side Rabbi Yosef Elboim spends his afternoons studying Talmud. When I ask Elboim a question he answers by jumping up and walking in quick bird-steps to the metal shelves, each with two rows of books, one behind the other, well-used volumes with faded gold lettering on the spines. He brings back a book and opens it and guides me through intricate logic. He wears a long black jacket and white shirt and round black homburg and has long gray sidecurls and speaks Yiddish to the handful of other men studying in the hall. To me he speaks Hebrew but to tell me a phone number he has to write it; numbers he stores in Yiddish.

In his mid-forties, Elboim studies for his living, which is normal among ultra-Orthodox men his age in Israel. He has never served in the army. That's also normal for Jews who believe they're spiritually in exile in the Jewish state: The state was created by Zionists who gave God a dismissal notice and sought redemption through practical action. Yet Yosef Elboim is a man of totally pragmatic spirit. So he regularly cites secular Zionist founder Theodor Herzl as his model as he seeks, step by practical step, to restore sacrifices and rebuild the Temple.

Ultra-Orthodox society lives by the rulings of the generation's great rabbis. Those rabbis forbid entering the Temple Mount. Yet every Tuesday, Yosef Elboim arrives at the ramp leading to the Mount's Mughrabi Gate. There he meets two, five, or twenty supporters from his Movement for the Establishment of the Temple. The cops at the guardpost collect their ID papers, checking for troublemakers. When I saw Elboim there, the police told him his people could enter two at a time. Elboim demanded my cell phone—imperious, like an ex–brigade commander who lacks civilian manners—and called a higher-ranking cop and said, "You know me, I don't cause problems." He got permission for groups of four. Behind him walked two Israeli cops and a Waqf guard, the Jews and the Muslim all portly, tired, unpromoted, fortyish, shlepping through the rituals of guard work. Elboim walked a loop along the edges of the Mount, avoiding the area where the Temple stood, a bone-thin man marking out his land claim in quick steps, and exited.

Elboim goes to the Mount to show that Jews can go inside, despite the rulings of the famous rabbis, despite the intent of Israeli authorities to keep Jewish and Muslim holy space separate. If he can get thousands to come, he'll establish that Jews belong there as much as Muslims. Then it would be time for sacrifices that, as he reads religious law, may be performed even before the Temple is built. I look at him under the synagogue's fluorescent lights and for a moment see him in olive-drab, no side curls, the same flame-blue eyes, the same impatience with philosophy, a brigadier's brass on his shoulder, leaning over a sand-table model of tank-battle terrain, explaining how to break each fortification.

This is a family business. His father Avigdor wrote a three-volume work, *The Torah of the Temple.* In it, he lists all the reasons given by great rabbis that the Temple cannot be built in our time: Sacrifices, for instance, may only be offered by members of the hereditary class of priests, *kohanim,* but we have no pedigree to prove that the Jews who claim that status today—men with last names like Cohen, Katz, Kahane, Cagan—are really descended from those who served in the Temple. The priests must wear garments prescribed in the Torah; we've forgotten how to make them. Bringing precedents from Jewish law, Avigdor Elboim rebuts each argument in order to prove that the Temple should be built.

Yet the book begs to be read against itself. The sages it cites use so many arguments to reach the same conclusion because they started from that conclusion. They cited technical reasons for not building the sanctuary, but were in fact making an existential statement: For nearly two thousand years, the Temple has belonged in Jewish thinking to an era when evil is over with, and you don't get to that time simply by starting to build. The Elboims reject that message. For them, as for many millennialists, symbol and reality are one. If the Temple can now be built, then redemption can be reached.

Yosef Elboim was thirteen when Israel took the Temple Mount. He was sure the Temple would quickly be rebuilt. "A few months went by and nothing moved. I figured there were committees, plans." He has no answer for why he and his family saw this differently than virtually all other ultra-Orthodox Jews. His uncle got him involved, he says.

When years passed and the Temple hadn't been built, Elboim sought people who shared his interest. He saw that Orthodox Jews were turned off by Gershon Salomon's secular stance, so he started the Movement for the Establishment of the Temple, aimed at the Orthodox. In the mid-eighties, the movement held a dinner for anyone interested in the Temple; thirty people came. The second time, in 1988, there were sixty. In February 1997, 1,200 people showed up, and the next time they switched to a convention format, sans supper, because they couldn't find a banquet hall big enough. Elboim claims 250 members paying monthly dues to his movement, ten thousand fellow travelers who have expressed support. That's a fraction of what you need to elect one Knesset member. It's also too many to dismiss.

To show that the priestly garments could be recreated, he and his uncle David spent years making a set. They paid craftsmen to make sacrificial utensils specified in ancient texts, to demonstrate it was possible. They'd disprove all the excuses. He went with Rabbi Ariel and Yehudah Etzion to see Melody, because she proved that finding a red heifer was possible.

As Elboim stringently interprets religious law, though, there's an obstacle to using a red heifer: It must be sacrificed by a priest, a *kohen*, past bar-mitzvah age, at least thirteen years old, who has never had contact with death, never stepped on a forgotten tomb, never been inside the same hospital as a corpse.

Elboim explains his plan to break that obstacle. He'll need to bring up boys in a place where they'll remain untainted. A structure will be built on columns, so that empty space will separate it from earth that could contain graves. "When they're born, an apartment would be enough. But we'd need to prepare a playing field"—also on columns—"so they can be there until bar-mitzvah age," he explains.

The mothers will come to the compound to give birth. Parents, he says, will live elsewhere, but will be able to take turns spending time with the boys. Once a cow is available and a boy comes of age, he'll be taken to perform the sacrifice. Isn't this cruel to the children, I ask. "When people want computer whizzes, they have kids sit for years in front of a screen. When it's nonsense, everyone knows it's important. But something *real*—then they start with ethics."

The thin man across the table is serious, and he is not alone. A West Bank settlement agreed to host the project, on condition that its name remained secret. He advertised in his newsletter and elsewhere for candidates. Eight couples signed up to give birth in the compound. Alas, that wasn't enough. Tests showed that four babies would be girls. And Elboim wanted a score of boys, so the kids would have friends. "If we'd said we were going to raise soccer players," he says bitterly, "people would have signed up." I'm struck by the other side: Eight families agreed to turn newborn sons over to be raised in isolation. The settlement is still prepared to go ahead, he says. All that's needed are children, whose childhood will be a small sacrifice to the redemption.

THE PRIESTLY GARMENTS are at his uncle's. Yosef Elboim takes me into a one-room apartment and peremptorily leaves me with someone I must assume is his uncle: a little man with a trimmed white beard, a black velvet skullcap nestled above his ring of white hair, a short-sleeved shirt with thin stripes on what must once have been a white background and is now between gray and beige. His eyes, once blue, are clouded. The room has one big window, a bathroom sink, a refrigerator, a single gas burner. Dividing the room in half are a big wooden hand loom and a square gold form that I recognize from a photo Yosef showed me as a model of an incense altar.

Without introduction, he tells me he has a message he wants me to publish. The Arabs aren't really from here, he says, they are descendants of the people brought here by the king of Assyria when he mixed up the nations, so unlike us they don't have a real right to be here.

"I wrote a letter to Bibi," he says. He shows me the letter to Benjamin Netanyahu. The top says "Dear Bibi." The bottom has no signature. It is about this point. He pulls out a Bible and reads to me from Kings in a Yiddish accent I can barely understand about the mixing up of the nations 2,700 years ago.

"Are you David Elboim?" I interrupt, impatient.

"Yes."

"I came to see the priest's clothes."

He goes behind the loom and calls me and hands me a green plastic trash can with a white lid. Only later do I realize that the clothes of the priests for the Third Temple are stored in it. He sits down at a tiny table. "I made them on that," he says, pointing to the loom. "It has 1,000 threads. No one knew how to do it. You need linen threads. And you need to weave it. It can't be knitted like a sweater. And there can't be a seam. The sleeves can be sewn on, but not the rest. It has to be like a firehose, which is woven and can't have a seam because it would burst. No one knew how to do any of it."

They don't raise flax in Israel, he tells me. It comes from Egypt. Someone in Tel Aviv imported it for shrouds, for the dead. He ordered it from the shroud people. "You had to bleach it. And you had to make the threads six-ply. With the help of heaven we did it." He lifts the trash can lid and I see big plastic bags.

He says: "I didn't know how to weave. One Sabbath I was walking, and I saw a place with a sign: 'Australian Institute for Handweaving.' I went back after the Sabbath. They made little rugs. They said they couldn't do it, I'd have to learn. Their looms weren't big enough, so I ordered this from America. It took a year, a year and a half to come." He speaks slowly, mixing words and saliva in his toothless mouth, moving his thin arms and big hands in wide, clumsy motions in the air. Yet he did the exacting work.

The loom came unassembled. A woman came from the institute to set it up and teach him to use it. The cloth, he says, had to be double, with a checked pattern woven in, and the woman was stumped. He found another teacher at the weaving department at the Israel Museum.

With shaking hands, he opens the plastic bags. Rolled up in a disk is a long strip of cloth. "This is the belt. It's thirty-two cubits." It's a handbreadth wide, the thread thick and rough. The priest would wrap it repeatedly around his waist. Elboim takes out the pants. The material is natural, heavy. The checked pattern, off-white on off-white, is created by one thread going under several cross-threads. He shows me proudly: The legs are seamless tubes connected seamlessly to the upper part, also a tube. He shows me the tunic, long and straight like a nightshirt. "Look," the little man says, "I made it as one piece in a circle." There's a hat too, a long strip meant to be wrapped as a turban, but he couldn't get the knack so he sewed it together like a stocking cap.

"There are a thousand threads in that machine," he says, pronouncing it *makhon*, "institute," instead of *mekhonah*, "machine." He came here after the Holocaust in 1946. Hebrew is still work. "It took a long time. Then I stopped. I grew up." He means, "I got old."

"These are the four garments the priest has to wear in the Temple," he says. "I made two sets. But if the Temple's built, there'll be a lot of priests. Rabbi Ariel brought a woman who wove for him. If the Temple's built, a lot of people will weave."

"How long did you weave?" I ask.

"Three years."

"All day?"

"No, no. I was also a carpenter. I had a workshop here." He pushes his face forward as if staring close up at threads, his clouded eyes popping, his hands up as if working. "You could go crazy from it if you worked on it all day."

Then he sounds thoughtful. "It was the experience of a lifetime, of a lifetime."

"Why did you make them?"

"We'd gone up to the Temple Mount. My nephew gave me the motivation," he says. "We spoke about building the Temple and offering sacrifices. But a priest who offers sacrifices without wearing the garments is subject to death. So I decided to do it. That Australian institute—it was sent by heaven."

I'm looking at an old man who spent years of his life weaving flaxen clothes in an ancient pattern for priests to wear and is tired now. He comes from an earliest generation of ultra-Orthodox Jews, he is more worldly than his nephew, he worked with his hands. But he is like some medieval monk working a lifetime on a manuscript; he has produced a strange garment for use in a nonexistent Temple.

He tells me he inspired Yisrael Ariel to open the Temple Institute and begin producing all the implements of sacrifice. "After I started, Rabbi Ariel got interested. It's like anything, one person starts small, another picks it up and does it big. In the beginning he took my garments. He had a group of Rabbi Kahane's fellows, he exhibited them all over the country." He pauses. "I didn't do it for honor or to make a living."

He looks like a lone eccentric. But Kahane and Ariel took from him the idea of creating the clothes and the implements to promote the Temple. Today busloads of schoolkids come to visit Ariel's institute. Ten thousand people are on Yosef Elboim's mailing list. One has to wonder if one day the work of the lone craftsmen laboring for God's glory will unintentionally inspire someone else to labor in explosives.

This isn't his home. He comes during the day for quiet, to study. Once he displayed Temple artifacts here. "Yeshivah students threw stones when I had the exhibition," he says. It's just like Poland before the war, he says, when the rabbis forbade Jews to go to the Land of Israel. If someone said he was going, they wouldn't let him be called to read from the Torah scroll in the synagogue and get a blessing before he left. "He'd have to go to the end of town," he says, "where the craftsmen had their synagogue. Today it's like that with the Temple Mount, the rabbis say it's forbidden to go there."

The subtext is agony. He obeyed those rabbis, or his parents did, and stayed in Poland. I don't know what he saw, who he lost, for listening to ultra-Orthodox rabbis who regarded returning to the land as rushing the redemption. Now, he's saying, they oppose taking human action by going to the Temple Mount or weaving priestly garments on a handloom.

Here, it seems, is the source of the family's activism, and a clue to how the Holocaust spurred messianism. David Elboim is not the only Jew to have learned from the catastrophe not to accept blindly what rabbinic authorities say. But his rebellion is more specific. He accepts that leaving Poland for Palestine in 1938 meant pursuing redemption, not simply seeking reasonable refuge. Therefore, it was a mistake not to pursue redemption. And as he sees it, there's no difference between fleeing Europe and building the Temple. So on this point, he chooses not to listen. This way, he can hold together the fabric of faith and still rebel. I leave him studying in his room.

■

A LONESOME WAIL sounds over the streetcorner, like a saxophone in mourning. A Brinks truck is pulled up on the downtown Jerusalem sidewalk. Next to it stand two blue-uniformed guards, a balding man with a ponytail who holds a long corkscrew horn that once belonged to a beast, a woman with a nightblack mane over the shoulder of an azure dress that says everything necessary about her figure, and Reuven Prager, master of ceremonies, wearing his recreated Temple-era tunic and shoulder-length sidecurls and big white smile. The man with the curling addax horn lifts it again, and lets loose with that wail, and a passerby says, "All right, Satchmo." As per Prager's request, the Brinks men are both *kohanim*. Despite the stench of a weeklong garbage strike, the guards and Prager and the dark-lipped woman named Lior and the musician all look happy. The Brinks men have just made their thrice-yearly pickup of a lockbox full of sacred half-shekel coins, guaranteed .999 pure silver and dedicated to the unbuilt Temple, and are about to deliver it to a safe in the Chief Rabbinate building. Everyone here has one foot into a different, imagined era where, presumably, city workers never need to strike for better pay.

The horn player lives a few blocks from me, a reasonable fellow, or so I thought thirteen years ago when he blew a lovely sax at my wedding. At the last shekel ceremony he gave me a book explaining how the Council for Foreign Relations was behind the Oslo Accords and the Rabin assassination—a strange Israeli adaptation of the usually anti-Semitic conspiracy theories of America's rabid right. At that moment it seemed that the appropriate soundtrack was not a shofar blast but the music I remember from childhood right before Rod Serling appeared on screen to tell us we were in the Twilight Zone. But conspiracy theories have a natural draw for those awaiting history's last act: They live in a great drama, and want to find the elusive villain.

The Brinks men mark the end of Prager's production, which began earlier, up one of the narrow nineteenth-century streets gentrified into crafts galleries and cafés, under the vine-covered arbor in the courtyard of the House of Harari harp shop. The Hararis, Micah and Shoshana, met as "seekers after the truth," as she puts it, in a Southern California beachtown in the early seventies, and later started reading the Bible in Colorado when a blizzard imprisoned them in a log cabin where they lived ten thousand feet up in the mountains. They discovered, she says, that they were "descended from kings and holy men and beautiful women" and that the prophets had foretold the ingathering of the exiles, so they ended up in Israel. The Aquarian dream of wandering footloose and naive into the Garden flowed seamlessly into the fantasy of a rebuilt Temple. In the shop are the biblical harps that Micah makes from maple and cypress, twenty-two-string triangular ones and ten-string ones whose sides look like two uplifted arms. A print spread covers a bamboo couch; incense vainly fights the smell of burning garbage; a painting shows a Temple courtyard where rows of Levites play harps and horns. In a framed photo, Shoshana Harari is kneeling in a field of anemones, playing a harp and wearing a flowing white dress that looks lifted from one of E. M. Lilien's drawings and was actually made for her by Reuven Prager. Like Lior's getup with the dark blue harp design on the chest and his own tunic, it's part of his concept that to make "the production" of rebuilding the Temple seem plausible, proper costuming is essential.

Prager began minting coins in 1997. When the Temple stood, every Jew was required to give a silver half-shekel annually to pay for sacrifices and upkeep. Prager, a coin collector in his Miami childhood, decided to revive the custom, with the idea that the Temple would come into existence the moment it owned something, before one stone was in place. A gilt-painted wooden chest sits in the Hararis' shop; coin customers are supposed to drop them in—or send them back, if they buy via the Internet, as most do. "The Exile Has Ended," Prager announced in a *Jerusalem Post* ad after the first coins were donated. In 1998 he sold five thousand coins, but he admits that only 10 percent came back. One reason: "A lot of Christians have bought them," he says. "There's a tremendous gentile interest in the Third Temple."

For the ceremony the gilt chest comes out into the courtyard. Prager begins reading an ancient description of how half-shekels were donated when the sanctuary stood. To remove the coins from the chest, you have to be descended from the tribe of Levi; Lior qualifies and Prager asks her forward—the first time in history, he proclaims, that a woman has performed the sacred task. A feminist revolution.

She crouches at the chest's low opening, asks the group's permission according to a traditional formula, and shovels a pile of silver coins into a wicker basket and then into the lockbox, while Prager and the pony-tail play a duet on corkscrew horns. At the Korean restaurant that shares the courtyard, a woman covers her ears. The well-armed gentlemen from Brinks arrive for the pickup.

Prager's face is picking up wrinkles; gray has touched his trim beard. He talks quickly, giggles too much, is sure he's at the center of world-changing events. He lives alone, months behind in his rent. It would be easy to laugh at him, but it would be like laughing at Job, a Job sans grandeur, who never had his children restored.

In 1977, a college kid from a nonreligious home, he came to Israel to study at a yeshivah of the Chabad hasidic movement, whose campus rabbis sought spiritually adrift Jewish students. Prager leapt into the new life; at twenty he was married. Within three years, he and his wife had three children—all sickly. "I buried the first and the third," he says. "By the time I was twenty-three, I was like an eighty-year-old man."

His marriage broke up. He kept Jewish dietary laws, but maintained little else of Jewish tradition. When the summer month of Av began, he had to decide whether to follow the Orthodox ban on shaving, in mourning for the Temple, or publicly show that he'd left religion. That night, he says, "I raised my hands to Heaven and said 'OK, You want to fight, You're on.' " He had decided that the Lord Himself was complacent, too willing to accept the ultra-Orthodox style of serving Him. For Prager, that kind of religion had become terribly insufficient. He would convince both God and the Jews that it was time for final redemption. The Jews had already returned to their land and regained sovereignty, so now it was time for the Temple. Prager decided to take the memories of Temple practices and make them *real*. He started with the fact he was descended from the tribe of Levi, a semi-priestly status with virtually no content since the Temple's destruction. He declared himself a "Levite on duty," responsible for revived rituals.

It was a one-man enactment of how messianism and millennialism often develop. Struck by upheaval, he could no longer accept religion as usual. It was inconceivable to go on worshiping God as if nothing had happened, and unimaginable that God would continue to allow such unfairness in His world. But he didn't want to give up faith. One part of the answer was to declare that God would simply have to establish His kingdom on earth. The second part was that religion would have to be returned to a pristine state appropriate for the messianic time. He could thereby insist that he was more loyal than anyone else to true faith—and rebel against conventional religion. The same logic has led Christian millennial movements to leave established churches and claim to restore Christianity to its original form.

Prager says politics don't concern him. It's a common "seeker" perspective: on the way to spiritual satisfaction, worldly problems will evaporate. "The Muslims believe in serving God. When God makes clear that it's time to build His house . . . the Muslims are going to dance [the Dome] off," he tells me. He says he takes part in all the meetings of Temple activists, though he adds: "God has not put together a very good marketing team for the Temple"—it includes too many "unthinking blow-up-the-mosque folks." He describes that as putting the cart before the horse. First one should create everything necessary for the Temple. Like the incense; he says he's identified all the ancient ingredients. Or like the right clothes: He started producing his Beged Ivri—"Hebrew Clothing"—fashions in the eighties, men's garments based on ancient sources, women's on his imagination. A marketing photo on the wall of his apartment shows a woman in a white handwoven dress, trimmed in gold brocade, with a deep décolletage: sacred cheesecake. He admits that ultra-Orthodox Jews have occasionally complained that his work is immodest, but he makes each piece to the customer's request. But the real point, it seems, is that his chesty model is posing pastorally beneath a spreading tree. Prager presents the illusion of an idyllic, sensuous past—and future.

Shoshana Harari, who says politics is "a very low form of spirituality," is a natural partner. Of late, she contributes a natural-healing column to the English-language *Your Jerusalem,* a former tourist monthly turned fringe-right tabloid, complete with front-page conspiracy theories. Harari describes the time of the rebuilt Temple as a "restored Garden of Eden"; she doesn't know how it will be achieved, but the harps her husband makes will be used there. Four of them are in the Temple Institute's collection.

Harari is unusual among Temple enthusiasts: most are male. Even Prager's desire to involve women in a ritual is exceptional. Ariel's Temple Haggadah stresses the point: A two-page painting shows a group eating a paschal offering at a Temple-time Passover meal—and all are men. Modern Judaism, including Orthodoxy, is an arena for women's demands for equality. To idealize the Temple era is to long for Judaism at its most patriarchal.

But there may be a subtler reason for the milieu's maleness: People who think the Temple will bring redemption offer an engineering solution to existential problems. Human evil? The potential for cruelty? The need for meaning? Let's locate where the altar stood, breed a red heifer, weave the priest's clothes. The idea that the Temple will bring world peace bears a family resemblance to, for instance, a claim that the Internet will end human loneliness. The techno-fallacy isn't burnt into the Y chromosome, but in modern society, it is more common among men.

The desire to recreate the Temple fits another pattern, known from another part of the globe. Beginning in the late nineteenth century, millennial movements known as "cargo cults" appeared among South Pacific islanders. Assaulted by European rule, by the ideas of Christian missionaries, by the sight of material wealth brought from afar, islanders turned to a vision: A new age would dawn with the arrival of great vessels, carrying their dead ancestors and Cargo—the wealth *they* deserved. Islanders built "docks" or "landing strips," assuming they would thereby bring the Cargo-bearing ships or planes. In his study of the phenomenon, *The Trumpet Shall Sound*, sociologist Pete Worsley stressed that the islanders weren't irrational: They reached reasonable conclusions from fragmented information. The Europeans they saw never worked; manufactured goods simply arrived at their docks and landing strips. And the powerful knowledge of the whites, conveyed by Christian missionaries, told of the millennium.

For some fundamentalists, Jewish and Christian—often educated people—the Temple has become the great Cargo ship. Looking for the lost Ark with radar, or minting silver half-shekels, is akin to building the dock. So are the scholarly prophecy conferences of Christian fundamentalists, the "intelligence briefings" and newsletters that line up verses of scripture with geopolitical developments. The outward form of practical action—even of think-tank-style analysis—is applied to salvation. Here, too, there's rational reasoning from misread facts: A mix of step-by-step activism and political forces has already brought developments that look like fulfilled prophecy. Therefore, more of the same will fulfill the rest, and bring (please check one) the Redemption of Israel or the Second Coming. The problem arises when you want to build your landing strip on the political mine field known as the Temple Mount, when you insist that the mines will vanish of their own accord.

I'm sitting in Reuven Prager's living room. He's told me we'll be interrupted; someone's coming to film him. He's showing me the Temple-period bridal sedan chair he spent nine years making, with the velvet interior and the draping of silk and gold brocade bought for him in Damascus by a non-Jew at $400 a meter from stock made for the Saudi royal family. To market the Temple, he believes in being theatrical. There's a knock. When Prager opens the door, Yehudah Etzion enters with a cameraman. He's making a film on Levites and *kohanim*. It's one more way to make the Temple seem real to people. Prager speaks to the camera.

SO THE MOVEMENT GROWS. The number of Jews in Israel caught by the dream of a rebuilt Temple can only be estimated. As one Orthodox rabbi who outspokenly opposes the phenomenon puts it, "there are people who quarter-believe and who half-believe," concentric circles of support. Over time, more Orthodox Jews have become willing to enter the Mount in order to stake a religious claim. The number ready to come to a convention or demonstration, once in the dozens, rose during the 1990s to hundreds and beyond. Yosef Elboim's list of ten thousand presumably does not include all the sympathizers. On the hardline side of the West Bank settlement movement, among the most bitter opponents of peace with the Palestinians, the Temple Mount has become a rallying call.

This is a small, radical minority. Its members see themselves as standing at the gate of redemption, and are stunned that most Jews don't want to join them in crossing the threshold. Its growth matters not because it is about to become a mass movement, but because numbers and enthusiasm increase its potential to aggravate conflict at the spot that symbolizes the dispute between Jews and Arabs.

But the Temple movement has another audience. For premillennialist Christians, what Reuven Prager calls the "the production" of rebuilding the Temple seems more than plausible. For them, indeed, the Temple activists are stars of a drama they do not understand themselves.

SEVEN

The
Divine Repertory
Theater Company

Bid the players make haste.

—WILLIAM SHAKESPEARE,
Hamlet, ACT III

THE CROWD OVERFLOWS the rectangular prayer area next to the Western Wall, filling the wide plaza behind, tens of thousands of men and women holding the hands of small children, and more keep pouring through the metal detectors at the entrance. The men grasp long palm fronds, making the plaza looks as if an oasis grove had uprooted itself from the desert and come on pilgrimage to Jerusalem. It's the autumn festival of Sukkot, and the fronds are for waving in celebration of God's life-giving.

Four guys with scruffy late-adolescent beards sit below the ramp that leads to Mughrabi Gate, waiting for Gershon Salomon. Sukkot, the Feast of Tabernacles, is one of several times of year when Salomon marches up the ramp with his Temple Mount Faithful, demands to enter the sacred precincts, and calls for replacing the Islamic shrines with the Third Temple. Standard turnout is around two dozen—aging ultranationalists alongside a few activists left over from Meir Kahane's

Kach movement and some teens from the fringe of religious Zionism. The myriads of Jews, to Salomon's outraged incomprehension, prefer to make pilgrimage to the Wall.

Though the Temple movement has grown, Jewish support for Salomon has faded. The extreme nationalism of soil, myth, and messianism no longer grabs Israeli secularists. Though Salomon now wears the skullcap of a religious Jew, he's still perceived in the Temple movement as a secularist, and "Orthodox Jews don't want to join an organization led by a person who's not religious," as one ex-ally says. When one of Salomon's gray-haired followers stands at the Wall plaza, shouting through a bullhorn at holiday worshipers to take the Mount from the Muslims, ultra-Orthodox men gather around to argue theology. "Until the messiah comes, it's forbidden to go up there," roars a yeshivah student.

"You're standing in the messiah's way," Salomon's man yells.

"You think this is redemption? Redemption is when you and I overcome our evil impulses."

"The Temple was always built by human beings."

"Great sages told them to, not a few media hounds."

This time, though, Salomon has reinforcements. Pastor John Small stands near the ramp with congregants from his Florida church. He's wearing a T-shirt that reads "Space Coast Prophecy Conference" and a nametag from the Feast of Tabernacles celebration run by the International Christian Embassy. The "Embassy" is a pro-Israel evangelical group formed in 1980; its annual gathering brings over five thousand people to the city to proclaim love for Israel, and to fulfill Zechariah's prophecy that in the Last Days all nations will come to Jerusalem to celebrate Sukkot. Salomon has spoken at Small's church. "We support building the Temple," Small says. "We support what he's doing. He's a *Zionist.*"

Salomon arrives, leaning on his cane. Someone hands out Temple Mount Faithful flags, blue and white with a yellow map of the Much Greater Land of Israel stretching from the Sinai to Iraq, and evangelical visitors grab them. At crowd's edge, I get a happy handshake from Texas oilman Hayseed Stephens, who hopes to fund the next Temple's construction after his well hits petroleum where the Bible told him, next to the Dead Sea. Wearing a brilliant white Stetson, he drawls, "Lots of people think Gershon is *meshuganeh,* they think I'm *meshuganeh.* The only way to tell is that if he builds the Temple he's not nuts, and if the Lord comes I'm not nuts."

A woman from Philadelphia tells me that for the last year, she's been raising money for the Faithful among Christians; at the Embassy celebration, giving is good. "I don't find much interest among Jews," whether Reform, Conservative, or Orthodox, she says. It probably doesn't help that her sales pitch includes catastrophic conflict on Israeli soil. "I think there's a war coming within a year or two," she tells me, smiling and citing Ezekiel 38. It's a reference to the invasion of Israel by the mythic forces of Magog, leading to the Last World War. "Then the way will be paved for the Temple. We're reaching the End of the Age."

Nearby, a Danish woman with a guitar tells me of writing the score for a musical, *The Temple Shall Be Built Again.* It will be performed at another Tabernacles gathering, organized by the International Christian Zionist Center, a breakaway from the Embassy. Finally, the group surges up the ramp, 150 people, perhaps 200. At the green gate at the top, the police commander recites his standard line to Salomon: "I'm sorry to say you can't enter. The Mount is closed today to visitors." The potent fumes of sanctity are in the air, and the cops don't want Salomon lighting any matches.

Stuck on the ramp, Salomon takes a megaphone and shouts in English, "Soon we shall see the rebuilding of the Temple . . . and the accomplishing of God's Endtime plan of the lion lying down with the lamb," to answers of "Yes," "Amen," and "Hallelujah." A nationalist in his native tongue, Salomon has absorbed a Last Days vocabulary in English that fits his evangelical audience's expectations. As everyone marches down the ramp and out of the Old City, a goateed American leads a group in singing a Hebrew song about brothers living in peace to the incongruous tune of "Battle Hymn of the Republic," then switches to a song about building the Temple. It hasn't been built today. Nor have the fumes been set afire, not this time. But today the Faithful had numbers.

IT MAKES SENSE for evangelical backers of Israel to take the unlikely figure of Gershon Salomon as the true representative of Zionism. From the start, dispensational premillennialists have seen Zionism as proof that prophecies of the End are coming true. News reports from the embattled Holy Land have been read as further evidence that the Rapture is near, that God and His oft-mocked faithful believers will soon be victorious.

So for those who accept dispensationalist doctrine, as so many evangelicals do, it's natural to proclaim love of the Jewish state. Israel's existence gives a believer the warm feeling that the world is behaving as he or she expects it to. Yet affection for Israel and "the Jew" doesn't keep dispensationalists from stressing Jews' failure to accept Jesus, or from predicting their vast suffering during the Tribulation. This is a curiously cold affection, for dispensationalists do not look at Jews as normal people. Rather, as premillennialist writer Randall Price puts it in his 1998 book *Jerusalem in Prophecy,* Jews are the "players . . . for the prophetic drama," or perhaps simply "the scenery," placed on the stage by the Director. Since they're in place, the "curtain call" of the End, as Price calls it, must be near.

An audience will give its greatest love to the actors who make the play progress toward its desired climax. If the state of Israel is exciting, all the more so are right-wing politicians who want to hold on to every inch of land that Israel has captured, and West Bank settlers who have staked their claim at places with Old Testament names like Hebron and Elon Moreh. Better yet is someone who seeks to build the Temple, who would finish setting the stage for history's final scenes. For most Israelis the Temple movement appears marginal; for many of the country's evangelical backers, the same movement is the ultimate expression of what Zionism is supposed to do. Only one other kind of Jew that can generate such excitement: the rare few who have accepted Jesus, as Jews are supposed to in the premillennialists' Last Days.

When someone is watching a play this important, the temptation is to cheer the heroes, even leap to the edge of the stage and join in. The same beliefs that spur support for Israel create enthusiasm for the Israeli right, and for settlers, and for Temple activists. They can also produce anger when Jews stray from the premillennialist script—for instance, by agreeing to trade land for peace.

And some on the stage, members of the divine repertory company, willingly accept the audience support. If other Jews do not back them sufficiently, let evangelicals help out. Secular politicians and far-right messianists have both accepted such assistance. The relationship presents a picture of missed meanings, ignored motives, mutually contradictory expectations.

IT'S THE OPENING NIGHT of the Christian Zionist Center's Tabernacles happening in Sultan's Pool, an Ottoman reservoir turned amphitheater outside the walls of Old Jerusalem. Introduced by blasts of rams' horns, backed by a band of keyboards, electric guitar, and drums, a singer belts out, "Let's go up to the mountain of the Lord," amplified by a gigawatt sound system and speakers. The crowd of a couple of thousand stands swaying, singing, swept away—the religious experience that usually hides a centimeter under the surface of a rock concert here daring to speak its proper name.

The International Christian Zionist Center was started by Jan Willem van der Hoeven, a tall, jowly minister who speaks in a constant storm of enthusiasm and enraged protest. Van der Hoeven grew up in the Netherlands; his hero was a Dutch woman who hid Jews during the Holocaust. In his book, *Babylon or Jerusalem?*, he attacks Christian anti-Semitism over the ages. But he also argues that the Nazi genocide was the Lord's way of convincing the recalcitrant Jews to return to their land—a justification of God that blames Jews for their own destruction.

Van der Hoeven moved to Jerusalem in 1967. When the Knesset's passage of the Jerusalem Law—a restatement of Israeli rule over the united city—sparked an exodus of foreign embassies to Tel Aviv, he helped found the International Christian Embassy, then served for years as its spokesman. The Dutch minister takes a stridently right-wing view of Israeli politics. "As long as the Bible doesn't say, 'I will bring My people from all over the world to half the land of their fathers,' " he says, he'll oppose territorial compromise.

He's most passionate when talking about the Temple Mount, sputtering about Jews who are satisfied "with a stupid Jewish Wailing Wall," who wait for the messiah to build the Temple. "The messiah will do it!" he says in mocking falsetto, then drops to bass: "Don't give me that crap. That is the crap that led six million Jews into the gas chambers." In America, he says, "You have many Christians, many preachers who say Jesus can come any time. I can tell you he's not coming in 2000. . . . What, he comes [through] the eastern gate of the Mosque of Omar and is greeted by the homosexual Yasser Arafat?" Even before the turn of the millennium, he has provided two explanations for those who expect the Rapture and will be disappointed: It didn't happen because of the Muslim presence on the Mount, and because of the Jews' refusal to rebuild the sanctuary.

Van der Hoeven's outspokenness is a key reason for his 1997 split with the Christian Embassy, where staffers acknowledge a preference for the Israeli right but publicly proclaim love for Israel no matter who's in power. Every year the Embassy asks Israel's prime minister to address its Tabernacles gathering; Netanyahu got the wildest applause, but Yitzhak Rabin also came. At the end of September 1999, a few months after Ehud Barak's landslide victory over Benjamin Netanyahu, the new leader has broken tradition and turned down the Embassy's invitation.

As for Van der Hoeven, his opening-night guest below the Old City walls is the man he regards as the once and future prime minister. Introducing Benjamin Netanyahu, Van der Hoeven compares him to other great men to whom the Jewish people failed to listen, such as Moses and "the rabbi from Nazareth." Voting out Netanyahu, in other words, was another proof of Jewish theological obtuseness. Van der Hoeven promises the ex–prime minister, "You have an army of Christians who want you to return" to power. Among Israelis, this is Netanyahu's political nadir—he's defeated and under police investigation for taking bribes. Here he gets a standing ovation and the once-familiar rhythmic cries, "Bi-*bi*, Bi-*bi*." After Netanyahu's speech, Van der Hoeven is back at the mike, promising, "My messiah is not going to come to a Mosque of Omar, but a Third Temple which God will let be built . . . I hope under your premiership."

As Van der Hoeven speaks, a woman steps next to me in the dark, whispers in American English, "Don't worry, I'm Jewish too," and hands me a business card introducing her as "Your Missionary to Israel," with New Testament verses in Hebrew and English to urge me to accept Jesus. Her pitch isn't part of the official program. Both Van der Hoeven and his ex-colleagues at the Christian Embassy stress that they don't seek to convert Jews. They know that's a condition for low-stress relations with Israelis: As far as Jews are concerned, Christian proselytizing historically has meant an assertion that the Jewish people has no right to exist any more. Virtually all Jews, including the most secular, reject the evangelical view that you can remain a Jew in the ethnic sense while accepting Christianity—indeed, the Israeli Supreme Court based a 1960s ruling on that consensus. To "support Israel" while actively seeking to convert the Jews is, in Jewish eyes, to couple a caress with a stab in the back.

Yet in the dispensationalist program, there's no contradiction: The Jews remain God's chosen nation, but their salvation depends on accepting Jesus. And among fervent evangelical supporters of Israel, missionary energy is impossible to suppress. The next morning at the Christian Embassy's Tabernacles celebration, fifteen hundred people show up for the morning's main event, an Irish couple's tag-team talk: Providing a headstart on 2000, he proclaims that the new millennium has begun with Rosh Hashanah, the Jewish new year, in September 1999; but the true proof that we're in "the last part of the Last Days" is Israel's 1967 conquest of Jerusalem. Then his partner announces that "it's glorious to have here" Jewish immigrants from the former Soviet Union "who have come to know Him as Yeshua"—Jesus' Hebrew name—and she urges the audience to "pray for our messianic believers here in Israel." The woman sitting in front of me weeps with joy.

Outside, a constant wail fills the lobby, customers testing rams' horns at souvenir stalls doing a raging business in Jewish ritual objects. Between them, half a dozen booths promote missionary efforts to Israelis. The laptop slideshow at Holyland Ministries shows evangelists handing out bread to destitute Jewish immigrants from Russia and exploiting the opportunity to engage them in Christian prayer. Next to the Maoz Ministries desk, a Hebrew-speaking man recognizes me as a compatriot and buttonholes me to "explain what we are doing in the body of Christ." Asked about the booths, softspoken Embassy spokesman David Parsons has to search for words: "We are evangelicals. . . . But we are not a missionary ministry to Israelis. In the booths, we say they can have [missionary material] to pick up, but they can't hand it out. We can't cut ourselves off from part of the body of believers."

Parsons's answer only underlines the point: "Bible-believing"

Christians' backing for Israel normally comes packaged with a firm belief in proselytizing to the Jews. Yes, some buy one component without the other. Yet even the Christian Embassy, perhaps the group most eager to please Israelis, would be able to evade the pattern only at the cost of much of its constituency.

The booth area also offers the option of helping West Bank settlements, as at the desk of the Christian Friends of Israeli Communities. That organization arranges for churches to adopt settlements and so to support "those pioneers now fulfilling the covenant to Abraham, Isaac, Jacob . . . regarding the restoration of *all* the land God has allotted to Israel," as a leaflet says. The group notes that it's "not an evangelistic ministry"—a tip that the purpose of raising funds for preschools or medical supplies is not to sell Christianity to West Bank settlers.

Still, the juxtaposition is a reminder: Converts and Israel's uncompromising right serve the same function here; they provide the eerie sense that Endtimes prophecies are coming true. That's the explicit message at another booth—promoting Project Shofar, an effort run by PR director Gary Cooperberg of the Nir Yeshivah in the West Bank's Kiryat Arba. Cooperberg, an ex–New Yorker, was once Meir Kahane's foreign press secretary. Even in the Gush Emunim culture, the rabbis who head Nir are known as hardliners. Rabbi Dov Lior, for instance, once wrote that Israel should use captured Arab terrorists as guinea pigs for medical experiments. Cooperberg says the yeshivah isn't "the type of group to go looking for Christians." But Christians who read "the Bible and the newspaper and see that they correlate" showed they were interested. And like them, Cooperberg is convinced that history is near its conclusion. "When the End of Days continues to unfold amid a host of powerful delusions," says a Shofar handout, "everyone of [God's] servants should be soberly anticipating . . . the culmination of Redemption." Some of the funds Shofar raises will support the yeshivah; the rest will go to efforts to convince U.S. Jews to move to Israel in fulfillment of Last Days prophecy. Politically, Cooperberg is at the far fringe of the Israeli right, but in soliciting evangelical support, he has company from the mainstream.

■

THE PHOTO FILLS your browser screen: A bearded, grinning Zola
Levitt poses next to Benjamin Netanyahu. It appears in the televangelist's website slide show from an Israel tour, and not by chance: In
1998, Levitt commented on the then–prime minister by pointing to
the meaning of his name in Hebrew: "I do support the policies of Netanyahu's government . . . Netanyahu is indeed, as his name states, the
gift of God."

Levitt's Internet site could be viewed as a caricature of premillennialist views of Jews and Israel; the shrill tones presumably reflect
the preacher's love-hate relationship with his own Jewish roots. The
teleministry's purpose, it announces, is to equip gentile viewers to
"witness" to their Jewish friends. In an online newsletter, Levitt blasts
Judaism as "the cockamamie rules and regulations invented by a
bunch of lawyers called rabbis." Demonstrating Levitt's "biblical" support for Israel, the newsletter opens with a current affairs article—a
screed against the Mideast peace process by Gary Cooperberg, with a
note that the Kiryat Arba Kahanist has also appeared on Levitt's show.

Yet Levitt's tilt toward the Israeli right is hardly unique. The ro-
mance between American evangelicals focused on prophecy and Israeli leaders first bloomed during the 1977–83 administration of
Menachem Begin, the first rightist elected the country's prime minister. Evangelicals' relationship to Israel turned ambivalent during the
1992–95 government of Yitzhak Rabin, who disdained biblical rhetoric and based his pro-peace policies on a hardnosed view of Israeli security needs. John Hagee's *Beginning of the End: The Assassination of
Yitzhak Rabin and the Coming Antichrist*—which topped Christian
bestseller lists in 1996—portrays the mixed feelings. Hagee, pastor of
a 15,000-member San Antonio church, starts by praising Rabin's brilliance and personal warmth. But then he gives the backdrop to Rabin's
murder. Israel, he says, is divided between religious Jews who think
they have a "holy deed to the land" and Jews who "put more faith in
man than in the God of their fathers." If his readers miss which side to
sympathize with, Hagee stresses that the word of God gives the Jews
the right to land stretching all the way across Iraq. And, he says,
Rabin's assassin, Yigal Amir, belonged to the religious side of Israel.
From there, readers are left to draw their own conclusions.

What bothered Hagee, writing right after the assassination, was that he expected it to speed the peace process, which he regarded as the work of the Antichrist. But that was OK: After the process leads to the "most devastating war Israel has ever known . . . the long-awaited Messiah will come." So everything would work out, even if Rabin was unknowingly on the side of darkness.

Ambivalence about Israel's leadership vanished when Netanyahu came to power in 1996. The secular leader of the right-wing Likud party was as adept at appealing to conservative Christians abroad as he was at playing to Orthodox Jews at home. Netanyahu and his chief policy adviser, David Bar-Illan, identified with American-style conservatism. Together, they courted evangelicals as allies against the Clinton administration and its effort to push ahead with the peace process.

The Netanyahu-evangelical alliance reached its most public display when Netanyahu came to Washington in January 1998 to discuss Israel's stalled withdrawal from parts of the West Bank under the Oslo Accords. Before sitting down with President Clinton, Netanyahu was feted at a rally organized by Voices United for Israel, a group bringing together conservative Christians and Jews, where the crowd greeted him with a chant of "Not one inch!" and speakers included Reverend Jerry Falwell. Then he met privately with Falwell, Hagee, and leaders of the Southern Baptist Convention—a denomination that had already angered Jews by publicly resolving to target them for conversion.

As a foreign leader visiting Washington, Netanyahu could hardly have been ruder to his host, the American president: On his own TV show, Falwell had been hawking a discredited video that accused Clinton of drug-peddling and involvement in political murders. But Falwell publicly promised evangelical lobbying against any more Israeli concessions in the West Bank: "There are about 200,000 evangelical pastors in America, and we're asking them all through e-mail, faxes, letters, telephone, to go into their pulpits and use their influence in support of the state of Israel and the prime minister."

Bar-Illan was Netanyahu's liaison to evangelicals. The adviser kept his door open to conservative Christian leaders; on occasion he'd take a particularly influential one, like Pat Robertson, in to meet the boss. The applause Netanyahu received at the Washington rally, and when he spoke to the Christian Embassy's Tabernacles gatherings, exceeded any reception he got from his own Likud party, Bar-Illan hap-pily told me in 1998. Evangelicals "are opposed to giving up any land. It belongs to the Jews. . . . They oppose aid to the Palestinians. Yes, they see the conflict here in black and white," he noted approvingly. And, he said, they "lobby, lobby, lobby" Congress to support those hawkish positions. Netanyahu and Bar-Illan saw their relations with the Clinton administration as a battle, to be fought in the American political arena. The Christian right was a solid ally: It shared an antipa-thy for Clinton; it shared Netanyahu's sense of being besieged in a lib-eral world.

Netanyahu's zigzag premiership lasted three years. Israelis de-bated whether he was a committed rightist trying to satisfy domestic moderates, or a moderate who played to more extreme supporters. But conservative Christians clearly loved him as a hardliner. The Bible promised that the Jews would return to their land; Netanyahu was in-sisting on the biblical claim to the full land of Israel.

Moreover, premillennialist preachers were wont to fit hardline Israeli positions into their apocalyptic scenarios. In *Jerusalem Be-trayed*, a 1997 book, Dallas pastor Mike Evans describes the peace process as "an international plot to steal Jerusalem from the Jews . . . behind the international cast of collaborators is a master conspirator who is directing the play," the as-yet-unrevealed Antichrist. (In a mass mailing, Evans urged believers to buy the book because "there are less than 1,000 days until the year 2000.")

Falwell may have done the most to show what lay behind support for the Israeli right. In January 1999, he told 1,500 people at a pastors' conference in Tennessee that the Antichrist was probably alive today and "must be male and Jewish." Justifiably, Jewish leaders accused Falwell of inciting anti-Semitism: The comment was an invitation to regard Jews as tied to demonic forces. When I asked Falwell about the remark, he insisted that "there is not an anti-Semitic bone in my body. I doubt the Jewish people and the State of Israel have a better friend outside their own community than Jerry Falwell." His point, he said, was that he expected the Second Coming soon; it would be preceded by the arrival of the Antichrist—who would have to be Jewish to con-vince people he was the real savior. Falwell was sincere in insisting he loves Israel. But that love, like the Antichrist comment, derives from expectations that Jews will fulfill their role in the premillennialist version of Christian myth.

And that myth can lead to a strange contradiction, even for a Netanyahu backer like Evans. In his book, he seeks to stir opposition to what he sees as a diabolical peace process. He predicts that it will lead to a final war on Israeli soil so terrible that blood will flow "down the Jordan River Valley, down the length of the Dead Sea, and thence . . . the entire length of the Negev to Eilat." Yet he sees that vision as the prelude to Jesus' return—and urges his audience "to pray earnestly for the fulfillment" of prophecy. Evans isn't alone: Chuck Missler, who's sure there's "more support for the State of Israel from fundamentalist Christians in America than from ethnic Jews," also argues that as bad as the Tribulation will be for everyone, it will be even worse for the Jews.

Such figures don't speak for all evangelical supporters of Israel. Christian Embassy spokesman David Parsons, for instance, says he strongly rejects "the die-or-convert scenarios" for Jews, adding: "It's a repulsive thing." Yet many of the people who have been most vocal in their backing for Israel, and most hawkish, happily look forward to just such a scenario.

Bar-Illan saw no problem with this alliance. "None of the people I've met ever engaged in missonary purposes," he said. As for their views of apocalypse, "I busy myself much less with what is in their mind than with what they do." He cited international relations—"any country makes alliances with regimes it does not relish." He met with Evans regularly, he said, but seemed surprised to hear of the preacher's predictions of catastrophe. "Mike gave me his book last time he was here," Bar-Illan told me as I stood to leave his office, "but I never read it."

Yet countries do, in fact, pay attention to what their allies hope to get out of an alliance in the long term. There are gradations: For some evangelicals, who simply identify with the Jews as God's chosen, the issue may not exist. But those who believe Israel should hold on to land because of biblical promises are judging its interests, and America's, on the basis of their religious vision, not of either country's practical needs. As for many on the Christian right, their support for Netanyahu was a foreign policy of apocalypse. The ultimate goal was Israel's good only if you consider the slaughter or conversion of the Jews to be in their own interest.

With the election victory of Ehud Barak, the relationship between Israel and conservative Christians went rocky. You could see it in Van der Hoeven hosting Netanyahu, and in Barak deciding he had nothing to say to five thousand evangelicals at the Christian Embassy's celebration. Just days afterward, the Christian Israel Public Affairs Committee—a small Washington lobbying group set up to focus Christian support for Israel—was sending out urgent calls to supporters: Phone, fax, e-mail your congressmen to vote against $1.6 billion in U.S. aid promised by Clinton to implement the Wye River accord, a step forward in the peace process. True, Netanyahu had signed the agreement, but unlike him, Barak appeared ready to implement it. The Israeli government sought a way to live without war; the U.S. administration saw an opportunity for Mideast stability; and at least some of Israel's Christian friends showed their affection by erecting whatever obstacles they could.

IF NETANYAHU is a gift from God in the eyes of "Bible-believing" Christians, then Gershon Salomon is close to a saint. "I've never met Salomon," Gwen Shaw tells me, "but they say he's a very holy man." Sister Gwen, as thousands of followers worldwide call her, is the founder and head of the End-Time Handmaidens, an Arkansas-based Pentecostal ministry. The state of Israel, and particularly West Bank settlers, she says, are signs that "a dispensation is coming to an end"— that is, that the Rapture is near. Of Salomon she adds, in a voice that could warm you up on an icy day: "He's a very fine man. He's not a crackpot, not a fanatic." Pat Robertson hosted Salomon on his *700 Club* television show. Calvary Chapel founder Chuck Smith speaks of having met "Rabbi Salomon"—a title that would be sure to provoke smiles among some of Salomon's fellow Temple activists.

Salomon is a man who lives to strut the stage. Unlike some Temple activists, he doesn't believe in entering the Temple Mount quietly. Street posters, ads, mailings announce his events. He informs the police, they bar his demonstrators from entering, he goes to court, the legal battle provides a few more newspaper inches. Once, recalls another far-right activist, he commented to Salomon that a demonstration was "one more failure"; Salomon said, "What do you mean? Now the whole world knows they won't let me on the Mount." Salomon is not a subversive; he wants the state of Israel to "liberate the Mount" from the Muslims and build the Temple; he follows the state's rules. The people he attracts aren't all so finicky. One early ally was Yoel Lerner, thrice convicted of plotting to blow up the Dome. But with a flair for street theater, with carefully nurtured press reports making him well-known among Palestinians as the man who'd seize Al-Aqsa, Salomon is quite capable of provoking havoc from inside the law.

That was most starkly demonstrated in 1990: Around Jerusalem, the Faithful put up posters announcing plans to lay a four-and-a-half-ton cornerstone for the Third Temple at Sukkot. It was a stage-whispered threat to seize the Mount. Word of the plan spread among Palestinians—but apparently not the news that the police had refused permission. It was a volatile time. The Intifada, the Palestinian uprising against Israeli rule, was in its third year. Saddam Hussein had conquered Kuwait; most Palestinians saw him as a new Saladin who would defeat the West. Unnoticed by Israelis, Palestinian expectations moved from the political to the apocalyptic. For many, the coming conflict in the Gulf was a sign that the Hour was near. Indeed, apocalyptic interpretations of the crisis were common across the Arab world. It's likely that those perceptions tinted Salomon's threat to Islam's shrines with a shade of the last battle between evil and good. Somehow, Israeli police missed the rank scent of trouble in the air. On October 8, thousands of Palestinians came to defend the Haram. Salomon's small group marched to an Arab neighborhood next to the Old City, for a "water libation" ceremony at the spring that once served ancient Jerusalem. On the Mount, the crowd apparently thought Salomon was approaching. Palestinians began hurling rocks at the twenty thousand Jewish worshipers gathered at the Wall below. An outnumbered force of a few dozen men from a police paramilitary unit opened up with live fire, killing a score of Palestinians. Riots spread through the occupied territories—and to the usually peaceful Arab towns in Israel. Salomon, unfazed by the bloodshed or the diplomatic damage to Israel, speaks proudly of how the cornerstone affair "set off a wave of interest . . . in the Christian world in the Temple Mount and our movement."

He'd found new fans, and he learned to cultivate the image they want. His speeches, and the messages he sends out to his Internet mailing list, are riddled with phrases like, "These are the godly, prophetic end-times and God is redeeming the people of Israel."

On a warm evening in May 1999, Salomon arrives to speak to Reverend Irvin Baxter's tour group at a Jerusalem hotel. Baxter tells his charges that "in my perspective it's highly likely" that the final seven years of history, the Tribulation, will start "in the next twelve months"—by the spring of 2000. The Jerusalem issue, he says, upbeat, "is going to throw Israel into the battle of Gog and Magog, of Armageddon. Before that happens, the Temple will be built." That's the cue for an ovation for Salomon, who asks everyone to pull their chairs close to him. The sixty or so Americans form tight circles, a caressing presence, around the silver-haired man who thanks "my brother Irvin Baxter" in slow, careful English. "We are the blessed generation which got chosen to be the generation of redemption. . . . In our lifetime will be built the Third Temple." The Dome of the Rock, he says, will be moved to Mecca. "Why didn't you all just blow it up when you had the chance?" he's asked, and he answers, "That's my question too." Someone wants to know about his experience of the Six-Day War; Salomon leaps back to the 1958 clash on the Syrian border when he was run over by a tank and lay near death in the battlefield, and "the Syrians themselves said after the battle to U.N. observers that they came to kill me . . . and they could not shoot me because thousands of angels of God Himself surrounded me." Baxter passes a plate, encouraging a love offering to the Temple Mount Faithful.

In his movement's office, Salomon shows me an example of the day's mail: "The Lord has convicted me to give you this bar of gold in order to help fulfill prophecy. I, too, am waiting for your (our) Messiah. I am not Jewish," reads the letter, to which is attached a small gold rectangle, an award inscribed with the words, "3 years No Lost Time Accidents." It's one example of thousands, he says; sometimes women send him their jewelry.

Salomon says most of his funds come from Jews, though a former activist in the Faithful says foreign Christians "are responsible for Gershon Salomon having a budget." The size of that budget is a mystery: Israeli nonprofit organizations are required to submit an annual financial statement with the state's Registrar of NPOs, but the Temple Mount Faithful hasn't filed since 1989. The group's main expenses, it would appear, are PR and the considerable legal costs of regular petitions to the Supreme Court against the police or other state authorities. Without backing from "Bible-believing" Christians, it appears that the Faithful would find it much harder to keep going.

Each summer, Salomon heads to America for a month or more, speaking at up to thirty churches. "At at normal prayer meeting, we have 100 to 150 people, says Laura O'Bryant of the Fellowship Church outside Orlando, Florida. When Salomon last came, "We had an overflow crowd of 250," and people drove in from as far away as Virginia to hear him. O'Bryant handles Salomon's speaking schedule. "I'm in a covenant to help him with whatever needs," she explains. "The Temple Mount has to be cleansed. We don't know how God is going to do it, by an earthquake or sending a group of people in, but we know it's going to be cleansed." O'Bryant's pastor, Ken Garrison, notes that the Florida church has also contributed to Kiryat Arba's Nir Yeshivah. Garrison indicates that he doesn't expect Jews to convert, but acknowledges that his is a maverick view.

Salomon is sensitive on that point. Once he objected to an article I'd written because I mentioned fundamentalist expectations that Jews will accept Jesus. It may be that there are Christians who expect Jews to convert en masse, he said, but "they're on the margins." The margins, in that case, include his "brother" Reverend Baxter, who says he expects a "a great Christian revival" among Israelis. And as for "my good friend Gershon," Baxter says, "if I ever feel like I can, I'll talk to him" about Christianity. While Salomon describes the Temple's restoration as the last act of the divine drama, Baxter acknowledges that he's eager to see it happen because it will be the next-to-last act: Afterward comes the Antichrist's desecration of the sanctuary, Armageddon, the Second Coming.

Here, in the warm relation of the two men, lies the mutually exploitative core of the ties between Christian believers in the End and Israeli rightists: The Jews accept political, financial, and moral support. Often they believe they are bringing the redemption, and disregard or downplay what their allies hope to see happen to Jews. The Christians millennialists believe the Jews have no idea of the catastrophic consequences of their actions—and encourage them to move forward. And perhaps it wouldn't matter, except that well-intentioned people warming themselves with the idea that Jews building the Temple will lead to the world's final salvation sometimes lend their hands to extremists who act, not in the realm of myth, but in a real country where real conflicts claim real lives.

A BLOOD-RED SUNRISE fills the screen. It's a visual refrain, appearing each time in the film that the Temple is about to be built in the course of Jewish history. Curiously, that's the closest we get to seeing blood in *And I Will Dwell Among You,* the Temple Institute's "inspirational video on the dream of the Holy Temple," even though the film promotes animal sacrifice. On screen, a man's hand holds a *mizrak,* a vessel for collecting a slaughtered beast's blood. Like seventy other sacrificial utensils—shovels for ashes, silver trumpets, a trident for turning animal innards on the fire—it has been recreated by the Temple Institute, ready for use. The hand turns the *mizrak* to show how the priest would empty it on the altar: no blood. The video is a professional PR job; the narrator is infectiously excited about the procession that brought water from a spring below Jerusalem to the sanctuary on Sukkot. The faraway memory of the Temple preserved in Jewish customs wakes up and comes alive. Up to a limit. Showing blood or intestines wouldn't be inspirational.

I'm watching the film in the screening room at the Temple Institute's Old City exhibition hall. "In the face of every crisis that the people endured, the Holy Temple was always *the* unifying factor," the narrator says, deleting centuries of strife from Jewish history. The Temple era was the Age of Innocence; it has to have been so that we can believe that rebuilding the sanctuary will restore innocence. The voice describes the Temple's destruction by Rome. It says, "The Temple Mount has stood in desolation for two thousand years," then explains: "The stone upon which the ark of the covenant stood in the Holy of Holies became a house of prayer for strangers." The camera sweeps the Mount, with the golden Dome at the center, and the narrator affirms, "Our hearts will only regain their strength with the re-building of the Holy Temple." The film ends without saying how we'll get from the "desolation" we've just seen to the Third Temple. The Temple Institute carefully stays silent on that point.

I wander through the exhibition. Next to the displayed *mizrak,* a broadshouldered young American bubbles enthusiastically to a couple about how the priests held a lottery each day for who would get which sacrificial task. "We're evangelicals, Bible-believing Christians," says the woman. "We consider the Jewish people our brothers and sisters. We want the Temple to be built." She speaks in a buttery southern accent; she and her husband, originally from Alabama, are campus ministers in Oregon. "When the Temple's rebuilt, it ushers in the Second Coming, but it also ushers in the Tribulation," says their friend, a former high-school pastor at Chuck Smith's Calvary Chapel. "This institute shows that God is working here. It means He will fulfill prophecy." Of course, they add, it's actually the Antichrist who'll build the Temple, but it will be a "landmark in time" showing that better things are coming.

The Institute gets a hundred thousand visitors a year. Their entrance fees, and purchases at the bookshop, provide nearly half its annual budget. The Institute's Rabbi Chaim Richman estimates that 60 percent of the visitors are non-Jews. Tour guides specializing in evangelical groups say the exhibition is a high point of visits to the Holy Land. Institute founder Yisrael Ariel has expressed his dismay that Christians are more interested than Jews in the Temple, say those who know him. Richman acknowledges that some donations, though not most, come from non-Jews. The bottom line: Ariel, Richman, and Co. would have a harder time staying in business were they not "a landmark in time" for Christian premillennialists.

But what business is the Temple Institute in? In 1997, then–PR director Chaim Jutkowitz told me the goal was purely to teach Jews what life *was* like back when the Temple stood. "Planning for the Third Temple is not part of our agenda," he insisted. A safe version for the secular press, and perhaps too for state-salaried educators. Field trips by public schools provide many of the Israeli visitors to the exhibition. Who could object to learning history? Except that in the Institute's bookstore, the luxuriously illustrated *Temple Book,* by Yisrael

Ariel, says: "The Temple Institute in Jerusalem was established with the purpose of *acting*. Its goal is to prepare the research, planning and organizational foundation for building the Third Temple." The statement comes just after a two-page photo montage of today's Jerusalem with the Temple in place of the Dome and Al-Aqsa.

Despite that picture, Richman says that the Institute doesn't deal with the Temple Mount issue; it's not a political organization. "As a Jew, I don't feel the perverse necessity, Woody Allenesque, to apologize" that the Temple belongs where the Muslim shrines are, Richman says. "That doesn't mean I'm a dangerous militant, it just means I'm not a *wimp*." But, he adds, "as we study the Bible, it becomes clear these things are not going to come about through aggression." Perhaps, he suggests, the Arabs will come down from the Mount one day and say "build it."

In the meantime, Richman says, the Institute's job is to fulfill the obligation to establish a Temple by doing what it can to prepare—create utensils, research technical issues, and teach people that once the Temple is built, "the most precious commodity is going to be the knowledge of God." Such spiritual perfection didn't exist in the days of the earlier Temples? "What went wrong was not the Temple, but the people," Richman answers. Besides, he asserts, "In the first forty years of King Solomon's Temple . . . there wasn't one military confrontation on the face of the globe." So perhaps the Institute is a version of the cargo cult: Make harps and a *mizrak,* and somehow the "house of prayers for strangers" will vanish, the Temple will be built, and war will end.

The Institute's 1984 registration as a nonprofit organization fills in more of the picture: The organization's long-range goal, it says, is building the Temple. Short-range aims include "learning the laws of the Temple" and "raising consciousness of the need and obligation of building the Temple . . ." Like other radical groups before it, the Institute has apparently been willing to downplay its final intent on occasion in order to soften up the public. Schoolkids come, adults buy prayerbooks showing how sacrifices were done, and perhaps some Orthodox Israelis who were satsified with today's Judaism of prayer, Torah study, charity will feel that the ancient religion must be resurrected.

The Institute may well expect God to solve the problem of the Mount. But as for its view of the "strangers" who now hold the site, a clue comes from the list of the eight founding members, who include Nir Yeshivah's Rabbi Dov Lior and Baruch Marzel, a prominent Kahane disciple—and Ariel himself, who ran for Knesset on Kahane's racist ticket.

In the mid and late eighties, Ariel was the central figure in the Tzfiyah (Expectation) ideological circle, established to voice support for the jailed members of the Jewish underground. The irregularly published *Tzfiyah* journal may have been the most poisonous set of pages ever published in Hebrew. In the first issue, Lior wrote that all of Israel's problems—from war to hyperinflation—were divine punishment for failing to build the Temple after 1967. Ariel outdid him: Angered that Gush Emunim rabbis and activists had condemned the underground, he asserted that the commandment "Thou shalt not murder" applies only to killing a Jew. Killing a non-Jew, he asserted, is a different sin, to be punished by God, not human courts. In the next issue, he attacked all religious Jews who hesitate to build the Temple. In the last issue, he wrote that both Christians and Muslims are idolators—and that Judaism forbids allowing them to dwell in the Land of Israel.

The Tzfiyah circle represented the radical edge, the worst potential of contemporary Jewish messianism taken to its bitter extreme. Ariel's view on killing gentiles is framed as an attack on the rest of the religious right, which to his amazement opposed the slaughter of Arabs. His article on the immediate need to build the Temple is a furious polemic against virtually the entire community of Orthodox Jews, who deny that the time is ripe, or that the sanctuary will be built by human effort, or that Judaism will ever return to sacrifices. He and the other writers testify better than anyone else could that they do not represent Israel or Judaism. But their radical group formed the ideological context for the Temple Institute.

I hoped to speak with Ariel, let him explain his views. I asked Temple Institute director Haim Makover to arrange a meeting. Makover asked if I was interviewing Arabs, if I'd spoken to the mufti of Jerusalem. Yes, I said. Rabbi Ariel, said the voice on the phone, "might not want to be interviewed for a book in which the mufti will be interviewed." Soon afterward, Chaim Richman told me he'd been in-structed not to speak to me again. Ariel, it appears, didn't want his in-stitution even to dwell in the same pages as Muslims.

It dwells, though, in the pages of Christian prophecy writers. For premillennialists, the Institute often looms immense on the Israeli Endtimes stage. "If you doubt that the Jewish people would ever at-tempt something so audacious" as replacing the Dome with the Tem-ple, writes John Hagee, "you need to know that some Jewish people are *already* planning for it . . ." Mike Evans, likewise, asserts that "the Jewish people" are "without a doubt" planning to build the Third Tem-ple. His evidence includes not just the Institute, but the Hararis' harp-making and Reuven Prager's search for the Temple incense—and they represent what the Jews as a people are up to.

The perspective is nearly as skewed in Randall Price's 1998 *Jerusalem in Prophecy,* whose cover shows the Temple superimposed on the contemporary city's landscape. Price describes three forces of apparently equal significance in Mideast politics: Israel's government rejects dividing Jerusalem; Yasser Arafat wants the Palestinian capital in the city; and "leaders in the Temple Movement . . . believe the time is at hand to rebuild the Jewish Temple."

Price, a Texas-based writer and lecturer, says he found faith as a high-school student while watching the Six-Day War on TV. Among prophecy writers, he stands out for stressing that the Temple will exist in the millennial kingdom—and that after all the centuries of rejecting animal sacrifices, Christianity will validate them. "People say sacrifice ended with the death of Jesus," he says. "I'm having to correct Christ-ian notions in that respect." That argument gets fuller treatment in *Messiah's Coming Temple,* by Oregon preachers John W. Schmitt and J. Carl Laney. In the rebuilt Temple, they say, animal sacrifices will serve to commemorate Jesus' shed blood. Of course, an obstacle will need to be removed first. "Someday . . . newspaper headlines around the world will announce the destruction of the Dome of the Rock. That event will prepare the way for the rebuilding of the Temple in fulfillment of biblical prophecy," the authors happily predict. Snap-shots show Laney with friends such as Yoel Lerner and Yisrael Ariel.

One can be evangelical, of course, without focusing on the End Times. Among the great many who do concern themselves with the

End, Israel can be just one piece of the picture; the supposed interest of Jews in building the Temple can be an exciting proof of prophecy, not a reason for taking any action. The number who have actively supported a Temple group, even come to hear Gershon Salomon speak, is far smaller.

And yet, among all those who have heard that the Temple is essential to prophecy, that Jesus will set his feet on the Mount of Olives and enter the rebuilt sanctuary through its eastern gate, one person or a handful could conclude that they are God's instrument for clearing the ground. And at the Temple Mount, even a spark can ignite disaster.

The very breadth of fundamentalist Christian interest in the Temple, even if often shallow, has the power to encourage Jewish extremists as well. Gershon Salomon stays on the stage of Jerusalem with evangelical help. The Temple Institute is able to continue spreading its message among Jews in part due to "Bible-believing" Christian interest.

Bit by bit, the Temple movement grows. Now and then, enough people gather to create the intoxicating feeling of numbers, of mass support. The danger is that someone—as anonymous as Yigal Amir was before he shot Yitzhak Rabin, as unknown to the general public as the underground members were before their arrest—will decide that enough Jews want the Temple, *now*.

SEPTEMBER 15, 1998: Pamphleteers work the crowd flowing into the Jerusalem Convention Center. Girls in maxiskirts advertise the Temple Mount Seminary, linked to a Kahanist yeshivah. Moshe Feiglin, a settler whose Zo Artzeinu ("It's Our Land") movement blocked roads to protest the Oslo Accords in the days before Yitzhak Rabin's assassination, gives away bumper stickers calling for "Jewish Leadership for Israel." "We don't have Jewish leaders?" asks a newsman. Feiglin gives a *"Nu,* come on," shake of his head.

It's the best turnout the Movement for the Establishment of the Temple has ever gotten for its annual convention. Activists look ecstatic. It helps that Hanan Porat—Gush Emunim founder turned Knesset member for the National Religious Party—sent out thousands of invitations on parliamentary stationery. As a partner in Benjamin Netanyahu's ruling coalition, Porat is chairman of the Knesset Law Committee; his effort is the rough equivalent of the chairman of the Senate Judicial Committee mailing out invitations to a militia convention. Ironically, it also helps that Netanyahu is about to leave for the Wye Plantation, to negotiate under American pressure to get the Oslo process moving again. The far right fears that the prime minister is about to turn more land over to the Palestinians. Demanding Jewish control of the Temple Mount represents a call to get the messianic process rolling again, and has brought all the extremists together. In the convention center lobby, someone hands me a pamphlet arguing that Jews should immediately offer sacrifices where the altar once stood, even if people get killed doing it.

The center's main hall seats 1,500; by the time the lights dim, it's nearly full. One of the first speakers is Dov Lior; the audience rises in respect as he steps to the dais. "A reporter just asked me, 'Why do you want to build the Temple? It's likely to plunge the Middle East into bloodshed,' " he recounts, then answers the question: "Building the Temple will bring peace, will bring security, will cure all the ills of society!" The MC introduces two musicians who will perform a piece on "light and darkness"—like our reality, he says, "of redemption and destruction." Reality, it seems, is confusing the messianists: The state that they expected to fulfill their vision has turned around and started making peace with the Palestinians.

Yisrael Ariel suggests an explanation. "If you see failures, if everything we do doesn't bear blessings, it's a sign . . . we aren't doing enough to build the Temple," he proclaims. The woman sitting next to me whispers, "Amen."

The rhetoric grows more strident. "We will remove the abominations that sully our holy mountain!" Gershon Salomon shouts. "We will liberate the Temple Mount, even if the political leadership doesn't want to. . . . Instead of the Dome of the Rock and mosques, the flag of Israel and the Temple!" The crowd answers with a hurricane of cheers and rhythmic clapping; for once Salomon has the adulation he dreams of, a prophet among his own people. Yet Yehudah Etzion outdoes his rhetoric, impatient not only with the government but with the Creator. "We shouldn't wait for God," he proclaims, "but, as it were, hurry

Him up. We should take up the burden first . . . and afterward He will agree and help us."

A video produced by Etzion's Hai Vekayam movement appears on the screen. One scene shows Muslims, distorted by a wide-angle lense, kneeling in prayer on the Mount. In the audience, people are shouting, booing at the screen, freed by numbers to speak their fury.

Here's where hope for the world's redemption has arrived: hatred at the others, the unbelievers, the people who stand in the way. Across the national and religious divide, the same hope has led to the same dark passions.

EIGHT

AWAITING THE HOUR

Oh the foes will rise, with the sleep still in their eyes . . .
The hour when the ship comes in.

– BOB DYLAN,
"When the Ship Comes In," 1964

IT WAS 8:35, and the hostess of Israel Radio's morning news-and-gab program was on the phone with a mother at Kfar Darom, an Israeli settlement in the Gaza Strip. The crackle of automatic weapons came clearly over the line. "There's a really serious exchange of fire," the woman said. "They're at the northern fence. They're throwing stones into the settlement. This is going on two hundred meters from the houses. The kids are in the houses . . ."

The siege of Kfar Darom started with hundreds of Palestinians hurling stones into the Israeli enclave of forty-three families, and escalated into a gun-battle between Israeli soldiers and Palestinian Authority policemen. Though bullets did hit the houses, none of the children were hurt. Other people were less lucky. Ambulances kept carrying away Palestinians, yet the crowd grew. An Israeli brigade commander arrived, took three bullets in the stomach and hip, and was helicoptered out. In five hours, twenty Palestinians were killed. The Israelis suffered eight wounded. It had been two years since the

Oslo peace accord between Israel and the Palestinians, but the last week of September 1996 looked nothing like peace. It looked like war, at least a spasm of war, a sudden, raging convulsion. The proximate cause was a hammer blow too close to Al-Aqsa.

It happened the night of September 23, just after Jews broke the Yom Kippur fast. Israeli police deployed around the Old City. Near midnight, in the Muslim Quarter, just north of the Temple Mount, on the stone-paved street known as Via Dolorosa, the route Jesus is said to have walked to Golgotha, workmen began knocking away a wall. That opened a stairway into a tunnel—a hidden piece of an aqueduct cut through the rock two thousand years before. The channel linked up to the modern-day passage dug by the Religious Affairs Ministry along the Mount's western side.

With the new opening, visitors could enter the tunnel at the Western Wall plaza, walk north next to the huge stones laid by Herod's builders, and emerge in the Muslim Quarter. Tourists had seen the tunnel before, but they'd had to return the way they came. Now the attraction would be more accessible. The passageway did not run under the Mount—though it did pass by the sealed gate through which rabbis Goren and Getz had hoped to delve beneath the Mount. And it was an indirect reminder of another incident, years before: During the excavations south of the Mount, Israeli archeologists had entered two ancient tunnels beneath Al-Aqsa—in one of them, penetrating one hundred feet. Under Muslim pressure, the government had sealed the passages. In the area of Al-Aqsa, any Israeli archeology translates as Muslim anxiety. What one side describes as "to dig" the other hears as "to undermine"—not just physically, but psychologically: Jews seek to reveal a past that Muslims would like to repress.

Opening the tunnel was a festive occasion. Jerusalem Mayor Ehud Olmert, a member of Benjamin Netanyahu's right-wing Likud party, swung a sledgehammer. Also there was Matti Dan, the key figure in efforts by the Ateret Cohanim yeshivah-cum-settlement organization to settle Jews in the Muslim Quarter. ("Every step taken to join the Jewish people to the land will bring blessing to the whole world," Ateret Cohanim's executive director told me, explaining why the group's efforts were good for Arabs.) Another guest was American millionaire Irving Moskowitz, a Netanyahu friend and campaign donor.

Moskowitz's best-known cause is bankrolling religious settlers to move into Arab areas of East Jerusalem. Some of the cash comes from the bingo hall his foundation runs in the California town of Hawaiian Gardens, under an agreement that the profits go to charity. In 1996, the foundation gave close to $1 million of what Hawaiian Gardens' low-income residents lost at bingo to Ateret Cohanim. Dan and Moskowitz's presence testified volumes: Netanyahu, elected prime minister three months, was satisfying supporters on the religious right. The tunnel would boost the Jewish presence in the Muslim Quarter—another step toward redemption.

Not that the tunnel was a new issue. In 1988, an entrance was cut elsewhere in the Muslim Quarter. Archeologist Aren Maeir, there to supervise the work, says he "was almost lynched by hundreds of Arabs. The muzzein [at Al-Aqsa] announced that the Jews are entering the Mount." Maier was standing on the street with a few workers and a half-dozen cops, and "suddenly the whole world came at us from all four directions." Disturbances spread across the West Bank, and the entrance was shut. Later on, Prime Ministers Rabin and Peres were willing to try again—but only if circumstances guaranteed low tensions with the Palestinians.

After Netanyahu's election, though, relations unraveled between Israel and the Palestinians Authority, which had been established under the Oslo Accords to rule parts of the West Bank and Gaza Strip. The accords required Israel to pull out of Hebron and other parts of the West Bank; talks on a permanent peace agreement were to begin. Netanyahu stonewalled. Security officials reportedly told the prime minister that the tunnel should wait till after the Hebron pullout. Netanyahu, a man cursed by self-confidence, ignored the advice. The decision to open the tunnel was reached at a mid-September meeting to which the military chief of staff and the head of military intelligence were not invited. The choice of midnight as H-Hour shows that Netanyahu knew there could be some trouble. His departure the next day for a swing through Europe shows that he didn't expect a major blow-up.

But the conflagration was already beginning. The next morning, Palestinian legislators and the mufti of Jerusalem led protesters through the Old City. In a Gaza Strip refugee camp, Palestinian Authority head Yasser Arafat began a speech with the Koranic call to holy war. An official statement of the Authority and the Palestinian Legislative Council called the tunnel opening "part of a Zionist-Israeli plot to Judaize the Holy City and damage Al-Aqsa mosque." An Arab League statement accused Israel of trying to undermine the mosque and build the Temple.

At first, the violence followed the old pattern of Palestinian protest: Young people hurled stones at Israeli soldiers or police, who answered with tear gas, rubber bullets, and sometimes live fire. That quickly changed: Outside the West Bank city of Ramallah, as troops clashed with protesters, Palestinian Authority police arrived—and soon were shooting at the Israelis.

The line between riot and pitched battle had been crossed. Israeli sources said the Palestinian police had opened up on them, rather than restraining the crowds. Palestinian police said they were defending their people against Israeli fire. Either way, the battle escalated. The third day was the worst. That's when Kfar Darom was attacked. In Nablus, ground zero was Joseph's Tomb, the supposed burial site of the figure whose story is told in both Genesis and the Koran. Years earlier, a group of Israeli settlers had established a yeshivah at the tomb complex, a Muslim place of pilgrimage as well. Under the Oslo Accords, the tomb remained an Israeli outpost even after the Palestinian Authority took over the city. That day a mob attacked the enclave; Israeli troops shot back; the Palestinian police opened fire. Once again, a place that two faiths considered sacred to their shared God was desecrated with blood.

Inside the war was a memory of peace, evidence of the developing human relations between Israelis and Palestinians that were nearly but not quite swept away by the tunnel incident: Palestinian ambulances evacuated wounded Israelis, a Palestinian journalist reported from inside the Israeli complex. Those were small signs of hope on a day when eleven Israelis and nearly seventy Palestinians were killed.

At last, Arafat broadcast orders to his men to hold their fire. But Palestinian anger came from the bottom up, not just from the top down, so the strife went on. On the Temple Mount, Israeli police and Muslim worshipers clashed after Friday prayers. The police said they used no live fire; three men somehow died of gunshot wounds.

One was an East Jerusalem carpenter's apprentice named Ayman Itkadik. I should remember his face: He was working on renovations in my apartment. He was due to be married the next week; he'd just finished making the furniture for his home. The first day of the fighting, I'd found brushes sticky with paint in my flat: The East Jerusalem workers had fled, terrified to be in a Jewish neighborhood. When I told a neighbor, he said, "I like that. I can't be in an Arab part of town without being afraid." Without noticing, he was celebrating that Jerusalem was more divided than it had ever been since 1967.

The tunnel opening ignited the worst clashes between Israelis and Palestinians since Israel's conquest of the West Bank and Gaza Strip, and fractured Israel's relations with its Arab peace partners. Political postmortems stressed Netanyahu's bid to stall the peace process and Palestinian frustration as reasons for the explosion. But the actual detonator must not be ignored: The crisis showed again that the Mount is a sacred blasting cap, that even shaking the ground nearby can set it off.

It's quite possible that Arafat knew the tunnel did not go under the Mount, that he manipulated fears. But the fears were there to be manipulated. In part, they reflected a failure of many Palestinians to distinguish between the small number of extremists who wanted to build the Temple and Israelis as a whole. Then again, Israel had helped blur the distinction: A chief rabbi, Shlomo Goren, had tried to dig under the Mount; the state's justice system was remarkably lenient in dealing with the Jewish underground. History, sanctity, justified fears, and outright paranoia all mixed at the Mount.

And there was another factor. The evidence of it could be found just meters above the tunnel itself, in Islamic bookstores near the gates of the Haram. There was Egyptian writer Sa'id Ayyub's *Al-Masih al-Dajjal*—that is, *The Antichrist*—which expands radically on the old Islamic idea that at history's finale a Jewish Antichrist will rule until Jesus, as Muslim prophet, returns to defeat him. The cover shows a hook-nosed man wearing a Star of David on his neck, an army coat with a U.S. flag and a hammer and sickle on the shoulders, and missiles on his back. Published in 1987, *Al-Masih al-Dajjal* spawned an entire genre of Islamic books on the End. They shared fascination with Al-Aqsa and certainty of Jewish plots focused on the mosque. In the same bookstores one could buy a 1991 book by Muhammad Isa Da'ud, warning that the Antichrist's forces were kidnaping children to raise underground as soldiers in a gigantic army. "Where?" writes Da'ud, and answers, "Under Al-Aqsa Mosque and nearby." If you'd read Ayyub, Da'ud, or others like them, news of a tunnel near Al-Aqsa could sound like prophecy fulfilled, and a call to the final battle.

"WHEN ISRAEL OCCUPIED JERUSALEM, I was fourteen. We believed the Arab states would liberate us. They spoke to us on the radio—in a few days, in a few hours, it would all be finished. Now it's thirty years later . . ." The man speaking is an ex-activist in Hamas, the fundamentalist Islamic Resistance Movement. He grew up in Jerusalem's Old City. In a set of staccato images, restraining rage, he tells what Israel's victory looked like from the other side. "The black picture in my mind is seeing an Israeli soldier enter Al-Aqsa. . . . Near the Wailing Wall, I saw a soldier step on the Koran. . . . A soldier told us it was forbidden to pray in Al-Aqsa . . ."

The shock of June 1967 had the the opposite meaning for Arabs as for Jews. Arabs expected triumph, and defeat defied reason. In Israel, the state, army, and national heroes gained a superhuman aura. On the other side, secular Arab nationalism appeared impotent; its prophets, like Gamal Abdel Nasser, had proven false. For many Jews, the war confirmed that a secular, Western-style state was fulfilling a divinely appointed role. For Arabs, the secular state could look like an empty shell. One response was to reject secularism and return to Islam. Al-Aqsa under the rule of unbelievers—even if they left it intact—was a potent symbol of faith under urgent threat.

Eventually, the trauma produced a new Islamic apocalyptic vision. Like its Jewish and Christian counterparts, it portrays present-day events as the opening scenes of a Last Days drama. In large degree, the Islamic story is a negative of the Christian one. It explains Jewish successes as supernatural—but as demonic, not divine.

Until the 1970s, says researcher David Cook, modern Muslim books on "the Hour"—the end of history—presented old traditions, not trying to line them up with current events. But a world stood on its head—the West's continued hegemony, the 1967 disaster—invited apocalyptic explanations. Classical Islamic material didn't meet the need. For one thing, it didn't say enough about Jews. There was the tradition of the Jewish Antichrist, and a saying that in the last battle, rocks and trees would cry out, "O Muslim, there is a Jew behind me, come and kill him!" To elevate the Arab-Israeli conflict to cosmic battle, more was needed.

One source discovered by Muslim writers, says Cook, was the poisonous literature of European anti-Semitic conspiracy theories, already translated into Arabic. In particular, there was *The Protocols of the Elders of Zion,* portraying a purported program by Jewish leaders to take over the world. To that, Sa'id Ayyub added another source: biblical prophecy as read by evangelical Christians. Ayyub "takes the Christian messianic fantasy . . . that these are the last days and Israel's existence is a sign of the End," Cook says, "and transforms it for his own purposes."

Cook is a surefooted explorer of this hallucinatory realm, which most Western scholars leave as terra incognita. In his thirties, with sandy-colored hair and a voice that oscillates between excited and exasperated, he hunts through the bookstalls of Cairo, East Jerusalem, Nablus, Amman for newly morphed visions of the End. Biography is half an explanation: Son of a conservative Baptist professor of theology, Cook is a believing evangelical who's unorthodox enough to become a scholar of Islam. Researchers of millennialism, I've found, often have a quirky, questioning faith—a fascination with religion's power and with its dangers. In high school in Oregon, Cook and his friends lived on Lindsey's *The Late Great Planet Earth.* When he read Ayyub, some pieces were bizarrely familiar.

In *Al-Masih al-Dajjal,* Ayyub makes a single narrative of the world's past and future. It's a particularly dark telling of the divine novel, dominated by the antagonist—the *dajjal,* the Antichrist, at once a person and a faceless force, center of a Jewish conspiracy whose machinations explain history. In Ayyub's telling, every pope was a Jew. So was Martin Luther—who sent Jews to colonize America. So the U.S. "is now the principal center for the Jews," Ayyub says, and, "History bears witness that the United States of America, which has been occupied in all areas by the beliefs of the *dajjal,* is the chief enemy of Islam . . ."

The Antichrist, Ayyub asserts, is the Jews' messiah. That idea also pops up in Christian prophecy writings, but mutedly—for "philo-Semitic" Christians it means that, alas, the Jews will again be deceived. Ayyub brings out the full anti-Semitic potential: The Jews, he says, "took a messiah in keeping with their deeds and in accordance with their desires"—that is, they follow evil incarnate because it fits their character.

As the drama of the Last Days unfolds, Ayyub writes, "The dwelling place of the Jewish Prophet"—the Antichrist—"will be in the Temple in Jerusalem. For this reason they sometimes try to burn Al-Aqsa, and try to conduct archaeological excavations, and even try to buy the ground through the Masons of America." Jewish messianism links the Temple to the messiah; Christian premillennialists say the Antichrist will demand to be worshiped in the Temple. Ayyub draws the third side of the triangle. For him, too, whatever happens at the Mount—real or imagined—shows the nearness of the Hour and the last battle.

In passing, Ayyub also sets a time for the drama to begin: "The building of [the Temple] according to their plans will begin after the destruction of Al-Aqsa Mosque," says a footnote, "and the planned date for this is 2000." That reveals his sources—2000 had no religious meaning for Jews and shouldn't matter to a Muslim. But Ayyub constructed his picture of the mythic Jew out of materials manufactured by Christian millennialists, who often suggested that the End might begin in that year.

Elsewhere Ayyub is explicit about his raw material: He quotes Daniel, Ezekiel, and Isaiah; he builds a commentary on Revelation. Islam regards the Bible as a corrupted record of God's revelation, and for a Muslim to cite it openly is a radical step. Ayyub is undeterred. He speaks of a battle of Armegeddon—a Christian term—between the Muslims and the *dajjal*'s forces of Jews and Christians. That's the prelude to the final struggle in Jerusalem, when the stones will speak and Jesus will lead Muslims to victory. The climax of Ayyub's myth is slaughter. It's a sad contrast, Cook stresses, to classical Islamic texts in which Jesus kills the *dajjal*—in mythic terms, truth killing deception—but without a bloodbath of the people he deceived. In Ayyub's bitter words, anti-Jewish paranoia becomes theology, and the believer's hope for a better world is transformed into unredeemed hatred.

Ayyub's book, Cook says, was a "runaway hit," despite attacks from conservative scholars of Cairo's Al-Azhar University, foremost center of religious study for Sunni Muslims. The conservatives don't like his use of non-Muslim sources. Nor do they appreciate taking the vague idea of the Hour and making it immediate—the religious establishment is part of the given order that Ayyub claims will soon be overthrown. But Ayyub kept writing. Other authors have followed him, by the end of the 1990s producing several hundred books preaching the same urgent message. Their work can be found in the three hundred stalls of Cairo's book bazaar, in shops near the Haram, in the selection of Islamic books on sale next to school supplies and housewares in a Ramallah department store. The books sometimes sell too fast for shops to meet demand.

Ayyub and his followers rebel against a world in which the community of Islam is weak and the infidel West is strong. Yet to map the present, they use European anti-Semitism; to write history of the future, they use Christian millennialism. Again, it's a reminder of cargo cults—an impression made stronger when Muhammad Isa Da'ud asserts in a 1997 book that to make peace with the *mahdi*—the Muslim Endtimes leader—Europe and the United States will agree to transfer their technology to his empire. The apocalyptic writers seek to make sense of the inexplicable power of people they regard as undeserving, and when their own tradition is insufficient, they use whatever intellectual jetsam of the West is within reach.

But they also mine Islam. A brief passage in the Koran describes how the Children of Israel "twice commit corruption in the land." The Israelites are punished once, regain their wealth and numbers, and sin again. So God sends an army "to afflict you, and enter the Mosque as they entered it the first time, and utterly destroy that which they conquered." The verses appear to be based on the destruction of the First and Second temples. One way or another, Koranic commentators always read them as history. Until recently: The new, apocalyptic reading is that the "second corruption" refers to the Jews "gathered today in Palestine." The word "mosque" really means mosque, not Temple, proving that the verse is about a time when there are Muslims in Jerusalem and Jews can "corrupt" their shrine. The Koran, therefore, has foreseen the state of Israel—and assured believers it will soon be destroyed. Another writer, Bashir Muhammad Abdallah, argues that

God's reason for gathering the Jews in one land is to take vengeance on them in the Last Days. Israel's existence becomes proof that God is preparing the triumph of Islam.

As for the timing, Ayyub's footnote on 2000 was the tiny key that unlocked the gate of predictions. During Iraq's invasion of Kuwait and the Gulf War, there were Muslims on both sides who identified the conflict as the start of the apocalypse, while disagreeing on who were the good guys and who the bad. A Palestinian newspaper published a purported tradition from the Prophet—probably produced, Cook says, by Saddam Hussein's propagandists. It says the Hour will come when "yellow-haired people, Byzantines and Franks" gather with Egyptians "in the wasteland against a man named Sadim." For Byzantines, read "Christians"; for "Franks," we're meant to understand "Westerners."

From there, it's been easy to find other signs of the End. Muhammad Da'ud points to the Intifada—the Palestinian uprising against Israel—and the 1990s wave of Soviet Jewish immigration to Israel. Amin Jamal al-Din—an Egyptian whose Al-Azhar education failed to teach him caution—cites a late medieval work saying the world will end by the Islamic year 1500, which is 2076 on the Western calendar. Since the apocalyptic events will last 120 years, Jamal al-Din calculates, we're in the Last Days. Ironically, the medieval text was meant to cool expectations of the End in the Islamic year 1000. Jamal al-Din expected the Antichrist to appear in 1998. Da'ud asserted it would happen in 2000, explaining that former Israeli military chief of staff Dan Shomron "said during one of his speeches to the graduates of the Jews in one of the war colleges in Tel Aviv that 'in the year 2000 we will see the growth of a new leadership.' " Even if the Shomron quotation is correct, Da'ud's interpretation is wondrous: "He meant by this the *dajjal*, since he is their messiah and their king, whom they are expecting in the year 2000 to build them the Temple."

In 1999, a thin volume called *The Great Events Preceding the Appearance of the Mahdi* appeared in the Islamic bookshops of East Jerusalem and the West Bank. The cover shows an aerial shot of the Haram, and a picture of the Temple. Its author is the previously unknown Palestinian writer Fa'iq Da'ud. Just as Christian prophecy writers exaggerate any hint of messianic expectation among Jews, Da'ud resonates with every vibration of Jewish messianism and Christian millennialism. As portents, he reprints Hebrew news items on the Concerned Christians, a Denver millennial sect whose members slipped into Israel, and on Israeli police fears that the group or others like it could attack the Temple Mount to hasten the End. In America, he tells readers, presidents are obligated to "do everything possible to hasten the messianic redemption . . . since Christians believe in the second coming of the messiah and the Jews believe in the first coming . . . so it was incumbent to abandon differences . . . so that Israel would be a state . . . and the Temple would be built." In fact, Christian fundamentalists do tell Jews that "we both believe the messiah is coming" as proof of common ground—but armed with conspiracy theory, Fa'iq Da'ud inserts this in the U.S. Constitution. "It would be a humiliation for both Christianity and Judaism," he adds, "if the messiah comes in 2000 and Al-Aqsa is on the site of the Temple on Mt. Moriah. So there is an absolutely necessity to build the Temple." Here and there a strident Christian premillennialist expresses almost this idea. The paranoia is in attributing it to all Christians and Jews. Yet Fa'iq Da'ud can find hope in the threat to Al-Aqsa; it heralds the *mahdi*.

The theater of the End is triangular, and in the eyes of apocalyptic believers on all three sides, the great drama has begun. The sound system is hope and fear; each time an actor speaks, his words reverberate wildly. Three scripts are being performed. The cast of Jewish messianists has starring roles in the Christian play; Jews and Christians alike have parts in the Muslim drama. What one sees as a flourish of rhetoric can be the other's cue for a battle scene.

For Muslims, Cook notes, Jerusalem is the arena of the apocalyptic battles, and capital of the perfected world. Bassam Jirrar, a leading religious teacher and writer in the West Bank, says succinctly that Islam began in Mecca and Medina and will end in Jerusalem. Yet today the city is ruled by Jews—whose faith Islam expected to supersede, and whose state is tied to the West. For many believing Muslims, Jerusalem's condition precisely expresses the distance between the world as it is and the world as it should be—the gap that the apocalypse is meant to close.

BASSAM JIRRAR was born in Ramallah in the year of what Palestinians call the *nakba*, the disaster—the creation of Israel. He'll be seventy-four when, according to his calculations, Israel comes to an end. Counted by the Islamic year of twelve lunar months or 354 days, both he and the Jewish state will be seventy-six.

Jirrar likes to stand at the edge of other people's definitions of him, neither in nor out. Since elementary school, he says, people have called him "sheikh," roughly like calling an eleven-year-old "reverend," because of his interest in Islam long before the Islamic revival began among Palestinians. Later he'd help create that revival, teaching in mosques and universities. But the man who hosts me at his Nun Center for Koranic Research in the West Bank town of Al-Birah isn't wearing a sheikh's long cloak or solemn demeanor. He's in black pants, black polo shirt, an elegant touch of gray in his close-cut black beard; he likes to throw one leg over the side of his bamboo armchair, or to leap out of it; he should be teaching jazz. In 1992, he was one of 415 radical Islamic leaders whom Israel temporarily deported to Lebanon; he's regularly described as a Hamas leader. His response: "Everyone religious they say is from Hamas or the Islamic Jihad," which is not quite a denial. He approves, he says, of Hamas attacks on Israeli soldiers, but the group's terror against civilians "doesn't serve Hamas interests"—making him a moderate, relatively speaking.

Jirrar's second youthful love was science. He studies the Koran with calculator in hand, searching for hidden mathematical patterns, "miracles of thought" that prove the author is God. One such pattern, he claims, is that the number 19 is woven into Jewish history and destiny. That, and the Koran's verses about the "two corruptions," underlie the book he wrote during the months he spent with other deportees in a Lebanese tent camp, *The End of Israel 2022—Prophecy or Coincidence?* The second "corruption" he identifies with the State of Israel. It's discussed in a Koranic passage of 1,443 words; on the Islamic calendar, the year 1443 is 76 years after the creation of Israel—which makes sense, Jirrar says, because 76 is 4 times 19. Those verses were revealed to Muhammad a year before the start of the Islamic calendar, or 1,444 years before Israel's expected destruction, which is 19 times 76. He's talking fast as he tells me this; he's writing on the board in his conference room; he's tapping his calculator. The northern kingdom of Israel in the Bible was conquered by Assyria in the reign of its nine-teenth king, in the year 722 B.C.E., which is half of 1,444. Now he's cal-culating the number of years from King Solomon's death until Muhammad's night journey to Jerusalem. Politely, I refrain from men-tioning that he's off by one because the Western calendar lacks a year 0, that he suffers from the Y0K bug. Modern Israel, he calculates, will cease to exist on March 5, 2022. "It's clear the action will be terrible," he says.

Yet among Muslim prophecy writers, Jirrar is a moderate. In *The End of Israel,* he refrains from anti-Semitic statements. Rather than fantasize about slaughter, he suggests that Jews will eventually accept Islam. Not that he proposes giving up struggle. Israel's strength can cause frustration, but "when prophecy says the Muslims will conquer the Jews, it gives people courage." Why settle for a Palestinian state in the West Bank when God promises that Israel will disappear? But Jir-rar is an ambiguous prophet. His promised salvation is just distant enough to be a cerebral hope, not a battle call. It could invite Pales-tinians to accept Israel's "unjust" existence for a breathing space that might create the habit of peace. Radicals could regard him as sell-ing out.

Jirrar's book has sold 30,000 copies, he says, "in Palestine"—by which he means the West Bank, Gaza Strip, and Israel's Arab popula-tion. That's equivalent to selling over 2 million copies in the United States. Elsewhere in the Arab world, he claims sales of hundreds of thousands. Secularists, he says, are convinced by his equations. The pious are less enthusiastic, because his method isn't traditional.

Jirrar isn't a herald of the Hour. He speaks only of the end of Is-rael, not of the world. Islamic prophets of doom, like Christian ones, are sure humanity is at a moral nadir. Jirrar disagrees: "All people—whether Christians, Muslims, or Jews—are moving toward religion. The situation is getting better, so the End is far off." The remark im-plies some value in other faiths, tolerance one wouldn't find in Sa'id Ayyub. Jirrar confesses that Ayyub is "influential," but says the Egyp-tian writer is "not a serious student of Koran." Half a prophet, Jirrar is also half an establishment cleric with disdain for the prophetic rabble. The fact that he's accepted pieces of their ideas points to the apocalyp-tic school's impact.

Not that there's a copy of Ayyub's *Al-Masih al-Dajjal* on every religious Muslim's shelf. Jamil Hamami, an East Jerusalem graduate of Al-Azhar, has never heard of Ayyub, and he rejects Jirrar's theories. Hamami was a Hamas founder; he left the organization in 1995, believing the time for "military struggle" against Israel ended with establishment of the Palestinian Authority. Rather than demonizing Jews, he stresses his interest in interfaith dialogue. Yet he doesn't deny that apocalypse is in the air. Interest among Palestinians in signs of the Hour can't be measured, he says, but there's no doubt that "people are talking about it, in universities, in schools."

Sheikh Ismail Jamil, the seventy-year-old mufti of Jericho, has read Ayyub. "He didn't come up with anything new. He read old books and put everything in one place," he asserts—a bizarre comment, since Ayyub is a radical innovator. It suggests that the new apocalyptic visions have become conventional wisdom so quickly that their authors appear to be repeating clichés.

Jamil owes his position in Jericho to the Palestinian Authority. On his office wall is a photo of Al-Aqsa, which makes it precisely like every other Palestinian office, except that Jamil's version of the picture has an inset photo of Arafat and a quote from the leader: "Our Jerusalem will be only for us, no matter what others say." The quote underlines the role Al-Aqsa has come to play as the emblem of Palestinian nationalism, not just of Islam. But in Jamil's office the combined picture of Arafat and the shrine has an additional message: This room is the home of state religion.

Perhaps twenty books grace the sheikh's bookcase. The most worn volume, the one Jamil's hand finds easily, is *A Note on the Status of the Dead and Final Matters,* a thirteenth-century compendium on the hereafter and the Last Days. "Anyone who says he knows the time of the Hour is lying," Jamil says—and then he lists traditional portents that are being fulfilled. " 'The Hour will not come until the Byzantines invade Hijaz,' " he recites, adding, "This exists today." Hijaz is the northwest slice of Saudi Arabia; the presence of American troops in the kingdom fulfills the prophecy, he says. " 'In the Last Days the Jews will occupy Palestine'—and this exists today," he goes on. "The killing of people in Al-Aqsa, the Israeli occupation of Al-Aqsa"—another sign. He glances through his book. "Today," he says, "the signs are very clear to us."

Jamil is considerably milder than the most senior Arafat-appointed clergyman—Sheikh Ekrima Sa'id Sabri, the grand mufti of Jerusalem and Palestine. For years after Israel conquered East Jerusalem, Jordan continued controlling the city's Islamic religious apparatus. Sabri represents the Palestinian Authority's success in pushing Jordan aside. Sabri's angularly trimmed gray beard makes his face look like a square stone block. His views are as rock hard. While Hamami, the ex-Hamas man, says he fears "religious extremists" will try to destroy the mosques and that he "respects moderate Israelis trying to control the extremists," Arafat's mufti regards all Israelis as the threat. "Destroying Al-Aqsa and making it a Jewish place is the concern of every Israeli," Sabri asserts.

The mufti hasn't read Ayyub, but he knows Fa'iq Da'ud's book. It has value because "it makes very clear the dangers to Al-Aqsa Mosque." Jirrar's calculations are "just theory," Sabri says. But he's convinced Israel will disappear, because "it's in the Holy Koran," in the passage on the two corruptions. Sabri rejects setting a date for the Hour. Indeed, he knows who plants the idea in the media that the Hour is near: "the international Zionists all over the world, who want to destroy Al-Aqsa." The Zionist lobby and wealthy Jews, he says, also turn America against Islam. He interrupts himself to ask my religion. Perhaps my answer is the reason he describes *The Protocols of the Elders of Zion* as an accurate portrayal of "the upper ranks of the Jews." Politely, he has left me out of the conspirators. "The Jews worldwide are just 15 million people. But they make trouble all in every place, every country," Sabri says, laughing. He is happy telling me this. He is a hospitable man; he doesn't resent me for belonging to the lower ranks of the people who are the world's misfortune.

Sabri's tie to the Palestinian Authority doesn't mean that Arafat or other top officials share his beliefs, any more than Israeli government leaders shared the ideas of the late chief rabbi Goren. The problem is the ease with which political leaders seek the support of religious figures while discounting the potential impact of their views.

There are no polls on how many Palestinians or other Arabs profess apocalyptic beliefs. Many secularists would laugh at Ayyub's visions, and many pious Muslims regard them as unorthodox. But promoters of the End have given Muslims free tickets to the theater of the apocalypse. They've added even more power to Al-Aqsa as icon of

Palestinian nationalism, center of the Islamic revival, locus of pride and anxiety.

THE MAIN DRAG OF UMM AL-FAHM looks like hand-me-down town. Square storefronts of stucco or bare concrete face onto cracked sidewalks. The street is dirty. The grass in the center island is ragged. It's the only grass in town. The cars and pickups have worked hard, a long time, and want to tell you about it. There's a muffler shop, an Al-Aqsa Garage: If Israeli Jews come here, it's for cut-rate auto work. Umm al-Fahm is painful testimony to the stepchild status of Israel's Arab citizens, one-sixth of the population: more poverty per capita, more crime, more kids per classroom, less government cash for streets, sewers, jobs.

The neglect helped the Islamic Movement move into Umm al-Fahm's town hall in the local elections of 1989, apparently for good. The fundamentalist movement was founded by Sheikh Abdallah Nimr Darwish, who did time in the early eighties for leading a small group of Israeli Arabs that burned Jewish fields and called for an "Islamic Arab Palestine." After his release, Darwish changed direction, becoming ever more passionate in rejecting violence. Like other Islamic fundamentalists, he argued that all Palestine is a sacred trust to Islam. Unlike them, he professed pragmatic, long-term acceptance of Israel. The movement he created urged Muslims to return to faith, set up daycare centers, and organized volunteer efforts to pave the dirt streets of Arab towns.

The Oslo Accord divided the Islamic Movement—moderates supported Arafat and the peace agreement; hardliners didn't. In Israel's May 1996 national election, Darwish insisted in running a candidate for Knesset. A minority faction rejected the step, apparently because it implied recognizing Israel's legitimacy. The movement split. The leader of the radical faction is Sheikh Ra'id Salah, Umm al-Fahm's mayor.

Ever since the 1996 tunnel crisis, Sheikh Ra'id holds an annual "Al-Aqsa Is in Danger" rally in Umm al-Fahm. Al-Aqsa is the standard he carries into politics. The logic is clear: If all Palestine is an Islamic trust, the sanctity emanates from the Haram in Jerusalem. The mosque, like his town, is under Israeli sovereignty—yet it is also de facto autonomous Islamic space. It represents both the reality and the dream. And it is an arena in which the sheikh's movement can shadow-fence with the Israeli government within the tournament rules of democracy—and in the same parry and thrust, parade as more Pales-tinian than Arafat's Palestinian Authority. At the September 1999 Al-Aqsa rally, Sheikh Ra'id reportedly said that "a very senior Israeli figure declared that a final-status settlement with the Palestinians will not be reached, particularly on the Jerusalem issue, until the Third Temple is built." The odds of anyone connected to the Barak govern-ment saying that are lower than those of a Democratic administration instituting biblical law in the U.S. Nevertheless, the mayor may be-lieve every word he said.

Through its Al-Aqsa Association, the movement has changed the face of the Haram. In charge of that effort is Ahmad Agbariya, an ex-teacher in his forties. When he was growing up in Umm al-Fahm, Agbariya says, "The spirit of Islam didn't hover over the families. We didn't pray, we didn't keep the commandments." One result: Until the 1980s, few Israeli Arabs came to Al-Aqsa. For that matter, he says that before 1967, West Bank Muslims didn't fill what he calls "the southern building"—the actual Al-Aqsa Mosque at the Haram's south end. "In the 1970s, people began to do what Islam wants," he says. Now, during Ramadan, row after row of worshipers extend from the back of the mosque, past the Dome of the Rock, to the Haram's northern edge. "It's because God hovers over the people," Agbariya explains the change. "Muhammad, peace be upon him, said that at the end of the world . . . a great many people will pray at Al-Aqsa."

Agbariya became religious as a young man, when he concluded that in the original "era of Islam" immediately after Muhammad's time, society was ideal: "There was no killing. People had good rela-tions with each other." He sees the past through Islamic tradition, taken absolutely literally. One reason for Al-Aqsa's sanctity, he ex-plains, is that it was the world's second mosque, built by Adam forty years after the mosque in Mecca. One of the Arabic terms he repeat-edly uses for the site, *bayt al-maqdis,* is virtually the same as the He-brew word for Temple. But he repeats the party line: Archeologists have found no sign there of the Jewish sanctuaries. To share history would risk sharing space.

In 1996, Ramadan fell during the coldest, rainiest days of the raw

Jerusalem winter. The Waqf authorities reportedly received a quiet OK from the Peres government to use the underground vaults known as Solomon's Stables as a prayer hall. The vaults support the southeast corner of the Mount esplanade; archeologists date them as far back as Herod's time. They got their name during Crusader rule of Jerusalem, when the Knights Templar used them as stables. After that, they remained silent recesses beneath the sacred square.

Within a year, the temporary shelter became permanent. The Al-Aqsa Association raised money for building materials; it published calls for volunteers among Israeli Muslims, large numbers of whom work in the building trades. "A thousand people would come on a single Saturday," says Agbariya, donating their day off from secular construction work.

What Muslims now call the Marwani Mosque, named for an early caliph, is 40,000 square feet, large enough for up to 7,000 people to pray. It has the look of a skillfully converted cellar: a set of long halls, like tunnels set next to each other, with arched stone ceilings and tiny windows at the end. Inexpensive fluorescent lights hang from above; red rugs with simple floral and geometric designs, donated by Egypt, cover the floor.

Bad weather wasn't the only reason for developing the space. Says Agbariya: "Information reached us that Jews wanted to take it for a synagogue." In fact, the idea of turning Solomon's Stables into a Jewish downstairs below the Muslim upstairs on the Mount was in the air for years. In the early eighties, Gideon Charlap, an architect and graduate of the far-right Nir Yeshivah, sent such a plan to Prime Minister Yitzhak Shamir. Shamir never answered. Activists raised the subject again in 1996 with then-chief rabbi Avraham Shapiro, and small items appeared in the Hebrew press; nothing came of it. But in a strange cause-and-effect, Jewish messianism again strengthened the Muslim tie to Al-Aqsa.

It's unclear what renovations at the Mount have been approved by Israeli authorities, and what they've simply accepted. Israel has never strictly enforced building laws at the Haram—just as it has refrained from enforcing safety regulations at the Church of the Holy Sepulcher. As custodian of sites sacred to hundreds of millions of people, where numerous foreign governments claim interests, Israel necessarily puts diplomatic concerns over regulations. Israeli law requires supervision by the government Antiquities Authority at any site of archeological value—but a loophole for holy places gives jurisdiction to a cabinet committee instead of archeologists. In practice, it's up to the prime minister to allow or stop changes that could harm the historic record written in stones and pottery shards. Waqf officials deny Israeli sovereignty. Yet they have sought agreement for some moves, even if they are politically bound to deny it publicly. And by most reports, the Waqf maintained a dialogue with Antiquities Authority archeologists until the tunnel crisis.

The next step was to restore what Muslims call Old Al-Aqsa—a pair of long vaults directly under the mosque building. Archeologists say they were built in Roman times, as passages that led from the Mount's southern gates into the Temple. A Waqf staffer who took me to see them insisted that they were built by the Ummayad dynasty of caliphs, early in the Islamic era. Agrabiya says the halls are the mosque that Adam built at the beginning of time. If so, there's a Roman style to Adam's stonework, like the pair of columns topped with floral capitals at one end of the passageway. By the end of 1999, with lights installed and prayer rugs on the floor, Old Al-Aqsa was open for worshipers.

THE OLD WINDOW, blocked up with stones, was at the end of Old Al-Aqsa, in the Mount's south wall. In August 1999, the stones were knocked out. According to Agbariya, the opening was meant only to let air and light into the underground mosque. Israeli police suspected it would serve as an entrance, with Muslim worshipers flowing through the Israeli archeological excavations and park next to the Mount. Ehud Barak's two-month-old administration saw it as a Palestinian bid to test the new government's will. Shlomo Ben-Ami, the dovish ex-diplomat turned police minister, said the status quo had been broken: The Muslims could make changes within the holy site, not around it. Israeli security sources, according to leaks to the press, had a different nuance: Islamic radicals, including Israeli Islamic Movement activists, were seeking to embarrass the Palestinian Authority. A window crisis would close any window of opportunity for peace talks created by the Israeli change of government.

The prime minister met top brass. During the night, emissaries were sent to tell the Palestinian Authority and the Jordanian government what Israel planned to do. (The diplomacy itself was half the message, the half Netanyahu had always skipped.) Police went on high alert. By early morning, the window was blocked up. There was the stillness of many people holding their breath. The day passed, the streets of East Jerusalem stayed quiet.

Pieces of the story were left unpublicized. Ben-Ami stepped up police dialogue with the Waqf, cross-town diplomacy. According to a source close to the government, the unwritten agreement was that the window would be closed, but the Waqf would be allowed to open a new entrance to the Marwani Mosque inside the Haram, since safety required a second doorway.

In the last November of the millennium, bulldozers arrived on the Mount. Over the next two months, they chewed out a thirty-foot-deep triangular pit: a long slope for steps, a vertical stone wall showing the arched vaults of Solomon's Stables. Two arches would become a wide entrance. In the soil cross-section on one side of the pit, the round bases of a half dozen stone columns, debris of an unknown period, could be seen. A horizontal row of stones testified, perhaps, to a forgotten floor or ceiling, sliced by the earthmovers.

Israeli Attorney General Elyakim Rubinstein erupted: "Remains of Jewish history are being crushed . . . the Waqf has to be told—we also have a history." Rubinstein is Orthodox and has roots in the religious right, but his post is a nonpartisan one and the yelp was out of character. Jerusalem Mayor Ehud Olmert, in character, demanded that the work stop, attempting to embarrass Barak. The Waqf—or the Islamic Movement, pulling the Waqf along—had stretched approval for an entrance beyond what the government expected. But Barak had approved an entrance and chose not to be dragged into sending cops and building inspectors to stop the work.

A series of Israeli archeologists decried the unsupervised digging. A few added that the Muslims had damaged the record of their own past, but had probably not reached Jewish remains. For decades, the archeologists had lived with the past being out of reach on the Mount. It was much harder to watch someone dig without looking for history. The scholars weren't going to riot. But their response mattered, because for many Israelis archeology is the science of cultivating Jews' tie to their land. The bulldozers unnecessarily exposed an old divide: What is a living holy place for Muslims is a historic symbol for Jews. The archeolgists' constituency is wider than that of the messianists, even if its interest is much shallower.

Still, the incident's strongest impact was on the religious right. As usual, timing mattered. The Barak government was pursuing peace agreements with both the Palestinians and Syria. Headlines spoke daily of a possible Israeli withdrawal from the Golan Heights. Negotiations with the Palestinians seemed likely to lead to further pullbacks in the West Bank, and perhaps a compromise in Jerusalem. The dream that settling the Land of Israel would speed redemption appeared close to dead. Nothing could symbolize the disappointment and frustration better than Muslims shoveling aside history to strengthen their hold on the Temple Mount—and the fact that most Israelis weren't willing to do anything about it.

An unsigned editorial in *Hatzofeh,* the daily newspaper of the National Religious Party, had the tone of barroom shouts the moment before someone breaks a bottle against a table edge. The paper accused Muslims of "systematic destruction of Jewish remains" at the Temple Mount, and complained that the judicial system refused to enforce the law out of fear of Arab violence. Much of the Israeli public, it admitted, didn't care. So the courts and attorney general, the editorial said, should know that "there are more and more Jews who also know how to be violent. . . . You haven't got a clue of what's going down on the street, and there's very high certainty of an insane Jewish outburst of violence" over the Mount. So much for the hopes of Zorach Warhaftig, of the same National Religious Party, to channel messianic fervor toward the Western Wall. Now the party-line paper was legitimizing violence, if not calling for it, as the way for Jews to press their claims to the Mount.

Meanwhile, Moshe Feiglin announced that his Zo Artzeinu movement was resuming public activity, for the first time since the stormy protests before Yitzhak Rabin's assassination. "If we want a struggle for the Golan Heights and the Land of Israel, it has to start at the heart, at the Temple Mount," Feiglin said. Politically, the argument was nonsense—the Golan was a security issue that moved far more Israelis. But Feiglin was speaking the logic of myth, in which controlling the Mount meant controlling the dynamo of redemption. A protest against the Waqf's earthworks brought 3,500 people to Mt. Scopus—the spot from which Moshe Dayan and Uzi Narkiss had looked at the Old City in June 1967. It was the largest demonstration Temple activists had ever pulled together, a sign of growing support on the radical wing of "redemptive Zionism."

For years, Jewish extremists had fanned Muslim fears with Al-Aqsa. The Islamic Movement's volunteer building workers were now stoking Jewish anxiety over the Mount. On both sides, the undertone was hope for God to step into history, and the unpronounceable fear that prophecy could fail.

NINE

the day
after the last

*The day the Temple was destroyed,
prophecy was taken from prophets
and given to fools and children.*

—Talmud, Tractate Bava Batra

*The earth is dilating to nine and three-quarters.
It's birthin' time.*

—Hayseed Stephens

EARLY ON THE MORNING of February 25, 1994, Baruch Goldstein rose, put on his army reservist's olive drab uniform, took his army-issue Galil rifle, and left his home in Kiryat Arba to pray at the Tomb of the Patriarchs in neighboring Hebron.

Goldstein was over six feet tall, with a thick beard and a hairline beginning to recede. Born in Brooklyn, he'd come to Kiryat Arba after finishing medical school in New York a decade before. He was well known in the West Bank settlement as an expert in emergency care, regularly alerted by the army to treat soldiers or settlers injured during the years of the Palestinian uprising. He was well known, too, as a passionate disciple of the late Meir Kahane, whose Kach party he'd represented on the town council. Kahane had officiated at his wedding to Miriam, also a Kach activist—on the ramp leading to the Temple Mount's Mughrabi Gate. In December 1993, Goldstein had been called to treat Mordechai Lapid, a close friend and prominent rightist, and his son Shalom, who were shot in a drive-by attack by Hamas terrorists seeking to foil the recently signed Oslo peace accord. Both father and son died. At a memorial gathering at Kiryat Arba's Nir Yeshivah, Goldstein delivered one of the eulogies, recalled Dan Be'eri, a one-time member of the 1980s Jewish underground: "He called for vengeance, and expressed in great sorrow his pained view that because we were apathetic and had refrained from vengeance, we were guilty of their deaths—not on the practical level of deterrence, but on the metaphysical level, before heaven." He'd learned Kahane's doctrine well: Violence was a sacrament.

That February morning was Purim, a sort of Jewish Mardi Gras comemorating the Jews' victory over the evil Haman, as told in the Book of Esther. When the Jewish service was over, Goldstein entered another hall of the Tomb of the Patriarchs, where Muslim prayers for the holy month of Ramadan were in progress, and hid behind a column. He waited until the Muslim worshipers prostrated themselves. Then he began shooting. Methodically, he emptied a magazine, pushed in another, again and again, firing over a hundred bullets. Within moments, he'd murdered twenty-nine Arabs and injured scores. The shooting stopped only when several Arabs managed to strike him with blunt objects and kill him. Goldstein apparently expected to die; he'd left a goodbye note.

The slaughter itself would have been enough to ignite Palestinian anger; that it took place at a holy place during prayer could only stoke the fury. In clashes with Israeli troops across the West Bank, more Palestinians were killed.

Speaking before the Knesset, Prime Minister Yitzhak Rabin confessed that he hadn't imagined such a crime in his worst dreams; he referred to Goldstein as "mentally ill." The government appointed an inquiry commission headed by former Supreme Court chief justice Meir Shamgar. Ehud Barak, then military chief of staff, said the massacre "struck us like thunder on a clear day." Major General Danny Yatom testified that no one could have expected the "insane deed." As he spoke, Yatom raised one hand beside his head and turned it, as if asking what had turned the switch from sanity to madness in the doctor's mind. The Shamgar Commission concentrated on security responsibility at the Tomb, not what was happening in Goldstein's community or how he came to believe that God wanted him to murder. One of its conclusions was that the doctor-killer had acted alone.

Technically, that was true. In a deeper sense, Goldstein was not alone. Nor was he insane. Israeli leaders should not have been taken by surprise. His crime sprang directly from his beliefs, and from the crisis of his community after the Oslo Accord. It was a classic, though terribly extreme, example of what human beings can do when reality defies belief in redemption.

In the half-year between the signing of the Oslo Accord and the Hebron massacre, Israeli scholars and journalists warned of impending Jewish terror. Two months before Goldstein's attack, Professor Ehud Sprinzak, the country's leading expert on the radical right, wrote in the daily *Ha'aretz* that "all my professional alarm lights are flashing nonstop" and begged Rabin and Barak to act. The plea got no response.

After his death, Goldstein gained sainthood status on the extreme edge of "redemptive Zionism." His funeral procession began at a Jerusalem mortuary hall; among those who eulogized him were Yeshua Ben-Shushan of the Jewish underground and the Temple Institute's Yisrael Ariel. "Did he kill innocent people? The same supposedly innocent people slaughtered innocents in 1929. . . . The whole city of Hebron slaughtered Jews then. Those are the 'innocent people' who were killed in the Tomb of the Patriarchs," said Ariel. From there the corpse was taken to Nir Yeshivah in Kiryat Arba, where Rabbi Dov Lior said Goldstein had acted "for the sake of Jewish honor and to sanctify the Name of Heaven." (Later, answering bitter criticism from another rabbi, Lior committed the obscenity of writing that Goldstein "should be called a martyr, like the martyrs of the Holocaust.") In driving rain, hundreds of people accompanied the body from the yeshivah to the grave.

Goldstein's friends and family insisted that he'd acted out of ideology, not insanity. His choice of time and place backs that up. While Purim is an uninhibited carnival for most religious Jews, in the upside-down Judaism of the Kahanists it's a celebration of revenge against the Jews' enemies, seen as a mythological entity: Haman, Hitler, and Arabs are made one. And in the fundamentalist mindset, dates aren't symbols chosen by human beings. Instead, a date can literally have a character, a power; it's as if time had a topography, and particular days were mountains or wellsprings. Goldstein also chose a place with power: a supposed source of divine energy where, as he would see it, Jews struggled with the enemy for control. Displaced from the Temple Mount to its little sister, the Tomb of the Patriarchs, Goldstein's act fits the same pattern as the Jewish underground's planned bombing of the Dome of the Rock: Strike at a holy spot, end a peace process, put redemption back on track.

The Temple Mount plot was born in the shock of the Camp David Accord, when Israel first gave up land it had taken in 1967. The Oslo Accord was as great a shock: This time Israel agreed to give up territory from the biblical core of the Land of Israel. What's more, West Bank settlers felt like a rejected minority, after years of believing that they were Israel's vanguard. The sense of abandonment grew as rejectionist Palestinian groups aimed their terror attacks at Israelis living in the West Bank: As settlers saw it, the rest of Israel didn't care about their suffering. Writing in the settler journal *Nekudah,* Dan Be'eri said that in the months after the agreement, "Visionaries have seen their vision torn asunder before their eyes."

For a Kahanist, the crisis was greater. Alone among Jewish messianists, Kahane had set an approximate date for redemption: 1988. The date passed—and instead of the world being redeemed, the "prophet" himself was murdered. Oslo was further proof that the machinery of salvation had stalled.

Nihilism is just one possible response to the failure of prophecy. It's the one Goldstein chose: to destroy himself and others, to be Samson. In the days before the massacre, he told friends he had a plan to stop the peace process. But his comments after the Lapids' deaths show that he regarded violence as a means not only of affecting this world, but of satisfying God. Through sacrificing himself and shedding others' blood, he may well have believed, he would convince heaven that Jews were worthy of being redeemed.

Goldstein left no explanations, even in his farewell note. But those close to him read his deed in the language of messianism. During the *shivah*—the Jewish week of mourning—*Newsday* correspondent Lisa Pevtzow slipped into the Goldstein apartment, joining the visitors who came to voice condolences and pay homage. In the living room was a photo of the Temple Mount, with the Temple in place of the Muslim shrines. The mass murderer's mother spoke of his sense that redemption was near: "Americans are practical. They think redemption is far off. It's coming soon, though. Especially for Baruch." Goldstein's fellow Kahanist, Gary Cooperberg, sent out a fax to journalists about the massacre. Goldstein's "desperate act of love for his people," Cooperberg concluded, "will some day be recognized by all Jews as the turning point which brought redemption upon us."

By ignoring the theological crisis set off by the Oslo Accord, Israeli authorities left themselves unprepared for Jewish terror. By regarding Goldstein as a madman, they avoided the urgent need to understand the religious rationale behind his action. The security forces apparently remained unprepared for ideological violence from others on the religious right. Hebron was not only a disaster in its own right, but a tragically missed warning.

For if Goldstein didn't bring redemption, he did prove that a single individual—driven by despair, acting at a sacred site—could alter political reality. Forty days after the massacre, at the end of the Muslim mourning period, Hamas began its campaign of terror in Israeli cities. Hebron inspired a radical escalation: The Islamic fundamentalist group began using suicide bombers, targeting civilians inside Israel. The worst wave of bombings began on February 25, 1996—the second anniversary of the massacre, underlining the magic meaning of dates for extremists. In the space of two years, suicide bombers murdered over 120 people in attacks in Israeli cities. Culpability isn't a coin; sharing it doesn't reduce a person's portion. The guilt of Islamic terrorists is not reduced by remembering that Goldstein sparked the suicide attacks.

Goldstein's admirers produced a book in his memory, *Baruch Hagever*. The Hebrew title means both "This Man, Baruch," and "Blessed Is the Man." Temple Mount plotter Yoel Lerner helped produce it; Yosef Elboim, of the Movement for the Establishment of the Temple, contributed an article. One person who acquired the book was law student Yigal Amir. It was an inspiration for his own act of "self-sacrifice": assassinating Prime Minister Yitzhak Rabin. The slaughter at the tomb; the terror bombings; Rabin's death—all helped crack the hopes that the Oslo Accords originally inspired. At this writing, it remains an open question whether Israelis and Palestinians can recover from the wounds of Goldstein's gunfire and complete the difficult process of making peace.

IF ISRAEL'S SECURITY PEOPLE ignored the explosive power of belief in the End, they had company. In a drama that began almost precisely a year before the Hebron massacre, their American counterparts made the same mistake. The immediate death toll was higher. And while the legal responsibility of federal agents was still the subject of a court battle and government inquiry seven years later, it's clear that the people whose job it is to keep the peace played a role in the tragedy of Waco, Texas.

The story is well known: In Act I, seventy-six agents of the Federal Bureau of Alcohol, Tobacco, and Firearms stormed the Mount Carmel compound of the Branch Davidian sect on February 28, 1993. The raid—planned as a "dynamic entry," an assault—was based on allegations that the group had illegal weapons. Who started shooting that morning was up for debate, but the death toll is known: four federal agents, six Branch Davidians. Still, the sect's 130 members, led by David Koresh, refused to surrender. In Act II, the FBI besieged the rural compound. The final act: After an FBI spokesman declared that negotiations had been stalled for a month and that Koresh wanted "a showdown with the government where massive casualties and deaths will take place," the government's men provided that final battle. They used tanks to pump tear gas into the wooden buildings, then began demolishing them. The compound burst into flame. When the fire died out, the bodies of more than seventy sect members were found inside. Among them were a score of children—a bitter irony, since allegations of child abuse helped stoke the confrontation.

The problem at Waco isn't just who lit the inferno, but why the confrontation began and why it took the form it did. Labeling the Branch Davidians a "cult" played a role: Across the Western world, that term takes a group out of the realm of religious legitimacy and toleration. Like the word "insane," it implies beliefs not worthy of being understood. An all-too-common connotation is that a "cult" is led by someone who doesn't believe the ideas he or she presents, but uses them for self-aggrandizement and "mind control" of members.

Yet the Branch Davidians are, in fact, one small branch of well-rooted American religion. Their history begins in the Great Disappointment of 1844, when William Miller's final date for the Second Coming turned out to be just another day in history. One group of his followers found an explanation: Final judgment had actually begun, but in heaven, with the judging of the dead. That group, led by new prophet Ellen White, became the Seventh Day Adventist church, whose tenets also included celebrating the sabbath on Saturday and the certainty of coming persecution by the government. As often happens with movements born in a flash of millennial hope, the Adventists learned to live in this world by keeping the hope burning as a steady, smaller flame. In the 1920s an Adventist named Victor Houteff tried to fan it back into burning expectation. Expelled from the denomination, he founded the Davidians, who still considered themselves Adventists. He also established the center outside Waco, calling it Mt. Carmel after the place where Elijah fought the prophets of Baal: His followers were choosing the true God over the false religion of earthly kings. David Koresh was only the latest, most idiosyncratic of Davidian prophets—a self-proclaimed messiah whose teachings included polygamy for himself, and celibacy for everyone in the sect but him and his partners. Koresh may have found a "scriptural" way to satisfy his own desires, but we can assume that he and his followers believed his doctrine: Both celibacy and free love are common in millennial movements—a tightening of rules or freedom from them as signs that the new age is dawning.

Koresh expected the End to come in 1995, in a final battle to take place in Jerusalem. His scenario was based on Revelation 6:11–13, describing the opening of the "fifth seal" on the heavenly book of the apocalypse. The verses describe the death of some of God's true believers, a pause of "a little season" or "a short while," and then the slaughter of the rest of the believers. Natural catastrophes and final judgment follow.

After the initial raid at Waco, the FBI defined its siege as a "Hostage/Rescue barricade situation." That would have seemed bizarre to Koresh's followers; they stayed in the compound voluntarily. Koresh's own reading was as incomprehensible to his adversaries: In a radio interview the night of the raid, he said, "We are now in the Fifth Seal."

One of the bitterest tellings of the Waco debacle comes from James Tabor and Eugene Gallagher in their book *Why Waco*. The bitterness makes sense: Tabor and another academic scholar of religion, Phillip Arnold, made a near-successful bid to end the Mt. Carmel standoff. Koresh, as Tabor and Gallagher explain, saw the raid as the start of the "fifth seal" death of believers at the hands of godless authorities. But the scenario had begun early, in the wrong place. Confused, Koresh awaited a word from God to understand what was happening. For the Davidians, the FBI siege was evidence that the "little season" would quickly pass and they too would die in the world's last battle. Cutting off electricity to Mt. Carmel, blasting the compound with loud music, flooding it with searchlights at night—the FBI's tactics—only told the Davidians that they must be ready for martyrdom. The FBI's way of saying "Surrender!" meant "Hold out!" in the language of the sect. Meanwhile, the FBI commander at the scene told negotiators not to let Koresh speak "Bible babble" to them. That left Koresh with no words at all.

Tabor and Arnold tried speaking to the Davidian leader in the language he knew. On a local radio show, they presented another interpretation of the "fifth seal" that would stretch the "little season" and oblige Koresh to surrender so he could present his message to the world. The Davidians asked for a tape of the talk. And on April 14, Koresh sent out a letter saying he'd received his word from God: As soon as he could write his explanation of Revelation, he would leave Mt. Carmel. In luminous contrast to what the FBI said, Koresh was actively negotiating. Yet five days later, the FBI attacked. The result was catastrophe.

Waco has a complex message. The Branch Davidians' faith in approaching apocalypse was in itself incendiary. It was built on hope for cataclysm and martyrdom; it was a radical misunderstanding of a world that wasn't ending. Yet the federal agents' reading of Koresh appears as misconceived. Ignoring his beliefs, refusing to hear or speak his language, the FBI unwittingly played out his script for the apocalypse. Confirming the expectations of millennial believers, it turns out, can be as dangerous as disproving them.

Such subtleties were largely ignored after Waco. On the American far right, the Waco disaster was seen as proof of the federal government's malevolence. Timothy McVeigh's bombing of the Oklahoma federal building took place on the second anniversary of the Mt. Carmel fire. But for much of the public, Waco was simply testimony to the dangers of "cults," particularly their incomprehensible but apparently inevitable trajectory toward destruction.

In the 1990s, the last decade of the millennium, there was other testimony. In October 1994, fifty-three members of the Solar Temple, a small French-speaking sect, were found dead at two spots in Switerzerland and another in Quebec—some suicides, some murdered. For the group, this wasn't death but "transit"—from an earth doomed to ecological apocalypse, to salvation on the star Sirius. Fear that the sect was unraveling apparently led its leader to decide on the finale, argues Swiss scholar of religion Jean-Francois Mayer. More Solar Temple believers performed "transit" in France in 1995, and another group in Quebec in March 1997. A few days after the last of those incidents, thirty-nine members of the Heaven's Gate sect made their own exit, in a mansion in Rancho Santa Fe in Southern California. For years the group had lived in celibacy while waiting for flying saucers to take them to "the level above human," otherwise known as the kingdom of heaven, before the earth was "spaded under." Finally, they shed their "vehicles," their bodies, in order to ascend; phenobarbital, vodka, and plastic bags over the head helped them make the trip. Japan's Aum Shinrikyo sect, in contrast, turned its violence outward. Aum mixed Buddhist and Hindu ideas with predictions from the Book of Revelation and a dose of anti-Semitic conspiracy theory. Its guru, Asahara Shokou, not only predicted Armageddon in 1999, he set followers to work producing chemical and biological weapons—including the sarin nerve gas used in Aum's 1995 attack on Tokyo's subways. Twelve people died; thousands were hurt.

Then in March 2000, the nightmare recurred: Over five hundred members of the Movement for the Restoration of the Ten Commandments crowded into their Ugandan church—and died in raging flames. Sect leaders had predicted the end of our world at the end of 1999. The movement's private apocalypse made its members the first known victims of failed hopes that 2000 was the date at the end of time.

It was easy to decipher such evidence as saying that anticipating the End of Days was the province of "cults," and that the belief necessarily led to violence. But that reading misses many shades of gray. The turn of the millennium quickened hopes of history's end in movements that include millions of people. There are also countless small, offbeat religious groups that never turn violent. Then again, so-called cults aren't as offbeat as they look at first glance. Beneath the sci-fi veneer, for instance, the Heaven's Gate dream of ascent to heaven looked a lot like the Rapture; its original two leaders presented themselves as versions of the two Last Days witnesses predicted in Revelation.

What's true is that at moments of crisis, belief in the apocalypse can morph into the attempt to make it happen. Dealing with that danger is a subtle business. One cause for crisis in a religious group is an attack, real or perceived, from mainstream society. A few months before the turn of the millennium, religion scholar Jean-Francois Mayer cautioned a conference of academics and American and Israeli law-enforcement officials that cases like Solar Temple created a risk of automatically labeling small religious movements as headed toward suicide. And yet, Japanese police apparently ignored Aum far too long out of legitimate unwillingness to harass a religious group. Finding the balance can only be tougher in Jerusalem.

THE TWO-STORY STONE HOUSE in suburban Mevasseret Tzion has a spectacular view of Jerusalem. When the combined police and Shin Bet team arrived on the first Sunday of 1999, the Holy City was fading into nightfall. After they took away the members of Denver's Concerned Christians sect and searched for evidence, they locked the home.

But the next day, the yard was open. On the porch, garden tools lay scattered—gloves, trowels, a child's toy hoe. The sect members may have been preparing a winter garden when the police swooped in—a disconcerting image next to the police statement that "police and Shin Bet assessments are that [the group] intended to carry out violent, extreme actions in the streets of Jerusalem toward the end of 1999 . . . to bring about the Second Coming."

There was something else on the porch, apparently overlooked by police: an envelope containing an audiocassette and a packet of charts meant as study aids. At the center of the first chart, under the title "Time of the End Series," is a picture of Charles Manson, whose California "family" perpetrated the 1969 Tate and LaBianca murders in hopes of igniting an apocalyptic race war in America. The droning voice on the tape has been identified as Concerned Christians leader Monte Kim Miller.

When Miller started the Concerned Christians in the mid-eighties, it was a fundamentalist Christian group opposed to what he saw as New Age influences. By 1989, he was publishing newsletters portraying an abyss between Christian faith and loyalty to America: "America is a nation that serves the purposes of Satan in Jesus' name," stressed one issue of his *Take Heed Update.* Another newsletter identified America as the Antichrist, and the Catholic church as the "false prophet" who will be in league with the Antichrist in the Last Days. Such ideas didn't make him unusual in America's fundamentalist subculture. But Miller did have a particular passion for finding fingerprints of God and the Devil in unexpected spots. The Fourth of July, he "revealed," was both a pagan festival and a tipoff to America's roots in "Satanic" Freemasonry.

Over time, Miller transformed the Concerned Christians into a sect that regarded him as a prophet who literally spoke in God's voice. He told his followers to end contact with outsiders, all of whom were destined for Hell. Yet some did keep in sporadic touch with their families. Miller, they said, prophesied that he and another member of the group would be the witnesses who, according to Revelation, will die in Jerusalem's streets and be resurrected three and a half days later. It would happen, he predicted, in December 1999. Miller had seized the Last Days script shared by millions of Christian premillennialists and cast himself in a starring role. In the fall of 1998, he and some eighty followers disappeared from Denver.

From the start, Miller used audiocassettes to get his word out. In recorded lectures, he transformed historical dates and names into evidence that apocalyptic prophecies were coming true. By the time he recorded the Manson tape, the exegesis turned hallucinatory. Miller describes Manson ambiguously as "a counterfeit, and sometimes a picture of Jesus Christ, the Son of Man." "The killing of Sharon Tate and her baby . . . represents the killing of Rosemary's baby which [is] a killing of the Roman anti-Christ by the Lord," he explains dispassionately. "The Manson murders foretell the slaying of . . . America itself by the Lord." From there, he links Manson's life to historical events— the bombing of Nagasaki, the birth of Bill Clinton. The strangest link of all is between the release of a Beach Boys song supposedly written by Manson and the breakup of the Soviet Union.

There's mad method in this exegesis. Literary critics can assert meaning in a character's name, or repeated use of a phrase, because they assume the text to have design. Prophecy writers such as Hal Lindsey tie major world events to scripture, asserting that history, too, has an author and plot. Miller lunges wildly beyond: His divine plan includes the Beach Boys, Manson, Tate's infant, her husband Roman Polanski's movie *Rosemary's Baby*—all the blather of supermarket tabloids. We roll our eyes, but the promise of meaning pulled a few souls into the sect's orbit.

On the tape, Miller never suggests that he'd follow Manson's example. But he does show fascination with a man who hoped murders would bring the End. And he describes the brutal strangling of a pregnant woman as a clue pointing to fulfillment of prophecy, even a representation of divine judgment.

The first of Miller's followers arrived in Israel early in 1998, renting a Jerusalem apartment. The plan, says a source close to the affair, was for the full group to come. The raid on the Mevasseret house and another suburban home netted eight adults and six children. Police believed those were all the Concerned Christians then in Israel— though the roster didn't include at least one family that had been in the country for months. The sect members were deported to Denver, where they again vanished. Miller's whereabouts remained an enigma. The sect settled outside Athens, though the same source says they were still eager to reach Israel. In December 1999, Greek authorities evicted twenty-five Concerned Christians for overstaying their visas; they landed in New York—and disappeared. When the sect reached the predicted date for martyrdom, they did nothing to make it happen: presumably, they'd expected God to take care of it. As prophet, Miller could rewrite the End. Or he could wait for a chance to slip into Israel. Years before, a sect member told her mother that "Miller had a read a book on losing your identity." In parts of the globe, passports are just a commodity.

Researchers of millennialism weren't surprised when the Concerned Christians affair began. They'd expected to see just this trajectory on their radar screens: a group taking off from fundamentalist Christianity, headed for Jerusalem, fueled by hopes that the End would come around 2000. The arrival of Miller's group was just one sign that the the turn of the millennium was increasing Jerusalem's gravitational pull.

By the start of 1999, for instance, over a hundred born-again Christians from around the world were living in the Arab neighborhoods on or near the Mount of Olives, on Jerusalem's east. For Christian literalists, the Mount of Olives is where Jesus will return. "I can hear his footsteps," a Pentacostal minister who called himself Brother David once told me. David came to Jerusalem from upstate New York in 1980 and shed his last name and passport, planning never to leave. But only in the mid-nineties did he move to the Mount of Olives, anticipating the End—possibly, he said, in 2000: "Scripture says a thousand years is like a day with the Lord. Preceding Christ there were four thousand years, and then two thousand years after. We're approaching the End of the sixth day. . . . On the seventh day, He rested." That day of rest would be the millennium. A loose-knit community of foreign evangelicals formed around David, who held Wednesday night prayer meetings in an upstairs flat on the main road of Palestinian Al-Azariya: a woman on autoharp leading "Amazing Grace," David preaching, one overseas TV crew or another filming the media-friendly millennialists.

Al-Azariya was also home to Winston Rose, aka Brother Solomon, who calculated the End by the dense math of Victor Houteff's Davidian Seventh-Day Adventists. Jamaican-born, Solomon was for decades the pastor of the First Temple of the House of David in Brooklyn. In 1993, after visiting Israel, he retired early from his New York City teaching job, "just to come back here, because I thought it was that important, rushing against time. . . . We believe that the Lord is coming." At least two dozen congregants joined him. In Jerusalem, Solomon republished Houteff's *The Shepherd's Rod.* David Koresh, he said, was "an opportunist" who took over the Waco community. Elegantly dressed in a black pin-stripe suit, Brother Solomon spoke of the End with sweeping gestures: "The U.N. will come . . . against Jerusalem. Houses will be robbed, women ravished. . . . There'll be a civil war . . . Jew against Jew." By his arithmetic, it would happen not in 2000, but in 2001.

The approach of 2000 also created an audience for a one-time California building contractor who claimed to be the biblical prophet Elijah, and who said he was in Jerusalem as one of the Last Days witnesses. A tall, bearded man with chest-length gray locks, "Elijah" had been in and out of Israel for a decade and a half. He could be spotted at downtown outdoor cafés, the black attaché case next to his chair labeled "Jesus is my Lord. Elijah" in big red letters. People claiming to be biblical figures are standard scenery in Jerusalem; the government's district psychiatrist recalls having three Virgin Marys in town during the same week in 1997. Elijah alone broke out of the role of solo eccentric; by summer 1999 he'd picked up at least a few followers among foreign Christians in Jerusalem, and support from an American End of Days website headlined "The Ministry of Elijah in Jerusalem NOW!" Elijah claimed to have prophesied the drought then affecting Israel, linking it to the fact that the government was "breaking Elohim's [God's] word by giving land to Arafat, an Islamic moon-god worshiper." Professor Richard Landes, founder of Boston Univerity's Center for Millennial Studies, notes that through history, a few individuals are always announcing the End; in times of millennial excitement, people stop treating them as nuts and start listening. Elijah fit that pattern: People accepted him as a "witness" because they were aching for someone to appear on the stage of the End.

Yet by the turn of the millennium, Elijah was off Jerusalem's stage, as were Brother David and Brother Solomon and their communities—all forced by Israeli authorities to exit. Elijah was picked up first and pressured to leave the country. The formal grounds were that he'd overstayed his visa, but police hadn't started a crackdown on

Western tourists with expired papers—just on those considered at risk for millennium-linked violence. Elijah had spoken of "needing to enter the Temple Mount to bring the Redemption," a police spokesman said. Or not quite: Moments later, the spokesman backtracked, saying that Elijah hadn't explicitly spoken of action on the Mount, "but our assessment was that he intended to act." Two months later, in October, Israeli police held a midnight raid in Al-Azariya, arresting those who were awaiting millennial epiphanies without valid visas. "Our assessment is that in certain circumstances they could endanger public safety," a police spokesman said. Leaks to police reporters spoke of concern about mass suicide or an attack at the Temple Mount "on the night of the millennium," meaning December 31, 1999. Brother David was among those deported.

The concerns about violent plans, a security source told me, were based on "exact information, totally clear" gathered over months. But because the deportations were an administrative step based on illegal residence, police never had to present their evidence in court. Nor did they have to explain how they'd interpreted that evidence. What's striking is that the police assessments were so similar in every case, despite the differences between the people involved. Unlike Monte Kim Miller, for instance, Brother David never assigned himself a central role in the Endtime drama. Unlike Miller, he didn't cut off contact with outsiders; David's group welcomed media coverage as proof that the "Gospel is being preached to all the world," as required before the Second Coming. In both respects, Miller was showing warning signs for potentially turning violent; David wasn't. Police descriptions ignored such contrasts. It seems that security officials decided, even before the Concerned Christians showed up, that belonging to a "doomsday cult" was reason enough to evict a foreigner, especially one without papers.

Israeli police woke up relatively late to the expectations of some fundamentalist Christians that the End would begin in 2000. In 1998, the Israeli national police force's intelligence branch began consulting experts on apocalyptic beliefs. The experts spoke of a range of risks: At the low end, fundamentalist Christians might cause tensions by proselytizing to religious Jews or Muslims; at the very highest end, there was the chance that disappointed believers might eventually commit suicide or attack a holy site. By the time those assessements reached top echelons, it was as if a pastel picture had been shoved through a fax and arrived solid black. At a top-level security discussion in the fall of '98, the millennium issue was on the agenda as "Christian radicalism linked to 2000, in which believers try to meet their end at holy sites." Soon after, newspapers cited police sources as warning that "hundreds or even thousands of members of extreme cults" would reach Israel, many "with one goal: to commit suicide on the last day of 1999 at one of the holy places in Jerusalem's Old City." By sleight-of-mind, the risks had been assigned to a single day, December 31.

So when people proclaiming the End showed up, it was easy to slide them into a ready-made category, regardless of differences between them. Whether because of police policy or not, the turn of the millennium passed peacefully. But the policy was fraught with risks for the long term. A sense of persecution can shove a religious movement in the direction of violence. Academic experts' advice had been to learn the lesson of Waco—to avoid confrontations, and instead to make contact through mediators who could speak the sect's language.

Waco hinted as well that millennialists are less isolated than they appear, and overreacting to them risks angering fellow-travelers. Israel's expulsion policy held a similar danger. Elijah's deportation, for instance, sparked a column blasting Israel's treatment of Christians on a Web news service catering to the hardcore American right. Who knows if a potential Tim McVeigh was reading?

Expectations of apocalypse should be handled gently precisely because they do pose very real dangers in Jerusalem. The risk didn't evaporate at the turn of the millennium. It is only likely to grow in the years to come—in part because so many people did hope that 2000 would be the beginning of the End.

HAROLD "HAYSEED" STEPHENS blew through Jerusalem on his sixty-third visit to Israel just after Rosh Hashanah in September 1999. He'd come this time to spend the Jewish New Year praying at the spot in the Judean Desert near the Dead Sea where he was preparing to drill 30,000 feet for oil—according, he said, to God's instructions.

Hayseed is big man, with shoulders that look several feet wide and carved straight across; even with his full head of gray hair it's not hard imagining him as the West Texas farm kid who played a season of pro football for the New York Titans in the early sixties. He wraps that build in a brilliantly white Western shirt, impeccable Levis, and cowboy boots. The name "Hayseed" is cut into the back of his tooled leather belt; the oval buckle in front, the size of Houston, is embossed with a six-pointed Star of David, in the middle of which a derrick gushes black gold; below the star is an open Bible and the word "Jesus." In the executive conference room atop his hotel, he presses a hundred-shekel bill—twenty-five dollars—on the waitress who brings him orange juice. Hayseed is a giver. When he was "in the world"— that is, before he was born again—he gave it away at Vegas tables. In those days, he couldn't resist gambling, drinking, and fighting; he was totally selfish, he says. Yet someone who doesn't share his theology might suggest that Hayseed Stephens achieved a certain sainthood before he found Jesus, back when the young man for whom "football was my god" quit the Titans before the end of his rookie season to help care for his wife's younger brother, lying in the hospital with a head injury from a car accident. If you don't like Hayseed, it's because you decided not to before meeting him and you don't bend easily.

On a visit to Israel in 1982, Hayseed says, two hours after a meeting of Christian businessmen with Prime Minister Menachem Begin at which he gave Begin his white Stetson, God told him that "the greatest oilfield in the world" was at the southwest of the Dead Sea. The theory has more than revelation behind it; asphalt seeps to the surface in the area. He has been able to find investors who don't care about his theology. Back in the eighties, Hayseed's first drilling attempt failed; he believes the oil was deeper than he could reach then, and "it wasn't God's time." Because finding the gusher, Hayseed says, will fulfill prophecy: It will make Israel "a lender, not a borrower," as Deuteronomy promises; it will provide the wealth that will be "the hook in the jaw" pulling the "hordes of the north" to invade Israel in the final war predicted by Ezekiel. Hayseed plans to use every cent he makes to be "a financial blessing to Israel," which will include "helping to finance the building of the Third Temple." So, he suggests, God delayed the discovery, in order that it would come in the first year of the world's seventh millennium, which by Hayseed's figuring began at Rosh Hashanah.

"That's why we went down to the drill site . . . and we had prayers as the sun was going down over the sixth millennium and ushered in the seventh millennium. . . . There are six millennia of labor and the seventh day—what did God do? He rested. So we believe that the seventh [millennium] is when we'll enter the Tribulation," he explains. Were we to meet again a year later, in September 2000, "We'd both say we never dreamed this was gonna happen this quickly. . . . The earth is dilating to nine and three-quarters. It's birthin' time." The distant sound of an ambulance siren drifts into the comfortable room. "I believe you'll hear that sound out there more and more this year," he says. He is a very caring man hoping for pain because, he says, "birthin' is always painful."

Pay attention to the dates: Hayseed assumed the standard calculation of Christian fundamentalists that the year 2000 was six thousand years since creation. The Jewish calendar, for those who care to take it literally, put the world's age in September 1999 at 5,760. Yet he made Rosh Hashanah the start of the crucial year: Unlike January 1, it's a date one can find in the Bible. One has to wonder: If Hayseed were a poorer man, if he'd expressed his confidence in the approaching End by moving to Al-Azariyah instead of investing millions in drilling for oil, would the police have packed him on a plane for Dallas?

For in the fall of 1999, Hayseed sounded even more willing to gamble on 2000 as the beginning of the End than Brother David was. Neither was unusual. True, plenty of premillennialist preachers warned against setting dates for the End. Yet for many evangelical Christians focused on the Rapture, the temptation to regard scripture and current events as coded books containing the true date was irresistible. Quite commonly the same person who insisted it was forbidden to guess God's time also stoked the expectations.

For instance, Jerry Falwell. When the one-time leader of the Moral Majority gave his January 1999 talk asserting that the Antichrist was probably already alive and "must be male and Jewish," his intent was to underline that the Second Coming was near. Interviewed at the time, Falwell stressed he wasn't tying the final events to a date: "I just happen to believe that the Lord could come very soon. . . . Anyone who declares 2000 as the year of the Lord's coming is unwise."

A short while before, Falwell opened a Sunday sermon on the same note, saying he wasn't one of the "self-appointed prophets" who proclaimed the Second Coming in 2000. Oh, but it was so hard not to!

For once past the disclaimer, Falwell explained the "six-day theory," attributing it to Orthodox Jews and early Christians. To that, Falwell added what he called the "three-day theory": "Jesus rose on the third day. Would the beginning of the third millennium . . . not be the likely time for His return to earth?" Falwell's tactics were clear: He'd said he was against predictions; he'd presented the ideas in other people's names; no one could say Jerry Falwell was wedded to a date for the End. He was just flirting with it, heavily, very publicly.

The three-day calculation was no more original with Falwell than the six-day one. John Hagee, for instance, used it to conclude his *Beginning of the End* in 1996: "We are coming to the end of the second day. And the third day is forming just below the horizon; it will dawn with the appearance of Messiah . . ." An old pattern: As historian Albert Baumgarten notes, millennial movements produce multiple calculations for the same appointed time. The more ways you prove it, the more you overcome the giggles of your neighbors and your own irritating memory that people before you have guessed wrong. Almost anything can turn into a portent of apocalypse.

Particularly anything having to do with Israel. In his 1997 book *Jerusalem Betrayed*, Mike Evans cited the standard idea that the generation that saw Israel's birth would see the End, then used this math: "The generation of people who saw this 'blossoming' of modern Israel were born between 1925 and 1935. Their lifespan will be roughly 70 years according to the Bible . . ." That leads you to 2000, but with room to push the date off a bit when the need arises. Despite hawkish views on Israel, Endtime enthusiasts could also embrace the peace process as a sign: Either a final status deal in 2000 would enable the Jews to build the Temple, or it would divide Jerusalem, fulfilling Zechariah's prophecy that "half the city shall go forth into captivity." A red heifer that would be ready for use in 1999 was more proof. For Irvin Baxter, a news report that the number of Jewish settlers in the West Bank had hit 144,000 was another message—Revelation describes exactly that number of "servants of God" being singled out from the tribes of Israel in the Last Days. Baxter raised money from subscribers of his *Endtime* magazine and sent out 35,000 copies of a special issue to settler households, warning them of dangers ahead according to the premillennialist picture of the End.

The cow sprouted white hairs; the settler population rose past the magic number. Expectations didn't die. As late as December 1999 Chuck Missler—who'd told me just weeks before that he placed no significance in the year 2000—published a long explanation of the six-millennium calculation in his *Personal Update* monthly magazine. Missler added, liberally using italics, that "the current Hebrew calendar may have an error: *the year 2000 might really be 6000 on the corrected Hebrew calendar.*" The Jews, he argued, apparently goofed by 239 years in their calcuation of the world's age. The sixth millennium would open on Rosh Hashanah of 2000.

The same issue of Missler's journal carried a final warning on Y2K: "Conservative estimates," said an article, were that 25 percent of world trade would stop due to computer breakdowns; oil supplies could be disrupted. "Don't waste your time, blindly assuming you can avoid God's deadline," writer Gordan McDonald summed up. In a sermon on the same subject in August 1998, Falwell had announced: "God may use Y2K to crush us and prepare us for revival!" Neither McDonald nor Falwell placed the end of history on January 1, 2000. The link was more in the state of mind. For people looking for signs, praying for cataclysm, it was hard to resist hyping the computer glitch. It promised a modern-day Tower of Babel story: Godless Western society undone by technological hubris. Fitting the conspiratorial mindset of millennialists, it allowed believers to get out "the real knowledge" that authorities were allegedly hiding.

But some went further, warning—which is to say hoping—that the great computer disaster would lead directly to the End of Days. Prophecy writer Grant Jeffrey's online Y2K jeremiad began: "At midnight, Dec. 31, 1999, millions of computers throughout the world will begin to crash. The lights will go out in many cities around the globe. . . . The failure to correct this massive problem before the Year 2000 deadline may threaten our jobs, our safety, our food, and our finances. . . . This crisis may set the stage for the creation of the coming world government that was prophesied to arise in the last days . . ."

Future historians, I suspect, will study the buildup to the very boring day when computers didn't crash as part of America's cultural, not technological, history. The point is not the glitch, but how strident the rhetoric was in a country saturated with millennial beliefs, relative to less religious societies elsewhere in the West.

For mainstream media and culture, the Y2K scare helped tie beliefs about the world's end to the civil date of January 1, 2000. Once the date passed, many assumed apocalyptic fever had abated. Confusion between the turn of the millennium and "the millennium" as a religious concept strengthened that illusion. Yet the computer bug was just one scrap of evidence seized by those looking for proof of the End. Among those hoping for the Rapture in 2000, most never gambled on a specific day. Those who did often put their money on a scriptural date—the first new moon of the spring, or the autumn holidays of Rosh Hashanah or Sukkot.

Betting on 2000 was itself part of a bigger story: premillennialists' certainty that Israel's birth marked the start of the "terminal generation." That faith has erupted before: in sudden hopes for Rapture in 1967, in predictions that 1988 would mark the End. Some who guessed wrong before are wary of setting new dates. "I believe that people who were alive when Israel was founded will still be alive when all of [prophecy] is fulfilled. That's a big time period," says Hal Lindsey. Others leap at the hope offered by the next prediction. After 2000, new dates are likely to pop up on prophecy websites: 2001, or 2007, marking forty years since the Six-Day War. Historian Richard Landes notes that after the year 1000 proved a letdown, believers focused on 1033, anniversary of the crucifixion. The same could happen this time. We live in an era of millennial dreams. As the "terminal" generation ticks away, both desperation and enthusiasm are likely to grow. Yet with each "prophetic" date that turns out to be another workday, the fracture of faith is more painful.

And the dissonance between hope and reality is what creates the greatest risks in Jerusalem. The day after the last is most dangerous. The danger is doubled because just as premillennialist Christians confront the failure of predictions, Jewish messianists may face the end of their dream of redemption born in 1967's conquests.

ALL MILLENNIAL MOVEMENTS share one thing: failure. The world doesn't end. But the ways in which believers face failure are many.

The first crisis may not break a group. William Miller's followers built their hopes on the Second Coming occurring by March 21, 1844;

when that date went by, they calculated a new one, seven months hence. The very fact of failure seems to have given believers new energy. Proselytizing continued; excitement rose. Only when the new date passed did the movement fragment. Some believers, such as those who formed the Seventh Day Adventists, knit new theologies to show that prophecy *had* been fulfilled that day—and again began proselytizing.

Pioneer social psychologist Leon Festinger made sense of that behavior in his 1950s study, *When Prophecy Fails.* Festinger and two colleagues closely followed a tiny American sect that predicted natural disasters from which the faithful would be saved by flying saucers. When the prophesied time passed, the small group of believers suddenly began trying to convince the world of their beliefs. Festinger's explanation: When a person believes in something, and the belief is clearly proved wrong, a gap opens between what the person sees and what he or she *knows* is true. You can shed the beliefs, but if you've staked a lot on them, that hurts. One medicine is an explanation proving that the belief is still true. And the best way to convince yourself is persuade others: "If more and more people can be convinced that the system of belief is correct, then clearly it must, after all, be correct."

Ergo, when a messianic figure dies or disappoints followers, or when a date set for the End passes, believers are likely to respond by evangelizing. At the least, they'll look for reassurance that they're right. That may explain why monthly sales of Left Behind books actually doubled in January 2000, after the Y2K bug failed to trigger the End.

How far someone will go to hold on to a belief depends on how much he or she has invested in it. Telling your friends of your faith, risking ridicule, is an investment. If you break with your family, or drop out of school, or leave home to live elsewhere among the believers, your investment is even higher. In the amphetamine times of millennial hope, there will always be people who give their souls to the dream, and others who simply share the expectation. But you can't really tell from the outside what someone has staked. Your quiet neighbor may have truly counted on the Rapture in 2000 to save her from her boss. On the other hand, some people bend, backtrack, change more easily than others.

So while Festinger suggests that "there is a limit beyond which belief will not withstand" contradictory reality, the limit varies from believer to believer. Some Western communists lost faith when the Soviet Union signed its 1939 nonagression pact with Nazi Germany, others after the invasion of Hungary in 1956. And the choices are sub-tler than staying or going. Some quit the party but remained leftists. Others stayed in it, holding on to hopes for a Marxist millennium and sacrificing the concerns that originally brought them to communism. When the sixties faded away without bringing the Age of Aquarius, many young people quietly accepted American middle-class life. Some, though, held tight to millennial hopes at the price of filling them with very different values, becoming born-again Christians.

When people hold a complex ideology, a crisis places one belief in conflict with another. As in the Israeli messianic right after the Oslo Accord: In the eyes of the faithful, the sacred state had agreed to give up sacred land, and a large part of the sacred nation supported this step. The pieces couldn't hold together. One Gush Emunim founder demonstratively left his settlement's synagogue on the Sabbath, rather than listen to the weekly Prayer for the State: The state had lost its sanctity. Meanwhile, in the settler journal *Nekudah,* attacks multiplied against secular Israelis, symbolized by the godless Tel Aviv culture of "pubs, discotheques, and beaches." That double delegitimation of the state and secular Jews helped open the way to the Rabin asassasina-tion. Afterward, some on the messianic right reached the opposite conclusion: Reconnecting with secular Israelis was more important than holding land. Another gambit was to delay gratification: In con-versations, settlers told me they now realized that redemption would take generations. To hold on to "the process of redemption," they sac-rificed belief that it would happen quickly, without setbacks.

Fury at secular Israelis reflected a common response of failed millennialists: Find a scapegoat, something or someone holding up God's plan. Millennialism presents a drama of the future; most of the actors are outside the group of millennial believers. The messianists of Gush Emunim devoted years to building settlements. But the script they'd learned from the rabbis Kook, father and son, promised that secular Jews would retain a love for the Land of Israel and would even-tually return to faith. When the drama turned out wrong, it was easy to be enraged with secularists for ignoring their cues. Yet other options were available—to rewrite the script, or even strip the roles from the actors and begin seeing them as people free to choose other beliefs.

Richard Landes sees a similar logic in the Crusades, which started after a century of millennial fever among Western Christians. Spurring the march eastward, Landes suggests, was the belief that Jesus had not returned because the Holy Land was in the hands of infidels. The slaughter of Jews along the way was spurred by the idea that they had held up the End by failing to convert. Given the place of Jews in Christian mythology and the expectation that they'll see the light, Landes argues, they are a readily available scapegoat for disappointed Christian millennialists. That dynamic is behind Martin Luther's infamous 1543 treatise on the Jews, says another historian, Andrew Gow: Luther had believed that the last judgment was near, which is why he didn't seek to establish a church. Behind Luther's *On the Jews and Their Lies,* Gow says, is the implication that the End hasn't come because the Jews have rejected Christianity and have even influenced Protestants with their interpretation of scripture. Synagogues should be burned, Luther says; Jews should be given the choice of conversion or expulsion from Christian polities. In the 1930s, Gow notes, the Nazis massively reprinted Luther's treatise.

The potential for anti-Semitism is clear today—precisely because the dispensationalism accepted by millions assigns Jews such a large part in the drama. As long as believers expect the End tomorrow, the result is love for Jews. Yet that love is akin to what a fan feels while stalking a movie star, unable to distinguish between the actress and the part she once played in a movie. When the "terminal" generation refuses to reach its terminus, an old frustration with Jews who won't play their role is all too likely to surface.

We can be safe in assuming, for instance, that droves of Jews aren't about to emulate Rabbi Tsion Ben-Judah of the Left Behind books and begin promoting born-again Christianity. But Jews may disappoint dispensationalists in other ways, too. Giving up land instead of pursuing "biblical" borders may be interpreted as a theological betrayal. All the more so the refusal of Jews to fulfill the prophecy that so many dispensationalists have made the linchpin of apocalypse: "There remains but one more event to . . . set the stage for Israel's part in the last great act of her historical drama. That is to rebuild the ancient Temple . . ." as Hal Lindsey wrote. There is a powerful potential to read the converse of that sentence as "the last act has not begun *because* the Jews have not built the Temple." Jesus didn't come, perhaps, because rabbis were too strict about the rules for a red heifer, or because Israeli voters didn't choose a sufficiently right-wing government to destroy the Dome of the Rock.

The theology of apocalypse popular in evangelical Christianity teaches love for Jews—and implies hostility toward the people who rejected Jesus. When believers face one disappointment more than they're able to ignore, the package is likely to come apart. That doesn't mean anti-Semitism is inevitable. Another choice is to give up mythic expectations of Jews, to see them as people. The direction a person takes will reflect which commitment is deeper, toward human beings or the grand millennial story.

AT THE EXTREME, disappointed believers can choose the dream of salvation over human life itself. The members of Heaven's Gate, comments millennialism scholar Stephen O'Leary, "had been making apocalyptic predictions for years. They couldn't sustain expectation forever, so they had to take irrevocable action." This is the ultimate dogmatism: Any price is worth paying save the price of admitting that the Idea was wrong.

The disappointed may direct their violence at themselves, as they did in Heaven's Gate. In other cases, they have struck former believers who gave up the dream. Solar Temple's body count included "apostates" who were murdered. Or the violence can be turned outward—often as terror.

Terror, says political scientist David Rapoport, an expert on the subject, is best defined as violence that "goes beyond the conventions" society places on the use of force. We have rules for war. Terrorists ignore them; they put bombs on buses, they ignore white flags. Millennial movements have resorted to terror ever since the Jewish Zealots who rebelled against Rome nearly two thousand years ago. Zealots assassinated Jewish priests on holy days; they slaughtered a Roman garrison to which they'd pledged safe passage. To choose terror,

Rapoport argues, believers must expect that redemption is very near, and that it depends on human action.

The choice of terror is even more likely when the End is overdue. Those unwilling to accept failure may conclude that God is waiting for them to act, or that the type of action they have already tried—be it proselytizing or building settlements—wasn't enough.

If you've stood on the doorstep of a new age, you don't want to go back. One way to show you've stepped into the new era is to proclaim that the old laws no longer apply. "Terror," writes Rapoport, "is attractive in itself to messianists just *because* it is outside the normal range of violence and for this reason represents a break with the past, epitomizing the . . . complete liberation which is the essence of messianic expectation."

When a millennial movement comes apart, the fragment least willing to accept defeat may also hope that extravagant violence will reawaken others. That dynamic, it seems, drove the Weather Underground at the end of the sixties: A few people with bombs would start the new American revolution that a decade of mass activism had failed to ignite.

Yehudah Etzion's motive for seeking to bomb the Dome of the Rock, likewise, was to arouse a "redemption movement" precisely at the moment when, as settlers saw it, Israel was retreating from redemption by giving up the Sinai. But there was a subtext in the Jewish underground's plan: It would also wake up God, who had inexplicably allowed history to stall. It was not a new gambit: During the rebellion against Rome, nineteen hundred years before, Zealots burned Jerusalem's food supplies, apparently to put their fate entirely in God's hand and force Him to act.

Still, people aren't chemical elements; they don't react according to precise laws. Just as poverty breeds crime, millennial disappointment breeds violence—but the generalization doesn't tell you who will start shooting. Baruch Goldstein was an obvious candidate—after the fact.

Neither can we know *when* someone will act: which disproof of prophecy will matter, how long it will take to respond. The common perception that millennial violence would occur on January 1, 2000, was a double error. It promoted fear on the date itself, and perhaps complacency afterward. Dennis Rohan apparently expected the End in 1967; it took two years before he decided that God had chosen him to build the Temple. Goldstein acted relatively soon after the Oslo signing—but the peace accord was only the latest sign that his teacher's prophecies had failed.

BUT THESE EXAMPLES do provide a warning: The Temple Mount beckons seductively to believers eager to restart redemption. For Christian millennialists and Jewish messianists alike, the Mount represents the prophetic dénouement that is maddeningly close and out of reach. The physical place, and most of all the glowing dome at its center, have taken the role of the roadblock to human salvation.

When Israel has moved toward trading land for peace, the most radical of the rightists have taken aim at a shared holy site. Yoel Lerner began weighing an attack on the Dome of the Rock in response to Israeli-Egyptian disengagement talks. The attempt by Etzion and company was an answer to the Camp David accord. Goldstein was unusual only in acting at the Tomb of the Patriarchs—and in succeeding in his act. He's the exception that proves the terrifying rule.

Peace settlements are agreements to live in an untidy world, to accept that not all goals will be reached. They threaten believers who seek total resolution. Israeli religious rightists sometimes dismiss peace arrangements Israel has reached because they do not offer "real peace." Real peace is the wolf dwelling with the lamb. To the person who wants no compromises, sacred space held by the Other is a microcosm of the imperfect world.

After 1967, Jewish messianists expected to progress steadily toward redemption. The Oslo process cracked that optimism: Instead of climbing toward salvation, God's people were descending. Some extremists look for a cataclysm that will reverse the direction. Gershon Salomon speaks of the war of Gog and Magog, citing the chapters in Ezekiel and Zechariah that his Christian supporters love. Yehudah Etzion isn't driving under that influence. But he too speaks of a "paradoxical reality": Israel is moving in the opposite direction of what he thinks is inevitable. That supports predictions, he says, that there will be "a correction via catastrophe," a disaster that will put Jews back on track. Not that he wants catastrophe, of course. But he foresees a con-flict between Arabs and Israelis over Jerusalem—perhaps over the Temple Mount.

Both men have people who listen to them. They are extreme, not isolated. If the idea spreads that a catastrophe could be corrective, it is all too possible that someone, today anonymous, will try to ignite it at the Mount.

At some stage diplomacy is likely to defy prophecy for Christian premillennialists as well. Whatever conflicts precede it, any final-status accord between Israel and the Palestinians will necessarily con-firm Muslim rights at Al-Haram al-Sharif. It will shout the message that premillennialists have been trying not to hear: Israel has no inten-tion of building a Temple. A preview of the frustration came in a newsletter of Jan Willem van der Hoeven's International Christian Zionist Center soon after Ehud Barak was elected prime minister. Re-sponding to rumors of a deal that would give the Palestinian Authority limited control of the Temple Mount, writer Stan Goodenough warned that "Satan is moving to entrench his position on God's holy hill." A political arrangement over thirty-five acres is described as a cosmological defeat of light by darkness.

But for premillennialists, the greatest challenge is simply the pas-sage of time. After 2000, many believers must live with disappoint-ment—including ones whose pastors and favorite mass media evangelists remembered to say "no man knows the day" before brightly explaining why it really *could* happen when the world is six thousand years old. As the generation that saw Israel born gets older, the incomprehension that the End hasn't come will be greater. Most believers will not capsize. What of the few who do? Some may have heard that Jesus could not return in 2000 because he couldn't come through the Eastern Gate to the Dome of the Rock. Some may have read a prophecy bestseller asserting that the Dome's destruction will set off the war of Armageddon—and describing the conflagration as the prelude to the Second Coming.

And as experience shows, much less than a bomb causes conflict at the Mount. Threatening to lay a cornerstone for the Temple has sparked bloodshed; opening a tunnel nearly undid the peace process. Attempts by Jewish extremists to worship on the Mount spur Islamic fundamentalists to dig and build and renovate, feeding fear among the Jewish messianists that the Mount is slipping out of grasp. Any incident at the site can spin out of control.

Precisely that potential may be seductive for some people who want the End. In 1998, Israeli police arrested two Christians who arrived at Ben-Gurion Airport via Italy, reportedly after warnings from a foreign security agency they planned an unspecified "provocation" on the Mount to bring their own deaths and ignite Armageddon. A report at the time said the two were deported rather than tried because of their advanced age. Because no open hearing was held, the story can't be confirmed. But the longer Armageddon dawdles, the greater the risk is of a provocative act intended to ignite strife.

A member of the 1980s Jewish underground that plotted to destroy the Dome told me they had no intention of killing anyone; they planned only to demolish the building. His argument was disingenuous. Someone who brings explosives to the Mount has decided to preserve a vision at the expense of human life, possibly a vast expense. "Any blow-up at the Temple Mount—be it a fire, destruction of a building, or bloodshed—will have a hundred times the impact it would in any other spot," says Shlomo Gazit, the former head of Israeli military intelligence.

The effect of an explosion at the golden dome is not measurable in advance. Internationally, ex–Shin Bet chief Carmi Gillon notes, an attack would shatter Israel's claim to be protecting Jerusalem's holy places. "I don't think anyone would refrain from putting the blame on Israel," he says. It would be likely to unite the Muslim world against Israel. It could set off attacks on Jews still living in Muslim countries, such as Iran and Morocco. The full effect, say strategic experts, would depend on relations between Israel, the Palestinians and other Muslim countries. In the most extreme case, says Gazit, it could serve as a casus belli. The abstraction "war" protects our imaginations: For each of the dead, this would, indeed, be the End of Days.

Diplomacy might make a difference. If peace efforts continue, Arab leaders could insist that they will not allow a few extremists to end progress toward a reconciliation. "The question is their true degree of control," says Gillon. "This would be a situation of loss of control, because there'd be something stronger than political leaders:

religion." After the Hebron massacre, the Palestinian Authority didn't abandon the peace process, but the fundamentalist Hamas began its terror campaign. An attack at the Mount could arouse militants from Algeria to Afghanistan.

And to those assessments another factor must be added: Muslim apostles of apocalypse have told their coreligionists to expect the Jews to attack Al-Aqsa. If that prediction comes true, it will seem to confirm the whole awful script of the Hour; it will be read as the call to the last battle. For those who have learned the conspiratorial vision of the apocalypse books, no explanation that a few extremists were at work will help: They see one demonic force behind all misfortunes.

The danger isn't going away. Not as long as people think they know what God has to do next and where He has to do it, and are terribly impatient for Him to begin.

TEN

AVOIÐING
The CAIN OPTION

The messiah will come only when he is no longer necessary.

— FRANZ KAFKA

T HE FUTURE IS CLEAR, say millennialists of all faiths. The novel of human history is written in advance. People don't write it. At best, they decipher it, perhaps discover their own role in it. And we are in the final chapter.

Were I a millennialist, I could tell you the end of the story of the Temple Mount.

The sense that history's end is as close and tangible as Jerusalem's stones has made the national and religious conflict over the city even more intractable than it would have been otherwise. It has spurred attempts to destroy sacred shrines. It has turned minor incidents into battles, and has turned thirty-five acres into the potential detonator of war. It has led fundamentalist Christians in far parts of the globe to read news from Israel as printouts from God's press office. The disappointment of the millennial dreams tied to the Temple Mount only increases the risk. But this story's next chapter (which won't be the last chapter of history) can yet take many forms. It will be written not only by millennial believers, but also by politicians, police, clergy, and ordinary people of faith who can choose what kind of faith to have.

■

IN THE AFTERMATH of the Six-Day War, Israel created a division of holy space at the Temple Mount. Al-Haram al-Sharif remained a place of Muslim worship; it was controlled by Islamic bodies tied for years to Jordan and, after Oslo, to the Palestinian Authority. Jews expressed their religious tie to the Mount at the Western Wall, and their historical ties through archeological excavations next to but not on the Mount. If annexing East Jerusalem to create Israel's "united and eternal capital" expressed triumphalism, cultivating the Wall as Israel's most sacred site instead of the Mount expressed acceptance that power had limits—that Jews were still living in history, not in the days of the messiah. The rabbinic consensus that Jews should not tread on the Mount hinted at the same message and was crucial for maintaining separation of worship.

But the division was de facto and half-articulated. The government policy of banning Jewish worship on the Mount was never given a firm foundation in law. It depended instead on the determination that Jewish prayer inside the Haram was likely to spark disturbances. It was publicly justified, that is, by religious conflict, not by coexistence. Muslim authorities enjoyed an ill-defined, unacknowledged degree of extraterritoriality at the Haram: They built without building permits, they cooperated for years with Israeli archeological officials without admitting to it. They acquiesced to non-Muslim tourists, including Jews, visiting the Haram. In principle, Palestinians still regarded the Western Wall as Al-Buraq al-Sharif, and claimed that the old restrictions on Jewish prayer there should still apply; in practice, they could do nothing about it.

The arrangement allowed each side to make larger concessions than it was willing to state publicly. Most of the time, it allowed a fragile calm. But the de facto nature of the division had a price. Intact by the whim of an unwelcome ruler, Al-Aqsa became the locus of Muslim anxiety. Every real or imagined threat served as proof that the Jews would yet seize the site. Anxiety helped make the holy site into the emblem of Palestinian nationalism and the symbol of Islamic revival. It also fed conspiracy theories and, eventually, apocalyptic permutations of Islam. The 1990 cornerstone riot and the tunnel crisis of 1996 exploded out of those fears.

At the same time, the Temple Mount was in Jewish hands, yet the hands could not close around it. That situation fostered the maddening combination of messianic expectations and their frustration among a segment of religious Jews. Over time, the undefined division of holy space was inherently unstable. It spurred Jewish extremists to think that if they could encourage enough Jews to visit the Mount, if they tried often enough to worship there, they could change the status quo. It pushed Muslim fundamentalists to "defend Al-Aqsa" with construction projects and occasionally with violence. The chance of even a small incident sparking bloodshed continued to grow.

The Oslo agreement put Jerusalem's future—and therefore the status of its holy places—on the negotiating table, though at the end of the peacemaking agenda. Out of the public eye, contacts took place between Israelis and Palestinians aimed at reaching a settlement. The proposal that received the most attention—though the text wasn't made public—was the so called "Beilin–Abu Mazen understandings" of 1995, a draft reached by negotiators under the aegis of Yossi Beilin, then Israel's deputy foreign minister, and Abu Mazen, Yasser Arafat's No. 2. One provision: The Haram would officially have extraterritorial status and the Palestinian flag would be flown there—but the site would not be under Palestinian sovereignty.

An assassin's bullets foiled Beilin's intent to present the draft to Yitzhak Rabin, and the unsigned "understandings" were rejected by Rabin's successor, Shimon Peres, and by Arafat. Peacemaking is a painfully uneven process; a ceremony doesn't mean it has succeeded; a breakdown doesn't mean it's over. At the turn of the millennium, academics acting as unofficial emissaries of Israeli and Palestinian officials were discussing new permutations of the plan. Its fate would depend on political developments in Israel and the Palestinian Authority, on the courage of leaders on both sides, and on the willingness of both peoples to accept compromise.

Yet a de jure division of holy space is not only a political concession. It should be seen, rather, as a religious achievement. There's a profit in getting less than everything. The symbolism of publicly affirming the partition of the holy places is that Islam and Judaism will live side by side, neither victorious over the other. The division demands of believing Muslims to accept that Jerusalem is a shared city, not a solely Islamic one—and yet that Al-Aqsa is not threatened. It asks religious Jews to regard the state of Israel as an achievement, but not a prologue to final redemption. A peace agreement on Jerusalem could eventually convince many believers that they must step back from the threshold of the End. That would be one more dividend of peace.

But the most extreme, those who have invested themselves most in the dream of salvation here and now, are likely to refuse to retreat. For some, the appeal of catastrophe could beckon. That could be true on the third side of the stage as well, among Christian millennialists. Whether the conflict over Jerusalem continues or peace is finally reached, those guarding the city can't afford to go to sleep.

A PARABLE from the Jewish mystical tradition known as hasidism: A man was once walking through a forest at night and came to a house. Looking through the window, he saw people flinging their arms and legs about in grotesque motions. How awful, he thought, they're having seizures, they must all have a terrible illness, or perhaps they're mad. But the man outside the window didn't hear the singing inside, and didn't know the people were dancing. If you don't hear the music of faith, says the story, you'll see the dance as disease. To take the point further, if you don't pay attention to the particular song being sung, you may notice only "seizures"—and not which dance you're seeing out of the many possible.

The parable can be read as a warning for law-enforcement officials. Even a concept as strange to outsiders as the immediacy of the End deserves careful listening; it has internal logic and many possible nuances. The FBI commander at Waco who refused to listen to "Bible babble" tuned out the music that made sense of the Branch Davidians' actions. Evaluations of David Koresh as a conman or as mentally ill turned his dance into seizures. Israeli security officials, it appears, made a similar error after Oslo: They didn't grasp the religious impact of the peace agreement, and so missed the danger of Jewish terror.

Before the turn of the millennium, Israeli police swung too far in the opposite direction: anyone speaking too insistently of the world ending was ushered to a plane. If there was evidence that any of the deportees had specific plans for violence, it was never made public.

Even in the Concerned Christians case, a reliable source told me, the police had no more than assessments of potential risk. They were hearing the music of millennialism—but labeling anyone who danced to it as fearsome.

That approach was flawed, in principle and practice. In an open society, belief should not be made the grounds for police action or deportation. Yet it must be stressed: The policy could be carried out not because Israel is unusual, but because "cults" have been delegitimated in so many countries.

And the policy could create a false sense of safety. Potential perpetrators of violence are not so easily identified. No one would have noticed Dennis Rohan before he acted. At the same time, by refusing to pay attention to the subtleties of belief, one risks radicalizing millennialist believers, especially those on the extreme edge. If a group already sees life as a conflict between the few who follow God's laws and the many who obey godless governments, any experience of persecution will confirm that belief. The Concerned Christians assigned themselves a crucial part in the End; after their deportation, American fundamentalism expert Brenda Brasher cautioned that "when the police treat them as having a pivotal role, it reinforces their belief and enhances the potential for violence."

Brasher added that the deportation could incense others on the fundamentalist fringe. Speaking on an American midwestern radio talk show after the arrests, she was asked by one caller, "Don't police in the Holy Land believe in God?" Hasty action against a few people may create antagonism in a much larger milieu. And, says Brasher, "if you create martyrs, you make more people want to be martyrs." Persecution has its glory.

The deportation policy, in any case, could be implemented against Christian millennialists because they were foreigners without visas. Similar methods can't be used to cope with the risk from Jewish messianists in Israel. In the years to come, Israeli security officials—and their Palestinian counterparts, who share the Holy Land beat—need to take a more subtle, nuanced approach toward the risk of millennial violence.

The Rabin assassination provides a lesson. After the killing, says Carmi Gillon, "People wanted to know why I hadn't put microphones at Bar-Ilan University," the Orthodox institution where assassin Yigal Amir was a law student and right-wing activist. "I answered . . . it's the price of democracy. You don't want to live in East Germany." Gillon is right. Yet it didn't take secret-police methods to read the theological crisis on the religious right, and the delegitimation of secular authority. If the agency was paying attention, it should have been better prepared for the possibility of an ideological assassin taking aim at the prime minister.

To cope with millennialism, law enforcement officials must not treat beliefs as criminal. But they do need to understand where those beliefs could lead. They should keep close watch on potential targets—like the Temple Mount. When Israel budgeted millions of dollars for new security measures, such as setting up TV cameras in the Old City, it was on the right track. And as the missed opportunity of Waco shows, police need mediators available who can speak the language of faith to religious extremists. A mishandled confrontation in the city holy to three faiths would cause far greater shock waves than one in the Texas countryside.

POLICE AND SPECIAL AGENTS are actually at the end of the line: They get the chance to mishandle millennialism after political and religious leaders have already done so.

For politicians, it's easy to treat religious extremists as nothing more than political allies or enemies, and to ignore the messy theology. For the believers, though, the theology is what's real. This is a conversation in which the words can have radically different meanings for speaker and listener. The mismatch is particularly great when the believers are millennialists. Normal politics is a business of tradeoffs, of settlements rather than total solutions. Politics cannot help but disappoint the believer expecting the victory of good over evil.

For years, secular rightists in Israel have joined forces with the redemptive Zionists of Gush Emunim. The alliance inflated messianists' expectations and their influence in the world of religious Judaism. The first crisis came when Menachem Begin agreed to withdraw from the Sinai, hoping to reduce pressure on Israel to give up the West Bank. For those expecting final redemption, such a tradeoff made no sense.

Settlers led the protests against withdrawal—and a few plotted to destroy the Dome.

But the true example of politician as sorcerer's apprentice was Benjamin Netanyahu. Calling up religious energies without understanding them was the mark of his career. As leader of the right-wing opposition after Oslo, Netanyahu appeared at the angry demonstrations organized by West Bank settlers. Those were the people prepared to protest, and Netanyahu was desperate to show that the public wanted new elections. But Netanyahu missed that he was speaking to crowds whose faith in the state and the political process had been shattered. Netanyahu was leader of a major party; his presence and his rhetoric granted confirmation to their views. At one protest, Netanyahu spoke from a balcony festooned with the words, "Death to Arafat." Eventually, the assassin who shot Rabin could convince himself not only that God wanted him to act, but that much of Israel agreed.

Netanyahu likewise ignored the meaning of his own actions for Muslims. As a candidate he endorsed Yehudah Etzion's demand for Jewish prayer on the Mount; as prime minister, he once presented the local Greek Orthodox archbishop with a silver relief of Jerusalem—showing the Temple in place of the Muslim shrines. Carelessly, he fed Muslim fears that the Israeli government itself had designs against Al-Aqsa.

That sets the context for Netanyahu's eager relationship with the Christian right abroad. As his adviser David Bar-Illan succinctly said, he was concerned with what evangelicals did for Israel, not what they believed. Yet the alliance fostered expectations of Israel that would inevitably be disappointed—as exemplified by hopes that Netanyahu would build the Temple. It's no accident that fundamentalist leaders bragged of their ties with Netanyahu: By doing so, they reminded followers of how prophecy was "coming true" in Israel, and placed themselves on the prophetic stage.

But making alliances with religious extremists is not the mistake of one side alone. Yasser Arafat appointed Sheikh Ekrima Sa'id Sabri as grand mufti of Jerusalem, the top clerical post he had to give out. Arafat presumably sought religious legitimacy for his regime, even among fundamentalists. In fact he provided an influential pulpit to a cleric convinced of conspiracy theories and the prophetic certainty of Israel's destruction.

Religion can be separate from the state. It can't be driven out of politics. Politicians have a responsibility to examine the meaning their actions are likely to take on in the arena of faith. By seeking the support of fundamentalists or millennialists, political leaders also grant support to their version of religion. Ironically, a frontal attack on those groups can have the same effect. Yitzhak Rabin made that mistake when he disparagingly dismissed settlers as irrelevant, deepening their sense that Israel's mainstream had abandoned them. For that matter, labeling millennialists as "forces of evil"—as John McCain did during the 2000 Republican primary campaign, in a comment about Jerry Falwell and Pat Robertson—is likely to confirm their view of a world divided between God's people and all the rest. In either case, politicians help drown out the more numerous but quieter voices speaking other kinds of faith. And in either case, the millennalist cycle of over-confidence and despair becomes more intense.

Israel's relationship with American Christian fundamentalists is a case study in hard choices. Israel is strategically dependent on the United States, and its leaders have reason to seek political support in the American arena. But people who see Israel through the lens of Endtimes prophecy are questionable allies, whose support should be elicited only in the last resort. In the long run, their apocalyptic agenda has no room for Israel as a normal country. Boosting their expectations could well increase the acrimony when Israel's real needs lead it to depart from the "prophetic" program.

THE RHETORIC THAT MATTERS MOST, though, is that of the clergy.

In February 1999, two weeks after Jerry Falwell asserted that the Antichrist would be Jewish, he said he was sorry. Speaking at a prayer breakfast for Israel, Falwell said he "should have known better," and explained: "I apologize not for what I believe, but for my lack of tact and judgment in making a statement that served no purpose whatsoever."

At first glance, that's a thin expression of regret. And yet, the point deserves attention: The fact that he thought something was true didn't mean he had to say it. He should have considered how others would hear it. Issuing the apology, Falwell had in mind Jews who interpreted the comment as anti-Semitic. The audience that should have concerned him was his own community. For at least some listeners, his comments were likely to link Jews with demonic forces. It was irrelevant that he hadn't intended to fan anti-Semitism.

Let's take Falwell's half-apology even more seriously, and ask a wider question: What's the price of preaching the End? The profits of prophecy can be immediate. If you can convince people that this morning's headlines were predicted in the Bible, you've convinced them that the Book is divine and literally true. Persuade them that time is running out, and they won't want to procrastinate about repentance. Millennialism pours urgent meaning into religious acts. If spreading the Gospel, say, will hasten the End, it's far more worth risking the embarrassment of witnessing to strangers, or to friends.

Constant anticipation, though, breeds desire to set a date, a climax to complete the excitement. To stoke the delicious enthusiasm of the Last Days is to invite the depression that follows. And as religion scholar Stephen O'Leary argues, popular premillennial preachers "provide the petri dish" in which sects like Denver's Concerned Christians flourish—groups that find themselves foretold in scripture, that demand of followers to jettison family and former lives, that keep raising their bets on the End. The established leaders insist that such sects are aberrations, if not heretics. They're right. Yet the aberrations are people who took their message deadly seriously.

Out of all the people who have heard that fulfilling one more prophecy is a prerequisite for the Last Days, one or three or five may decide that God has chosen them to clear the ground for the Temple. Before Yitzhak Rabin's assassination, rightist rabbis suggested that giving up territory might be tantamount to a capital offense. Later they'd insist that was a metaphor: They intended only to emphasize the moral severity of the government's actions. But one man took the metaphors literally.

I mention to Carmi Gillon a rabbi's article in the far-right monthly *Your Jerusalem*, arguing that all Israel's troubles are punishment for not building the Temple since 1967. "You want to be a rabbi?" says the thoughtful man who resigned as Shin Bet chief after his agency's bodyguards failed to prevent Rabin's assassination. "It's a huge responsibility. You have to think not only about what you intend to say, you have to think about what people will understand you as saying." In that way, a clergyman is like a politician—except, says Gillon, that "a political leader is a passing shadow." A religious leader, in his followers' eyes, "is in touch with eternity."

Incitement need not be with malice aforethought, Gillon adds. "If a rabbi has something to say, let him say it, but he has to keep in mind that in the eighteenth row there's that one student who's interpreting his words."

But then, the trumpeters of the End are not about to lower their horns suddenly and silence their manic melody. The audience also has to make a choice: whether to listen to that fanfare, or to hear other, more sober melodies of faith.

WHITE PLASTIC CHAIRS have been set up in rows on a lawn shadowed by pines. There's a lectern under a grape arbor. A vague late-afternoon breeze whispers across Mount Zion and flutters the long jumpers of young women whose light skin and pale hair hint that they come from countries where the sun does not strike with Jerusalem's impossible intensity. The most common language that they and the young men with them speak is English. We're just outside the Old City's high walls, in the courtyard of Jerusalem University College, a place where young evangelicals come to study Bible. The setting is right for a graduation ceremony or wedding. It is hard to imagine, as the organizers of the Reconciliation Walk would like us to, that precisely nine hundred years before, in July of 1099, the Christian warriors of the First Crusade were methodically slaughtering the Muslims and Jews of Jerusalem in the name of Jesus.

The young men and women have walked the last leg of a pilgrimage that began three years before in Cologne, with the task of apologizing to people along the way for the atrocities of the Crusaders. Over two thousand Western Christians, mostly evangelicals, have taken part in the long march; today, here, at the gates of the city, the pilgrimage comes to its end. I've come to listen with a notebook and a large measure of cynicism. The fashion of asking forgiveness for historical crimes,

I again tell the friend sitting next to me, has reached absurdity: What can it possibly mean to confess the sins of people nine hundred years dead; what can it mean for the Jewish and Muslim and Greek Orthodox clerics near the podium to take turns accepting such atonement?

It takes Matthew Hand, one of the walk's organizers, about ninety seconds at the lectern to begin evaporating my cynicism. We could dismiss the murderousness of the Crusades as belonging to long ago, he says, if the end of the twentieth century hadn't witnessed the rise of religious wars, and of ethnic conflicts with a religious edge. To resist the slide back into the Middle Ages, Hand argues, we must understand the theology that drove the Crusaders. The average soldier of that day believed that "Christ's promised kingdom could be established . . . through military action"; he believed that "every Muslim he cut down represented a step nearer to Paradise," Hand says. "Our call is . . . to consider carefully our current views. Do we harbor a millenarian vision that is willing to sacrifice Jewish, Muslim, or Eastern Christian lives for the sake of an eschatological timetable?" The point of the apology is to renounce the motives of the Crusaders, he says; it's to affirm that Jesus saw the image of God in every person he met. This isn't about history, he's reminding the people he brought here, just past being kids. It's about what a person of faith is right now.

Afterward on the lawn I talk with another organizer, Cathy Nobles, an evangelical from Austin, Texas. She has been in charge of the lectures that groups of marchers get before setting out. She tells them that nine centuries ago, common people sought signs of the End—comets, unusual weather. As she lectures, she says, she can see in their faces that it hits them: Things haven't changed much. The marchers were sent to stand on street corners in Turkey and Lebanon, to offer their apology to passersby and shopkeepers. In form, it's a ritual they knew from hitting the streets to witness for Jesus. Except they weren't insisting they had the story that unbelievers had to hear. To apologize is to tell yourself that the other person has a story that's different from yours. The meaning of the ritual has been reversed, which is a mechanism for renewing a religion.

There are Jews, I suspect, who'd be unhappy with the Reconciliation Walk's impact: ones who count on evangelical backing for Israel keeping West Bank territory, or for Temple-building. Nobles speaks of Walk participants who have come to the project supporting Israel "as a step in the millennial plan," and who learn instead to see both Jews and Palestinians as people. There are Jews who'd rather be actors in a mythic drama, as long as they wear white hats and the Palestinians wear black. The pay, in political support, is good. And for a few, who have also convinced themselves that the drama of the End is underway, there's a basic empathy with Christian Endtimes believers, no matter how much they disagree on the final scene. I'd prefer to take the chance of political criticism, shed the role, and regain humanity. Cathy Nobles and Matthew Hand use a different religious vocabulary than mine; I would not make light of the differences in our commitments; but listening to them, I feel a basic empathy.

A theology fitting for the Reconciliation Walk can be found in Darrell Fasching's *The Coming of the Millennium: Good News for the Whole Human Race*. The book's title is a feint; Fasching, a professor of religious ethics who might best be described as dissident evangelical, scathingly attacks millennialism. People are not just storytellers, Fasching says, but "story dwellers," shaped by and living out the tales they tell. The tale of apocalypse is one of blessed catastrophe, in which the children of light gain bliss and the children of darkness burn. The story was acted out most fully by Hitler, a self-proclaimed messiah, Fasching says: "The Nazi vision of heaven was that of a village of pure German Aryans, eating, drinking and making merry, while next door the fires of hell, the death camps, transformed Jewish bodies into smoke . . ." And the tale is still being told by contemporary prophecy writers, exemplified by Hal Lindsey: "Lindsey, like Hitler . . . taps the all too human desire for uniformity and it leads him to a vision, similar to Hitler's, of apocalyptic purification of the earth through violence and death." Lindsey suggests that Armageddon will come through nuclear holocaust. Wishing for cataclysm, Fasching demonstrates, becomes Lindsey's test for being a good Christian, and the wish awaits someone who will try to make it come true. Against that vision, Fasching argues for a Christianity whose essential value is welcoming the stranger, the person unlike yourself. Instead of assigning the Other a part in a Christian drama of the End, Fasching calls for Christians to open themselves to the story that people of other faiths tell.

I mention Fasching's book, and the Reconciliation Walk, as small reminders: Religions have many voices. Even in a movement where millennialism is mainstream, it cannot have a monopoly. Fundamentalists and "near-fundamentalists," Fasching tells me, "think they have a corner on scripture." He wrote his book, he says, in order to show that a careful reading of the Bible can lead in other directions.

The point bears underlining: We live in a time when extremism is confused with religious authenticity, and not just in Protestantism. Purveyors of "literal" readings of sacred books claim to represent old-time religion, unadulterated by modernity. Yet literalism, apparently a mark of the conservative, is often the method of millennialists who look forward to an entirely new world. They place prophetic texts at the center of religion—and insist that the words must be read as factual, tactile accounts of the future.

So Jerusalem architect Gideon Charlap told me that the Jewish liturgy refers to the reestablishment of the Temple, and "if we're not going to build the Temple, we have to get rid of that prayer." And so, say premillennialist prophecy writers, if Zechariah speaks of a siege of Jerusalem, there will be a siege of Jerusalem; if Revelation tells that the fourth horseman of apocalypse has "power over the fourth part of the earth, to kill with the sword, and with hunger, and with death, and with beasts of the earth," well then, the good Lord has a working plan for 25 percent of the global population to perish as part of His salvation. As a mark of the End, Jesus says "the abomination of desolation" will "stand in the holy place," phrases that are less transparent, but premillennial literalists read them as referring to a point in the future when the Temple will be descrated. Therefore, blueprints for a new Temple must be in God's drawer of plans. Ezekiel lists nations such as Magog, Meshech, and Gomer. By the time we get to Hal Lindsey deciphering those names in 1970 as referring to Russia and the "Iron Curtain countries," who will invade Israel and might be destroyed by nuclear weapons, we have reason to wonder what is literal about this reading. The man who says, "I *hate* those who read their ideas into the scripture by using allegory," seems as capable as any allegorist of reading what he wants into scripture.

The literalism, rather, is in the millennialists' certainty that a sacred text is speaking entirely of physical places, dateable events—that it is describing the future in the manner of a cruise itinerary on the

travel agent's desk, even if the date is blurry and we don't quite remember the geographical names from fourth grade. Follow the itinerary, and the last stop is the renewed Garden, where human beings can
no longer do evil and need no longer suffer.

To read a religious work in this manner is the equivalent of reading Blake's lines in "The Tyger":

> *What the hammer? what the chain?*
> *In what furnace was thy brain?*
> *What the anvil? what dread grasp*
> *Dare its deadly terrors clasp?*

and then go looking for the anvil God used to make tigers. This isn't a
new problem. For centuries religions have seen debates between
those looking for a single, certain meaning in Holy Writ and those insisting on its infinite metaphoric possibilities. Yet literalism resonates
particularly well in an age of science and technology, despite the anti-
scientific conclusions that religious literalists can reach on matters
such as evolution. Our culture promotes confidence that technology
will solve our problems. A man or woman can be highly educated and
still expect all writing to aim for the single meanings of an anatomy
text, where ambiguity represents a mistake, not an opening. In content, millennialism appears as the opposite of science; in form, it repeats the promise of scientific salvation.

Sacred texts aim for meanings words can't get themselves around.
They admit countless interpretations. Within one tradition, the interpretations bang up against each other in loud contradictions. Literalism seductively promises that you'll know just what God wants of you.
But in reality everyone chooses an interpretation, and its moral consequences. "The way Hal Lindsey reads the Bible is unethical," states
Darrell Fasching.

To which millennialism's philosophical defenders would answer:
Millennialism is ethically essential. That defense can be heard from
academic scholars of religion and of politics; I've heard it as well from
old friends, politically active, whose messianism is purely secular. The
dream of the perfected kingdom underlies every radical hope to transform the world, says this argument. The effort to realize the millen-

nium is the engine of human progress, it says. The political alternative is conservatism; the religious alternative is accepting suffering.

The binary choice, 1 for millennium, 0 for status quo, has to be rejected. The resurgent religious millennialism of recent years may be only the afterwave of the political messianism that shook the world in the twentieth century, and the price of both must be faced.

"If a person expects a total solution, he's willing to kill 30 million people—that's Stalin," argues Jerusalem rabbi and Orthodox philosopher David Hartman. Hartman is also a dissident voice, a religious Zionist who rejects messianism. The Six-Day War, he says, brought the feeling among Orthodox Zionists that they were the instruments of redemption. The mistake that leads to is the feeling that "if I am an instrument for redeeming the world, I can't be doing evil. I'm ushering in a new era in history, and therefore I don't see what I'm doing to Arabs, I don't see what I'm doing to the country."

The function of the messianic vision is to serve as a criticism of the world as it is. The crucial error is to believe that we can reach the perfected era. As Hartman argues: "If you think the world should be a place without war and without poverty, that is a catalyst for enormous moral energy. But it's not a description of a condition in history."

The purveyors of the millennium, in religious or political garb, say that we will really get there. They promise to transform human nature so that people are free of daily choices between good and evil. After the revolution, you won't need to be afraid of pickpockets. You won't have to be afraid of yourself. In the new era, either sexual desire will end, or sexual jealousy will. It is a beautiful promise, and it is always broken.

People are story dwellers. In particular, they live in stories passed down, rewritten, and preserved by long cultural tradition. As a story acted out by people seeking great political change, millennialism is likely to end in despair: Total transformation doesn't come, and those who sought it may feel that politics itself is a deceiver, or that the dream of a better world is inherently treacherous. But millennialism is certainly not the only story of change embedded in Western culture.

In fact, as political philosopher Michael Walzer demonstrates in his *Exodus and Revolution,* the messianic story is a manic retelling of an older tale of deliverance: the Israelites' exodus from Egypt. In that drama, a people leave bondage, wander in the desert, accept laws, and enter the promised land. This is a model for politics of hope—but a different hope from what millennialism offers. The Israelites are liberated from slavery, not from history. They're free, but accept laws, because they know they need them; they have not become angels. They enter a promised land, a better place than Egypt—but not a perfect place: Canaan isn't Eden. If they're not careful they can lose their freedom—or become pharaohs themselves. The Exodus is not the end; it is the start of a new chapter, whose outcome is not forewritten.

As Walzer shows, the liberation from Egypt has repeatedly served political radicals, but fosters a more sober radicalism. "There is no ultimate struggle, but a long series of decisions, backslidings, and reforms," Walzer says. Because it does not offer absolute deliverance, Exodus politics does not justify absolute means. It abjures catastrophe because we will still be in this world and we don't want it ruined.

If we want great changes, we still have a choice of which story to live in. It's a point I take personally: In Jerusalem, I live on a stage where both stories have been acted out for a century or more, and it's up to both actors and audience to decide which one is in progress. Exodus politics and messianism, as Walzer argues, have been "radically entangled" in Zionism. For most Zionists, probably, the account that fits better, if and when they consider the matter, is the Exodus: Jews have left many Egypts and come to their own land. After that liberation, all the hard choices that come with having power begin.

As we've seen, though, images of final redemption were woven into Zionism from the start. And for some on the political right, messianism was more than a thread; it was the whole fabric. Yet political messianism gained its greatest legitimacy and widest support when it merged with religious messianism. The conquests of 1967 were the catalyst: For redemptive Zionists, physically possessing Hebron, Jericho, Shiloh, Old Jerusalem, and the Temple Mount proved that the final act was under way. Watched through a very different theological lens, the conquest had the same meaning for premillennialist Christians in front-row seats. Both literalism and the false hope of history's end fed the enthusiasm. Those two fallacies were joined with a third ancient error: that God could be owned by owning a place.

I'M SITTING IN A CAFÉ on Emek Refa'im Street in Jerusalem with Rabbi Shmuel Reiner. Emek Refa'im is where King David defeated the Philistines; I could find some meaning in that were I inclined to, but I'm not. You've got to weed out a lot of history and prophecy to get through a day in this town. Stick to now: This is the street for sitting in sidewalk cafés and catching old friends from grad school or other newspapers as they stroll past, the way you do in places where the world is not about to end. I'm nearly at the same table where I sat with Shmaria Shore months before, listening to him discuss whether raising a red heifer played any part in redemption.

Reiner speaks with many pauses, as if he's looking over each word carefully before putting it into play. "Redemption" isn't one of his words. "I'm a rabbi of continuity," he tells me, which means: not of radical historic breaks. That doesn't make him a defender of status quos. The yeshivah he heads, at a religious kibbutz on Mount Gilboa, is on the liberal edge of Israeli Orthodoxy. All the energy that religious Zionism has poured into nationalism he would like to pour into ethical demands. Years ago, it was Reiner who warned me of growing interest in Temple-building.

The Orthodox prayerbook has prayers for the Temple, I point out, as devil's advocate. Religion isn't printed words, he answers. It's how you interpret them; a rabbi chooses what values will guide his interpretation. Reiner could be quoting Darrell Fasching. Once I edited an article Reiner wrote on the Passover sacrifice. He did not suggest that today's Jews live in a warped reality because they can't make that offering. Working his way through the verses, he came to the demand that Jews struggle against the exploitation of illegal immigrants, because "ye were strangers in the land of Egypt."

Sacrifices aside, he says, half-surprising me, the symbol of the Temple has a value. "Sometimes I feel that to get up and go to a place that's outside all routine is an experience we need. . . . But the need is enough. There's a kind of thing you dream of, but the moment the dream comes true, it's not *it.*" A summary of what millennialists forget: There are things worth wanting that you cannot possibly acquire.

Eighteen hundred years ago, Rabbi Levi retold the story of Cain and Abel: The brothers agreed to divide the world—and then each claimed the place where the Temple would be built. They fought, Cain killed Abel, and bloodshed entered the world. You can read that as meaning: They thought they could corner a monopoly on truth, and it was worth killing for. It can mean: They thought they could own the Temple Mount, and have the gate to heaven. Or it can mean: Each thought that if he owned the place, he would have the key to the End. Rabbi Levi put the story at the beginning of time in order to say that it's engraved in human beings. It is a challenge we must continually contend with: Every day, Cain could kill Abel for the Temple Mount—or resist the impulse and lower his hand.

acknowledgments

THIS BOOK would not have been possible without the help and patience of my wife, Myra Noveck, my son, Yehonatan, and my daughters Elisheva and Shir-Raz. Besides putting up with a man possessed, my wife constantly helped sharpen my thoughts and assisted in the research; both she and my son read the manuscript as I wrote.

I began exploring the story told here in my writing for *The Jerusalem Report* and *The New Republic.* I'm grateful for the support and assistance of *Report* editor David Horovitz, founder Hirsh Goodman, and my fellow staffers, and of Martin Peretz at *The New Republic.*

Sharon Ashley, friend and colleague, read the entire manuscript. Parts were read by David Cook, Joseph Heller, Chris Lehmann, and Menachem Klein. Sometimes I was wise enough to accept their suggestions.

During my research, I've spent countless hours in conversation with people whose names appear in the text, and with some whose names are absent by their request. They include millennial believers and Temple activists and their opponents, government officials, and others. I'm appreciative of their willingness to share their time, and often their deepest concerns and hopes.

I've had the opportunity to learn from many scholars. Richard Landes of the Center for Millennial Studies originally focused my attention on the place of the Temple Mount in the visions of three religions, and has constantly given me insights since. David Cook shared with me his knowledge of Muslim apocalyptic thought and allowed me to make use of his writing on the subject before publication. Ehud Sprinzak not only provided his knowledge of political extremism, but allowed me access to invaluable documents. Menachem

Klein, Stephen O'Leary, Albert Baumgarten, Joseph Heller, Aren Maeir, Chip Berlet, Andrew Gow, Jean-Francois Mayer, Catherine Wessinger, Michael Barkun, Amnon Ramon, Ifrach Zilberman, Moshe Idel, Avi Ravitsky, Elchanan Reiner, Yaakov Ariel, Nancy Ammerman, Lynn Collette and others gave of their time and expertise. Naturally, I am solely responsible for how I have chosen to interpret their ideas.

In exploring Jerusalem's geography and past, I had the invaluable assistance of David Eisenstadt. Attorney Daniel Seidemann helped me research the financing of right-wing groups. Jerusalem District Psychiatrist Yair Bar-El was always ready to discuss the city's self-appointed prophets. Yigal Carmon shared his research on millennial disappointment. Rabbi David Rosen, director of the Jerusalem office of the Anti-Defamation League, added to my understanding of Christian-Jewish relations.

In telling a story that ties Jerusalem to distant places, I've enjoyed much help from colleagues in the media. Charlie Brennan of the *Denver Rocky Mountain News,* Christina Yao of KCNC-TV, and Elaine Ruth Fletcher of the Religion News Service pooled resources with me in covering the Concerned Christians. Michael Kaufman and David Cay Johnston at *The New York Times,* Larry Cohler-Esses and Eric Greenberg at *The Jewish Week,* and Cecile Holmes at the *Houston Chronicle* helped me with information, contacts, and understandings, as did others. Special thanks go to *Jerusalem Report* archivist Freda Covitz. I'm also indebted to Richard Reynolds at *Mother Jones,* and to archivists at *Kol Ha'ir* and *The Jerusalem Post* for access to news reports available on no computer.

Ora Ahimeir and Hamutal Appel at the Jerusalem Institute for Israel Studies and David Kessler at the Center for Millennial Studies helped with research materials and contacts with scholars. Tia Sumler at People for the American Way provided material on the American religious right; Susan Stawick at the Internal Revenue Service helped me receive financial reports of nonprofit organizations, as did state officials in New York and California, and the staff of Israel's NPO registrar.

Last, but certainly not least, I'm grateful to Sidney Bernstein for his encouragement, to my agent Lisa Bankoff, and to my editors Alys Yablon and Paul Golob at The Free Press.

Jerusalem, April 2000

NOTES

Much of the story told in this book is based on extensive interviews—with the people described here and others, some of whom asked to remain anonymous—and on my own observation of some of the events described. The notes below list selected documentary sources.

Introduction

1   *The bell tolled:* Material on the Movement for the Restoration of the Ten Commandments drawn from reports published March 18, 2000, and after by *The New York Times, The Washington Post,* Associated Press, and Reuters, and from the Kampala newspapers *New Vision* and *The Monitor,* accessed via the website of the Center for Studies on New Religions, *http://www.cesnur.org/testi/uganda_updates.htm.* For previous dates for the End, see Karl Vick, "Ugandan Cult Orchestrated Doomsday," *The Washington Post,* April 1, 2000; report on Credonia as charlatan: "Ugandans Seek Answers to Mass Murder," AP, April 1, 2000.

6   *A Jewish text records:* Breshit Rabbah 22:7.

One: CATTLEMEN OF THE APOCALYPSE

8   *one U.S. evangelical website:* Ashes of the Red Heifer," *http://www.direct.ca/trinity/ashes.html.*

8   *The Mishneh Torah:* Mose Maimonides, *Mishneh Torah,* Parah Adumah 3:4.

9   *his son ran home:* Shore attributed this account to the Israeli ultra-Orthodox press.

9   *The next day, a newspaper:* The story appeared in *Ha'aretz,* March 20, 1997; *The Boston Globe,* April 6, 1997; *Chicago Tribune,* May 29, 1997. Shore told me of Zik's radio report.

10 *On the opinion page:* David Landau, "A Red Heifer—It's Not Funny," *Ha'aretz,* March 26, 1997.

11 *The rite of the red heifer:* Baruch Schwartz, "Beyond Comprehension?" in *Seventy Facets: A Commentary on the Torah from the Pages of the Jerusalem Report,* Gershom Gorenberg, ed. (Northvale, N.J.: Jason Aronson, 1996).

11 *Yohanan ben Zakkai asserted:* Bemidbar Rabbah 19:8.

13 *The statement issued:* "Announcement and Warning," Jerusalem, 1967.

14 *We are stardust:* Joni Mitchell, "Woodstock," Siquomb Publishing Co., 1969.

15 *One of the group's:* Yeshua Ben-Shushan's confession; Judge Ya'akov Bazak's verdict, p. 18.

15 *In a verdict:* File 84/203, Dan Be'eri, verdict of Judge Tzvi Cohen, p. 3.

15 *Interior Minister Eli:* quoted in "Suissa: Annex Areas East of Jerusalem and Increase Its Jewish Majority," *Ha'aretz,* April 17, 1997.

16 *Reverend Irvin Baxter:* Irvin Baxter, Jr., "The World's Most Famous Cow," *Endtime,* July/August 1997.

16 *The televangelist Jack Van Impe:* "Holy Cow!" http://www.jvim.com/IntelligenceBriefing/jul1997/cover.html.

16 *In his Internet newsletter:* http://www.levitt.com/ *Levitt Letter,* July 1997: Vol. 19, No. 7 "A Note From Zola."

17 *Deflecting the Arrows:* Jamal al-Din, Amin Muhammad, *Radd al-siham 'an kitab 'Umr ummat al-Islam.* Cairo: al-Maktaba al-Tawfiqiyya, n.d., pp 47–48, translation courtesy of David Cook.

20 *The cows on the screen:* "Cattle on Ranch in O'Neil, Nebraska" (video), Canaan Land Restoration of Israel, Inc., Waverly, Tenn. Additional sources on the Lott-Richman red heifer project include "Rev Clyde Lott: Gulf Shores AL" (video), Canaan Land Restoration of Israel, Inc., Waverly, Tenn.; Chaim Richman, *The Mystery of the Red Heifer: Divine Promise of Purity* (Jerusalem, 1997); and correspondence and other documents provided by Reverend Guy Garner.

21 *I will pass:* Genesis 30:32.

23 *That's not the only:* B. Talmud, Kedushin 31a; Jerusalem Talmud, Pe'ah 3a; other rabbinic sources.

Two: THE HISTORY OF THE FUTURE

30 *Nicolae: The Rise of Antichrist:* Tim LaHaye and Jerry B. Jenkins (Wheaton, Ill.: Tyndale House, 1997). Other books in the series: *Left Behind,* 1995; *Tribulation Force,* 1996; *Soul Harvest,* 1998; *Apollyon,* 1999; *Assassins,* 1999; *The Indwelling: The Beast Takes Possession,* 2000. Information on Jenkins from *http://www.jerryjenkins.com/.* Sources on LaHaye include David Cantor, *The Religious Right: The Assault on Tolerance and Pluralism in America* (New York: Anti-Defamation League, 1994); Megan Rosenfeld, "All Around, the Sound of Celebration," *The Washington Post,* Jan. 22, 1985; "Catholicism Is 'False,' Kemp Backer Writes," *Houston Chronicle,* Dec. 5, 1987, reprinted from the *Baltimore Sun;* Maralee Schwartz et al., "Controversial Evangelist Leaves Kemp's Campaign," *The Washington Post,* Tuesday, Dec. 8, 1987; Don Lattin, "Same Religious, Political Flock but Far from Birds of a Feather," *Houston Chronicle,* April 21, 1985.

33 *The "Rapture of:* Sources on Darby and dispensationalism include Paul Boyer, *When Time Shall Be No More* (Cambridge and London: Harvard University Press, 1992); Timothy P. Weber, *Living in the Shadow of the Second Coming* (Chicago: University of Chicago Press, 1983); Randall Balmer, *Mine Eyes Have Seen the Glory* (New York and Oxford: Oxford University Press, 1993).

33 *the Lord shall descend:* I Thessalonians 4:16–17.

33 *this corruptible shall:* I Corinthians 15:53.

36 *Those millions of readers:* On the strength of evangelicalism and pre-millennialism, see Brenda E. Brasher, "When Your Friend is Your Enemy: American Christian Fundamentalists and Israel at the New Millennium," in Martha F. Lee, ed., *Millennial Visions: Essays on Twentieth-Century Millenarianism* (Greenwood Publishing Group, 2000); Boyer, op. cit., Balmer, op. cit., Damian Thompson, *The End of Time: Faith and Fear in the Shadow of the Millennium* (Hanover and London: University Press of New England, 1996).

39 *Mao assured: Quotations from Chairman Mao Tse-Tung* (Peking: Foreign Language Press, 1967), p. 23.

39 *rulers of Sodom:* Isaiah 1:10.

39 *the end of days:* Isaiah 2:2.

39 *a day of the Lord:* Isaiah 13:9.

39 *Zechariah detailed:* Zechariah 14.

40 *catastrophic millennialism:* Catherine Wessinger, "The Interacting Dynamics of Millennial Beliefs, Persecution, and Violence," in Catherine Wessinger, ed., *Millennialism, Persecution, and Violence: Historical Cases* (Syracuse: Syracuse University Press, 2000).

40   *In the second century B.C.E.:* Elias Bickerman, *From Ezra to the Last of the Maccabees* (New York: Schocken, 1962); Boyer, op. cit.

41   *Another sage, speaking:* Jerusalem Talmud, Ta'anit 4.

41   *nine-tenths of Judea's Jews:* Yehoshafat Harkabi, *Betokef Hametziut (Facing Reality: Lessons from Jeremiah, The Destruction of the Second Temple and Bar Kochva's Rebellion),* (Jerusalem: Van Leer Jerusalem Foundation, 1981).

42   *The kingdom of God:* Mark 1:15.

42   *If we're wondering:* Mark Galli, "Sliver in a Forest," *Christianity Today,* No. 61.

42   *sign of thy coming:* Matthew 24:3.

42   *abomination of desolation:* Matthew 24:15.

42   *In a passage:* B. Talmud, Sanhedrin 97a–99a.

43   *a third version:* On Islam and apocalypse, see David Cook, "Islam and Apocalyptic," at *http://www.mille.org;* David Cook, *"The Hour Will Not Arrive Until . . .": Studies in Muslim Apocalyptic* (Darwin Press, forthcoming); David Cook, "Muslim Fears of the Year 2000," *Middle East Quarterly,* June 1998; "al-Mahdi," "Isa," "Sa'a," and "al-Dadjdjal," *Encyclopaedia of Islam* (new edition), H. A. R. Gibb, E. Levi-Provencal, et al., eds. (Leiden: E.J.Brill, 1960–).

44   *the faithful city:* Isaiah 1:21.

44   *the mountain of the Lord's:* Isaiah 2:2–3.

46   *The most daring theodicy:* Stephen D. O'Leary, *Arguing the Apocalypse: A Theory of Millennial Rhetoric* (Oxford University Press, 1998).

47   *weighed in the balance:* Daniel 5:27.

47   *time of Shabtai Tzvi:* Sources include the following books by Gershom Scholem: *Sabbatai Sevi: The Mystical Messiah* (Princeton: Princeton University Press, 1973); *The Messianic Idea in Judaism* (New York: Schocken, 1971); *Kabbalah* (New York: Quadrangle/New York Times, 1974).

49   *England of the time:* Barbara W. Tuchman, *Bible and Sword: England and Palestine from the Bronze Age to Balfour* (New York: New York University Press, 1956)

50   *The lead article:* "Return of the Jews," *The Signs of the Times,* June 1, 1842. On the Millerites: Boyer, op. cit.; Thompson, op. cit.

53   *When we watch:* Chuck Missler, *The Coming Temple Update* (Audio-cassettes, Coeur d'Alene, Idaho: Koinonia House, 1995).

Three: THE GATE OF HEAVEN

56   *inscriptions from the Koran:* On the Dome and Haram, see *The Dome of the Rock,* text by Oleg Grabar, photography by Said Nuseibeh (New York: Rizzoli, 1996).

56   *Lindsey once thought:* Hal Lindsey with C. C. Carlson, *The Late Great Planet Earth* (originally published by Zondervan Publishing House, 1970).

60   *A Talmudic legend:* Mishnah Yoma 5:2; B. Talmud Yoma 54b.

60   *Another legend moves:* Breshit Rabbah 14:8.

60   *Not only was Adam:* Mishneh Torah, Beit Habehirah 2:1–2.

60   *Mount Moriah:* II Chronicles 3:1.

61   *priest of God:* Genesis 14:18.

62   *brutish and a stranger:* Josephus, *Antiquities of the Jews,* XVI 5:4.

62   *An alternative reading:* Meir Ben-Dov, *In the Shadow of the Temple: The Discovery of Ancient Jerusalem* (Jerusalem: Keter, 1985).

62   *a few aristocrats:* Louis Finkelstein, ed., *The Jews: Their History* (New York: Schocken, 1970).

62   *a rich man shall:* Matthew 19:23.

62   *Instead, he built:* Ben-Dov, op. cit.

63   *A fourth-century traveler:* Quoted in Dan Bahat, *The Illustrated Atlas of Jerusalem* (Jerusalem: Carta, 1990), pp. 65–66.

65   *he argued in the Biblical:* Asher Kaufman, "Where the Ancient Temple of Jerusalem Stood, *Biblical Archaeological Review,* March/April 1983, pp. 41–59.

68   *the Gospels quote:* Mark 13:1–2, Matthew 24:1–2, Luke 21:6.

68   *Forty years before:* B. Talmud Yoma 39b.

68   *hidden in a coffin:* B. Talmud Gittin 56a–b.

68   *Before, the ram's horn:* Mishnah Rosh Hashanah 4:1, and see Lee I. A. Levine, "Judaism from the Destruction of Jerusalem to the End of the Second Jewish Revolt: 70–135 CE," in Hershel Shanks, *Christianity and Rabbinic Judaism: A Parallel History of Their Origins and Early Development* (Washington, D.C.: Biblical Archaeology Society, 1992); Elchanan Reiner, "Temple, Destruction and Sacred Place: A Medieval Concept of Sacred Places," in *Sefer Hayovel Likhvod Felix Posen* (Tel Aviv: Alma Hebrew College, forthcoming).

69   *prophecy was taken:* B. Talmud Bava Batra 12b.

69   *the pleasure of sex:* Babylonian Talmud Sanhedrin 75a.

69   *If you have a sapling:* See Levine, op. cit., pp. 134–35.

69   *Christian philosopher Justin:* Dialogue of Justin, Philosopher and Martyr with Trypho, a Jew, Chaps. 21–26.

70   *what Muslims today:* Grabar, pp. 43, 47; private communication from David Cook, summarizing al-Tabari, *Jami' al-bayan* XV, pp. 1–18.

71   *"Glory be to Him:* Koran 17:1.

71   *The troops of the caliph:* On the conquest, sources include "Al-Kuds" in *Encyclopaedia of Islam,* op. cit.; Shlomo D. Gotein, "Jerusalem in the Arab Period (638–1099)," in L. Levine, *The Jerusalem Cathedra* (Jerusalem, 1982); Moshe Gil, "The Political History of Jerusalem During the Early Muslim Period," in Ben-Shammai and Prawer, *The*

Political History of Jerusalem: The Early Muslim Period (638–1099), 1996.

72   *Muslim texts praising:* Cook, *The Hour Will Not Come Until,* op. cit.

78   *To locate the Temple, Ritmeyer:* Leen Ritmeyer, "Locating the Original Temple Mount," *Biblical Archaeological Review,* March–April 1992; "The Ark of the Covenant: Where It Stood in Solomon's Temple, *Biblical Archaeological Review,* Jan.-Feb.,1996.

80   *The idea was popular:* Tuchman, op. cit.

Four: FOR GOD AND COUNTRY

81   *For Muslims, that:* Description of the 1929 riots based on Tom Segev, *Yemei Hakalaniot (Palestine Under the British)* (Jerusalem: Keter, 1999); Y. Porath, *The Emergence of the Palestinian-Arab National Movement 1918–1929* (London: Frank Cass, 1974); *Report of the Commission on the Palestine Disturbances of August 1929* (London, 1939); Ann Mosely Lesch, "The Palestine Arab Nationalist Movement Under the Mandate," in William B. Quandt et al., *The Politics of Palestinian Nationalism* (Berkeley: University of California Press, 1973); Yigal Lusin, *Amud Ha'esh* (Jerusalem: Shikmonah, 1982); Fred J. Khouri, *The Arab-Israeli Dilemma* (Syracuse: Syracuse University Press, 1968).

81   *A photo of a few:* Appears in Lusin, op. cit., p. 163.

82   *A girl named Rivka:* Quoted in Lusin, op. cit., p. 167.

83   *A 1998 report:* "Jerusalem, Our Capital," *http://www.pna.net/jerusalem/jeru_in_danger.htm.*

83   *Pro-Israeli histories often:* For example, Binyamin Eliav, ed., *The Jewish National Home from the Balfour Declaration to Independence* (Jerusalem: Keter, 1976).

84   *Start with the British:* On millennialism and the Balfour Declaration, see Tuchman, op. cit.

85   *despite all his zeal:* Ibid., p. 115.

86   *unmindful of the service:* Ibid., p. 202.

86   *Weizmann "kept bringing":* Ibid., p. 206.

86   *The harnessing of religious:* On Herzl's pragmatic Zionism, see Arthur Hertzberg's introduction in his *The Zionist Idea* (New York: Atheneum, 1973).

87   *house which is to shelter:* Herzl's address to the first Zionist Congress, quoted in Howard M. Sachar, *A History of Israel: From the Rise of Zionism to Our Time* (New York: Knopf, 1979).

87   *Yet Jews found it easy:* Illustrations described here and below appear in Rachel Arbel, ed., *Kahol Lavan Bitzva'im: Dimui'im Hazuti'im shel Hatzionut 1897–1947* (Tel Aviv: Am Oved/Beth Hatefutsoth, 1996);

Igal Avidan, "The Watch on the Rhine," *The Jerusalem Report,* June 12, 1997.

87 *A 1912 photo:* In Nachum T. Gidal, *Land of Promise: Photographs from Palestine 1850–1948* (Tel Aviv: Steimatzky, 1985).

88 *The alternative was developed:* See Aviezer Ravitsky, *Hatketz Hameguleh Umedinat Hayehudim (Messianism, Zionism and Jewish Religious Radicalism)* (Tel Aviv: Am Oved, 1993); Yosef Avivi, "Historiah Tzorekh Gavo'ah," in Moshe Ben-Asher, ed., *Sefer Hayovel Lerav Mordechai Breuer* (Jerusalem: Akademon, 1992), Vol. II.

89 *Let us swear that:* Quoted in Segev, op. cit., p. 250.

90 *Hajj Amin al-Husseini was appointed:* On al-Husseini's appointment and role in the 1929 disturbances, see Porath, op. cit.

91 *Avraham Stern was:* On Stern and Lehi, see Sachar, op. cit.; Jehuda Wallach, *Carta's Atlas of Palestine from Zionism to Statehood* (Jerusalem: Carta, 1972, 1974).

92 *Eldad, after the biblical:* Numbers 11:26.

92 *the group's veterans republished: Lohamei Herut Yisrael: Ketavim* (Hava'ad Lehotza'at Kitvei Lehi), Vol. I.

92 *Shaltiel was forty-five:* Shaltiel's biography based on an interview with his widow and Larry Collins and Dominique Lapierre, *O Jerusalem* (London: Pan, 1973).

94 *commander of the Lehi:* Collins and Lapierre, op. cit.; Nadav Shragai, *Har Hamerivah: Hama'avak Al Har Habayit (The Temple Mount Conflict)* (Jerusalem: Keter, 1995).

94 *And the heart imagines:* Yisrael Eldad (Scheib), *Ma'aser Rishon: Pirkei Zikhronot Umusar Heskel,* p. 363.

95 *In his 1996 book:* John Hagee, *Beginning of the End: The Assassination of Yitzhak Rabin and the Coming Antichrist* (Nashville: Thomas Nelson, 1996).

95 *Learn a parable:* Matthew 24:32–34.

96 *Where is our Hebron:* Kook's speech republished in *Nekudah* (Jerusalem), No. 86, April 1985.

96 *Jerusalem of Gold:* Hebrew lyrics appear at *http://www.israel-mfa.gov.il/mfa/go.asp?MFAG005e0.* The story about Rabin appears at *http://www.jerusalemofgold.co.il/thesong.html.*

97 *For Israelis, the three:* On the buildup to war, see Sachar, op. cit.; Khouri, op. cit.; Jehuda Wallach, *Carta's Atlas of Israel's Second Decade 1961–1971* (in Hebrew) (Jerusalem: Carta, 1980).

98 *When Colonel Mordechai Gur:* On the battle for the Old City, see Motta [Mordechai] Gur, *Har Habayit Beyadenu* (Ma'arakhot, 1973); Uzi Narkiss, *Ahat Yerushalayim (The Liberation of Jerusalem)* (Tel Aviv: Am Oved, 1975); Yisrael Harel and Motta [Mordechai] Gur, eds., *Sha'ar Ha'arayot: Hakrav Al Yerushalayim Behavayat Lohamei Hati-*

vat Hatzanhanim (Ma'arakhot); Uzi Benziman, *Yerushalayim: Ir Lelo Homah* (Jerusalem and Tel Aviv: Schocken, 1973).

98   *all that Vatican:* Narkiss, op. cit., p. 215.

100   *There was one incident:* Nadav Shragai, "Rabbi, Stop," *Ha'aretz,* Dec. 31, 1997.

100   *Ariel would later:* Shragai, *Har Hamerivah,* op. cit.; Haggai Segal, *Dear Brothers: The West Bank Jewish Underground* (Woodmere, N.Y.: Beit-Shammai, 1988).

101   *of an Orthodox paratrooper:* See Harel and Gur, op. cit.

101   *it came from Goren:* interview with a rabbinic colleague of Kook who requested anonymity, supported by Zorach Warhaftig's description of the two as being in "Goren's vehicle."

101   *Zorach Warhaftig heard:* Sources include Zorach Warhaftig, *Hamishim Shanah Veshanah* (Jerusalem: Yad Shapira, 1998).

102   *That night the bulldozers:* See Amnon Barzilai, "How the Mughrabi Quarter Was Razed," *Ha'aretz,* May 13, 1999; Teddy Kollek, *For Jerusalem: A Life* (New York: Random House, 1978).

103   *On the Saturday:* Benziman, op. cit.; Moshe Dayan, *Story of My Life* (London: Weidenfeld and Nicolson, 1976).

Five: A TASTE OF PARADISE

107   *Dennis Michael Rohan:* Sources on Rohan include *The State of Israel v. Dennis Michael Rohan, 173/69,* verdict and testimony; Nadav Shragai, *Har Hamerivah,* op. cit.; Abraham Rabinovich, "Rohan, 'King of Jerusalem,'" *The Jerusalem Post,* August 20, 1999; Benziman, op. cit.; reports of *The New York Times* and *The Times* of London, Aug. 24–26, 1969.

109   *premillennialist writer Randall:* Randall Price, *Jerusalem in Prophecy: God's Stage for the Final Drama* (Eugene, Ore.: Harvest House, 1998), p. 355.

112   *Kook and his disciples:* Ravitsky, op. cit.

113   *Secular politicans and intellectuals:* See Ehud Sprinzak, *The Ascendance of Israel's Radical Right* (New York and Oxford: Oxford University Press, 1991).

113   *The first Orthodox group:* On settlement and Gush Emunim, see Sprinzak, op. cit.; Segal, op. cit.

114   *When Israel's parliament:* Segal, op. cit., p. 43.

114   *In the first days:* Benziman, op. cit., p. 157.

115   *The government worked:* On legal status of Jewish prayer on the Mount, see Shmuel Berkovits, *Hama'amad Hamishpati shel Mekomot Hakedoshim Biyerushalayim* (Jerusalem: Jerusalem Institute for Israel Studies, 1997); Shragai, *Har Hamerivah,* op. cit.; Menachem

Klein, *Yonim Bishmei Yerushalayim (Doves in the Jerusalem Sky)* (Jerusalem: Jerusalem Institute for Israel Studies, 1999).

116   *Israel's chief rabbis:* "Announcement and Warning," Jerusalem, 1967.

116   *he set a limit:* See Shlomo Haim Hakohen Aviner, *Shalhevetyah: Pirkei Kodesh Umikdash* (Jerusalem: 1989).

116   *Shabtai Ben-Dov filed:* Shragai, op. cit.; Segal, op. cit.

116   *Lehi ideologue Yisrael Eldad:* Berkovitz, op. cit.; Shragai, op. cit.

116   *Ben-Dov's form:* Shabtai Ben-Dov, *Ge'ulat Yisrael Bemashber Hamedinah (The Redemption of Israel in the Crisis of the State)* (Safed, Israel: Hamatmid, 1960). Additional sources: Ehud Sprinzak, *Brother Against Brother: Violence and Extremism in Israeli Politics from Altalena to the Rabin Assassination* (New York: The Free Press, 1999); Segal, op. cit.

117   *Etzion didn't join:* Sources on the Temple Mount plot and Jewish underground include investigation documents and verdicts in the case and Sprinzak, *The Ascendance of Israel's Radical Right* and *Brother Against Brother,* op. cit.; Segal, op. cit.

118   *If you want:* Segal, op. cit., pp. 56–57.

120   *one printed product: The Gospel of John,* paraphrased by Chuck Smith, illustrations by Rick Griffin (Costa Mesa, Calif.: The Word for Today, 1980).

120   *tape on Revelation:* Chuck Smith, *Rev. 11* (Costa Mesa, Calif.: The Word for Today).

120   *The sixties, as the writer John Judis:* "The Spirit Of '68," *The New Republic,* Aug. 31, 1998.

121   *McGuire was baptized:* Devlin Donaldson, "Barry McGuire," *http://www.ccmcom.com/ccmmag/96apr/0496rewind.html.*

121   *Two years later, Lindsey:* Lindsey, *The Late Great Planet Earth,* op. cit., quotations taken from HarperPaperbacks edition, 1992.

122   *The Last Days of the Late, Great State of California:* By Curt Gentry (New York: G.P. Putnam's Sons, 1968).

124   *Based in Los Angeles:* Barbara and Michael Ledeen, "The Temple Mount Plot," *The New Republic,* June 18, 1984; Robert I. Friedman, "Terror on Sacred Ground," *Mother Jones,* Aug.–Sept. 1987.

124   *the radar affair:* Lambert Dolphin, "Geophysics and the Temple Mount," *http://www.best.com/~dolphin/tempgeophy.html;* Abraham Rabinovich, "Electronic Probes Aid the Archeologists," *The Jerusalem Post,* Aug. 1, 1983.

125   *The tunnel had its:* Yediot Aharonot and *The Jerusalem Post,* Aug. 28–Sept. 3, 1981.

128   *Kahane's ideas provided:* Yael Admoni, "Lo Mitzta'er, Lo Mitharet" ("No Regrets"), *Yediot Aharonot,* Oct. 10, 1997.

129   *Gush activist Yisrael Harel:* "Kahane the Outsider," *The Jerusalem Report,* Nov. 22, 1990.

130   *In the mid-sixties:* Michael T. Kaufman, "The Complex Past of Meir Kahane," *The New York Times,* Jan. 24, 1971; Michael T. Kaufman, "Remembering Kahane, and the Woman on the Bridge," *The New York Times,* March 6, 1994.

130   *for Kahane, God's reputation:* Meir Kahane, *Listen World, Listen Jew* (Tuscon, Ariz.: Institute of the Jewish Idea, 1978), pp. 118–23.

130   *In a 1983 book:* Meir Kahane, *Forty Years* (Miami Beach, Fla.: The Institute of the Jewish Idea, 1983).

131   *88 Reasons Why:* Edgar C. Whisenant, *88 Reasons Why The Rapture Could Be in 1988* (Nashville, Tenn.: World Bible Society).

131   *In one attempt:* Shragai, op. cit.; Ledeen, op. cit.; *The Jerusalem Post,* Jan. 29, 1984.

132   *They met nearly:* Sources on the underground listed above at note on *"Yehudah Etzion didn't join."*

134   *They could not completely:* Segal, op. cit.

Six: CONSTRUCTION WORKERS OF THE LORD

141   *Charles Krauthammer, defending:* "A Desecration of the Truth," *Time,* Oct. 14, 1996.

144   *His father Avigdor:* Avigdor Elboim, *Sefer Torat Habayit* (Jerusalem: Yeshivat Torat Habayit, 1992).

154   *The Trumpet Shall:* Pete Worsley, *The Trumpet Shall Sound: A Study of "Cargo Cults" in Melanesia* (London: Paladin, 1970).

Seven: THE DIVINE REPERTORY THEATER COMPANY

161   *Babylon or Jerusalem?:* Jan Willem van der Hoeven, *Babylon or Jerusalem?* (Shippensburg, Penn.: Destiny Image, 1993).

165   *The photo fills:* "Israel Slide Show" at *http://www.levitt.com.* Statement of purpose: *http://www.levitt.com/watiszlm.html.* Newsletter quotations: "Levitt Letter," September 1999: Vol. 21, No. 9, *http://www.levitt.com/newsletters/1999–09.html.* Comment on Netanyahu's name: fax interview with *The Jerusalem Report.*

165   *John Hagee's Beginning:* Hagee, op. cit.

166   *The Netanyahu-evangelical alliance:* *The New York Times,* Jan. 21, 1998; *The Washington Post,* Jan. 22, 1998.

167   *Jerusalem Betrayed:* Mike Evans, *Jerusalem Betrayed: Ancient Prophecy and Modern Conspiracy Collide in the Holy City* (Dallas: World Publishing, 1997).

167 *In January 1999:* "Falwell Says Antichrist Probably Is on Earth Now," AP, Jan. 15, 1999.

170 *Around Jerusalem, the Faithful: Ha'aretz,* Sept. 29, 1990; *Ha'aretz* and *Yediot Aharonot,* Oct. 9–15, 1990. On Muslim apocalyptic readings of the Gulf crisis, see Cook, "Muslim Fears of the Year 2000," op. cit.

175 *The Temple Institute in Jerusalem:* Yisrael Ariel, *Sefer Hamikdash (The Temple Book)* (Jerusalem: Pirsumei Yisrael and Makhon Hamikdash, n.d.), p. 125.

176 *Ariel was the central:* Sprinzak, *Radical Right,* op. cit.

176 *Tzfiyah journal:* Volumes I and II, 1985; Volume III, 1988.

177 *"If you doubt:* Hagee, op. cit., pp. 142–43.

177 *Mike Evans, likewise:* Evans, op. cit., pp. 234–43.

177 *Jerusalem in Prophecy:* Price, op. cit.

177 *Messiah's Coming Temple:* John W. Schmitt and J. Carl Laney, *Messiah's Coming Temple: Ezekiel's Prophecy of the Future Temple* (Grand Rapids, Mich.: Kregel, 1997).

Eight: AWAITING THE HOUR

181 *It was 8:35:* Sources on the tunnel crisis include reports in *Ha'aretz, Ma'ariv, Yediot Aharonot,* and *The New York Times,* Sept. 24–Oct. 1, 1996.

182 *a hidden piece:* On the tunnel, see Abraham Rabinovich, "Tunnel Vision," *The Jerusalem Post,* Sept. 27, 1996; Nadav Shragai, "The Tunnel—Part of an Aqueduct Uncovered in the Last Century and Rediscovered in '87," *Ha'aretz,* Sept. 25, 1996.

182 *millionaire, Irving Moskowitz:* Sources on Moskowitz include Leslie Susser, "The Mayor and the Millionaire," *The Jerusalem Report,* Oct. 16, 1997; Serge Schmemann and James Brooke, "U.S. Doctor's Donations Fuel Mideast Storms," *The New York Times,* Sept. 29, 1997; and other press reports. Figures on Irving Moskowitz Foundation from tax reports submitted to the State of California.

185 *there was another factor:* On modern Islamic apocalyptic thinking, sources include David Cook, "Muslim Fears of the Year 2000," op. cit., and forthcoming articles by Cook: "Modern Muslim Apocalyptic Literature Part I: Arabic Material"; "Jerusalem in Modern Muslim Apocalyptic Writings"; "From Banu Isra'il to the State of Israel: The Changing Exegesis of Qur'an 17:4–8" and "America, The Second 'Ad: Prophecies About the Downfall of the United States." Citations below from Arabic sources courtesy of David Cook.

185 *Sa'id Ayyub's Al-Massih al-Dajjal:* Cairo: al-Fath li-l-I'lam al-'Arabi, 1987.

186   *book by Muhammad Isa Da'ud: Ihdharu al-masih al-Dajjal yaghzu al-'alam min muthallath Bermuda.* Cairo: al-Mukhtar al-Islami, 1991.
187   *History bears witness:* Ayyub, op. cit., p. 64.
188   *a messiah in keeping:* Ibid., p. 32.
188   *The dwelling place:* Ibid., p. 106.
188   *The building of [the Temple]:* Ibid., p. 28, n. 6.
189   *Muhammad Isa Da'ud asserts in: Al-Mahdi al-muntazar 'ala al-abwab* (Cairo: al-'Arabiyya li-l-Tiba'a wa-l-Nashr, 1997).
189   *A brief passage:* Koran 17:4–8.
189   *Another writer, Bashir Muhummad Abdallah:* In his *Zilzal al-ard al-'azim* (Cairo: Dar al-Tiba'a al-Haditha, 1994).
190   *A Palestinian newspaper:* Al-Nahar, Dec. 15, 1990.
190   *Amin Jamal al-Din: Radd al-siham 'an kitab 'Umr ummat al-Islam.* (Cairo: al-Maktaba al-Tawfiqiyya, n.d.).
190   *Dan Shomron "said:* Muhammad Isa Da'ud, *Ihdharu,* op. cit., pp. 141–42.
190   *The Great Events Preceding:* Da'ud, Fa'iq Muhammad, *al-Umur al-'izam qabla zuhur al-Imam al-Mahdi* (1999).
192   *The End of Israel:* Jirrar, Bassam, *Zawal Isra'il 'amm 2022* (Beirut: Maktabat al-Biqa' al-Haditha, 1995).
193   *refrains from anti-Semitic:* Cook, "From Banu Isra'il to the State of Israel," op. cit.
196   *Sheikh Abdallah Nimr Darwish:* See Yossi Klein Halevi, "A Moderate Fundamentalist," *The Jerusalem Report,* Oct. 11, 1999.
196   *The Oslo Accord divided:* Yosef Algazi, "Accepting Israel and Linked to Hamas and the Islamic Jihad," *Ha'aretz,* Sept. 30, 1999.
197   *a very senior Israeli:* Yosef Algazi, "Tens of Thousands Came to the Islamic Movement's Rally 'to Save Al-Aqsa,' " *Ha'aretz,* Sept. 19, 1999.
198   *Israel has never:* Berkovits, op. cit.
199   *The old window:* Ha'aretz, Ma'ariv, Yediot Aharonot, Aug. 10, 1999; Kol Ha'ir, Aug. 6, 1999.
200   *Israeli Attorney General:* Ha'aretz, Dec. 2, 1999; reports in the Hebrew press over the following weeks.
201   *An unsigned editorial:* "For the Information of the State Prosecutor: There's High Certainty of Jewish Violence," *Hatzofeh,* Jan. 9, 2000.
201   *Moshe Feiglin announced:* Ha'aretz, Dec. 16, 1999.
202   *A protest against:* Ha'aretz, Dec. 28, 1999.

Nine: THE DAY AFTER THE LAST

203   *Early on the morning:* Sources on the Hebron massacre include extensive reports in the Hebrew press, and Yossi Klein Halevi, "Kahane's Murderous Legacy," *The Jerusalem Report,* March 24, 1994; Vivienne

Walt, "Heart of Darkness," *Newsday*, March 4, 1994. Be'eri's comments on Goldstein's eulogy and Oslo appeared in *Nekudah*, March 1994. Responses by Rabin, Barak, and Yatom to the massacre: See *Ha'aretz*, March 1, 1994, *Yediot Aharonot*, March 9, 1994; *Ma'ariv*, March 24, 1994. Shamgar Commssion conclusions: Commission of Inquiry into the Masacre at the Tomb of the Patriarchs in Hebron, report, 1994. Advance warnings: See Ehud Sprinzak, "What's He Waiting For," *Ha'aretz*, Dec. 16, 1993. Goldstein's funeral: See *Ha'aretz* and *Yediot Aharonot*, Feb. 28, 1994. Dov Lior's comment appeared in *Meimad* No. 1, June 1994. Scene at Goldstein *shivah:* Lisa Pevtzow, "Doctor Tried to Be Like Lubavitchers' Leader," *Newsday*, March 2, 1994. Memorial volume: Michael Ben-Horin, ed., *Baruch Hagever: Sefer Zikaron Lekadosh Dr. Baruch Goldstein* (Jerusalem: Yehudah, 5755). Goldstein as an inspiration for Yigal Amir: David Horovitz, ed., *Shalom Friend: The Life and Legacy of Yitzhak Rabin* (New York: Newmarket, 1996).

208   *The story is well:* Sources on Waco include James Tabor and Eugene V. Gallagher, *Why Waco? Cults and the Battle for Religious Freedom in America* (Berkeley: University of California Press, 1995); Thompson, op. cit.; Wessinger, op. cit.; and press reports. Comment on Koresh wanting "a showdown" from Ross E. Milloy, "Death in Waco: A Fiery End," *The New York Times*, April 20, 1993.

211   *there was other testimony:* Sources on millennialist violence include Wessinger, op. cit.; Jean-François Mayer, " 'Our Terrestrial Journey is Coming to an End': The Last Voyage of the Solar Temple," *Nova Religio*, Vol. 2, No. 2, April 1999; Gustav Niebuhr, "Death in a Cult: the Beliefs," *The New York Times*, March 28, 1997; David E. Kaplan and Andrew Marshall, *The Cult at the End of the World: The Incredible Story of Aum,* (London: Arrow, 1997). On the Uganda tragedy, see sources listed in notes on Introduction, above.

212   *The two-story stone:* Sources on the Concerned Christians include Charlie Brennan's extensive reports in the *Denver Rocky Mountain News*. The tape on Manson carries the title "Time of the End—Series #18. I Am the Lawmaker. Tape 30." The tape and packet of charts were found by journalist Elaine Ruth Fletcher. Concerned Christian newsletters: *Take Heed Update*, Sept.–Oct. 1989; *Report from Concerned Christians*, May–June 1990.

213   *the witnesses who according to Revelation:* Revelation 11:7–11.

216   *The Ministry of Elijah in Jerusalem NOW!:* http://www.dccsa.com/greatjoy/Elijmin.htm.

217   *Leaks to police reporters:* See, for example, "The Police Were Concerned About Mass Suicide or an Attack on the Temple Mount," *Ha'aretz*, Oct. 26, 1999.

218   *Soon after, newspapers:* The first wave of such reports appeared in the Hebrew press at the end of November 1998.

219   *the hook in the jaw:* Ezekiel 38:1–8, quoted by Stephens in *Oil in Israel: The End-Time Annointing* (video) (Jerusalem: Israel Vision, n.d.).

220   *must be male:* "Falwell Says Antichrist Probably Is on Earth Now," AP, Jan. 15, 1999. Falwell's sermon on 2000: "Ten Things I See In 99," Jan. 3, 1999, *http://www.trbc.org/sermons/990103.html.*

221   *John Hagee, for instance:* Hagee, op. cit.

221   *Mike Evans cited:* Evans, op. cit.

221   *"half the city:* Zechariah 14:2.

222   *As late as December:* "The Seventh Millennium," *Personal Update,* Dec. 1999.

222   *a final warning:* Gordan McDonald, "What Y2K Will Be," *Personal Update,* Dec. 1999.

222   *in August 1998, Falwell:* "Y2K Computer Crisis," Aug. 30, 1998, downloaded via *http://www.trbc.org/sermons/.* As of April 2000, the site no longer provided this sermon.

222   *Grant Jeffrey's online:* "The Millennium Meltdown," downloaded via *http://www.GrantJeffrey.com/.*

223   *William Miller's followers:* Tabor and Gallagher, op. cit.

224   *pioneer social psychologist:* Leon Festinger et al., *When Prophecy Fails* (University of Minnesota Press, 1956).

225   *eyes of the faithful:* See David Horovitz, op. cit.; Arye Heskin, "Judea and Israel Will Not Be Divided Again," *Nekudah,* Dec. 1993.

226   *There remains but one:* Lindsey, op. cit.

227   *Terror, says the political scientist David Rapoport:* "Messianic Sanctions for Terror," *Comparative Politics,* Vol. 20, No. 2, 1988.

228   *When a millennial:* See Ehud Sprinzak, "Extreme Left Terrorism in a Democracy: The Case of the Weathermen," in Walter Reich, ed., *The Origins of Terrorism* (New York: Cambridge University Press, 1990).

230   *Satan is moving:* Stan Goodenough, "Barak-Arafat 'Jerusalem Deal' would be major victory for Islam," *International Christian Zionist Center,* Aug. 1999.

Ten: AVOIDING THE CAIN OPTION

235   *The Oslo agreement put:* See Menachem Klein, op. cit.

237   *If a group already:* Wessinger, op. cit.

239   *As leader of the right-wing:* The demonstrations were widely covered in the Hebrew press. For a summary, see Horovitz, op. cit.

239   *he once presented:* Yosef Algazi, "Prime Minister's Present to the Head of the Greek Church: A Relief of Jerusalem Without the Islamic Shrines," *Ha'aretz,* Jan. 12, 1997.

240   *forces of evil:* David S. Broder, "Next Tuesday May Be Senator's Last Chance," *The Washington Post,* March 1, 2000.

240   *In February 1999:* "Fallwell Says He Regrets Saying Antichrist Is a Jew," AP, Feb. 2, 1999.

241   *a rabbi's article:* David Bar Hayim, "Not Yet Time?" *Your Jerusalem,* Aug. 1999.

243   *every Muslim he cut:* Hand quoted this phrase from John France, "The Capture of Jerusalem," *History Today,* April 1997.

244   *A theology fitting for:* Darrell Fasching, *The Coming of the Millennium: Good News for the Whole Human Race* (Valley Forge, Pa.: Trinity Press International, 1996).

245   *if Zechariah speaks:* Zechariah 12:2.

245   *the fourth horseman:* Revelation 6:8.

245   *Jesus says "the abomination":* Matthew 24:15, Mark 13:14.

245   *Ezekiel lists nations:* Ezekiel 38:2–6.

245   *Hal Lindsey deciphering:* Lindsey, op. cit.

246   *Yet literalism resonates:* O'Leary, op. cit.

247   *Exodus and Revolution:* Michael Walzer, *Exodus and Revolution* (New York: Basic Books, 1985).

249   *an article Reiner:* Shmuel Reiner, "Outsiders," *The Jerusalem Report,* Feb. 5, 1999.

249   *Rabbi Levi retold:* Breshit Rabbah 22:7.

iNDEX